WATERCOLOR THIS BOOK

Beautiful Butterflies & Flowers

20
Step-by-Step, No-Sketch Projects on Watercolor Paper

CHITHRA SHAAN
of Littleheartcreates

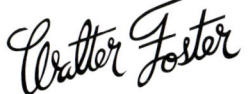

CONTENTS

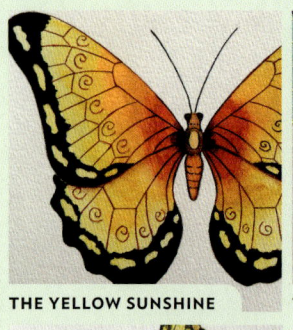

THE YELLOW SUNSHINE

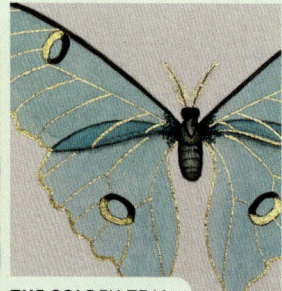

THE GOLDEN TEAL

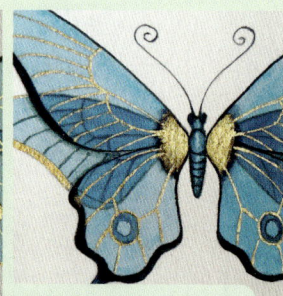

LONG-TAILED BUTTERFLY

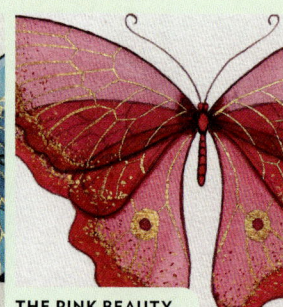

THE PINK BEAUTY

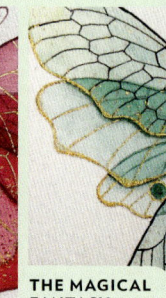

THE MAGICAL FANTASY

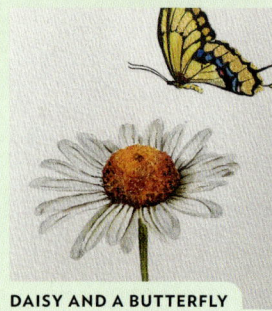

DAISY AND A BUTTERFLY

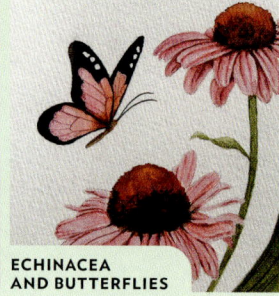

ECHINACEA AND BUTTERFLIES

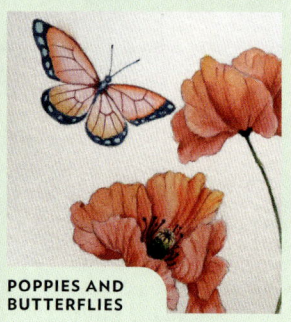

POPPIES AND BUTTERFLIES

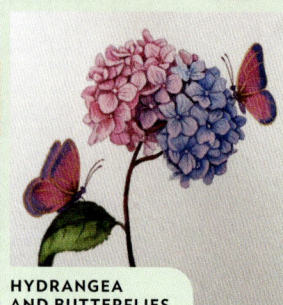

HYDRANGEA AND BUTTERFLIES

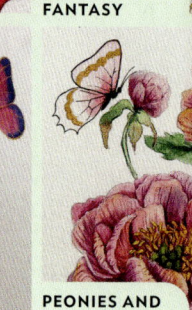

PEONIES AND BUTTERFLIES

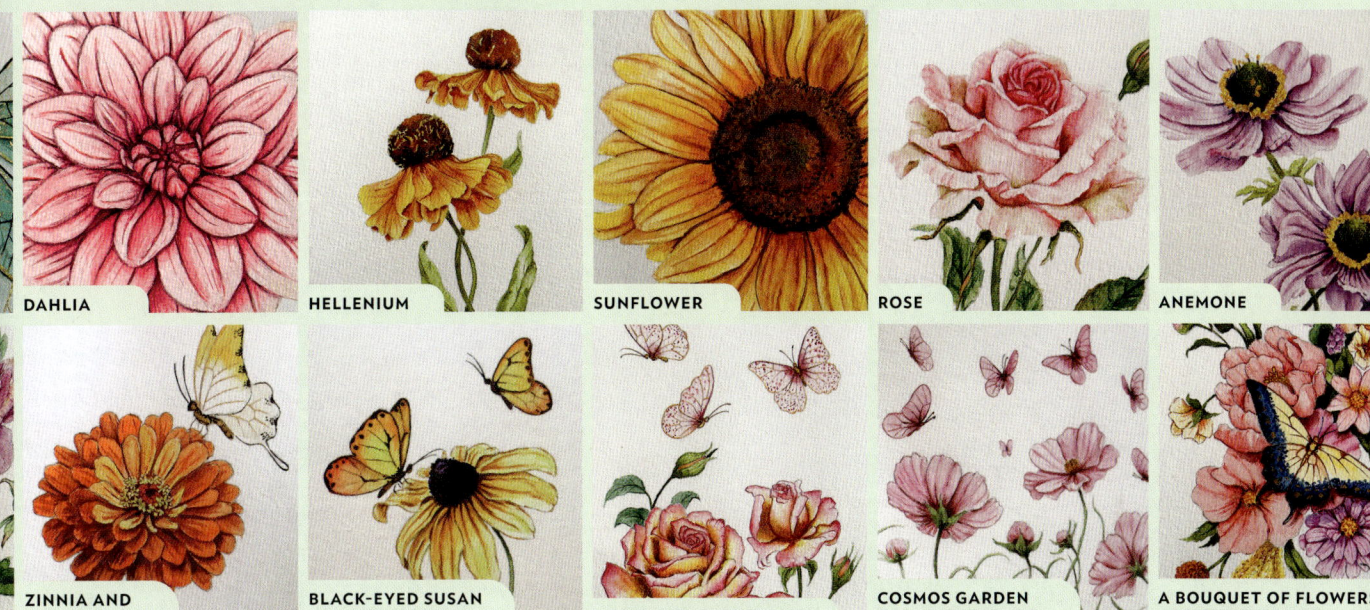

DAHLIA

HELLENIUM

SUNFLOWER

ROSE

ANEMONE

ZINNIA AND BUTTERFLIES

BLACK-EYED SUSAN AND BUTTERFLIES

ROSES AND BUTTERFLIES

COSMOS GARDEN AND BUTTERFLIES

A BOUQUET OF FLOWERS AND BUTTERFLIES

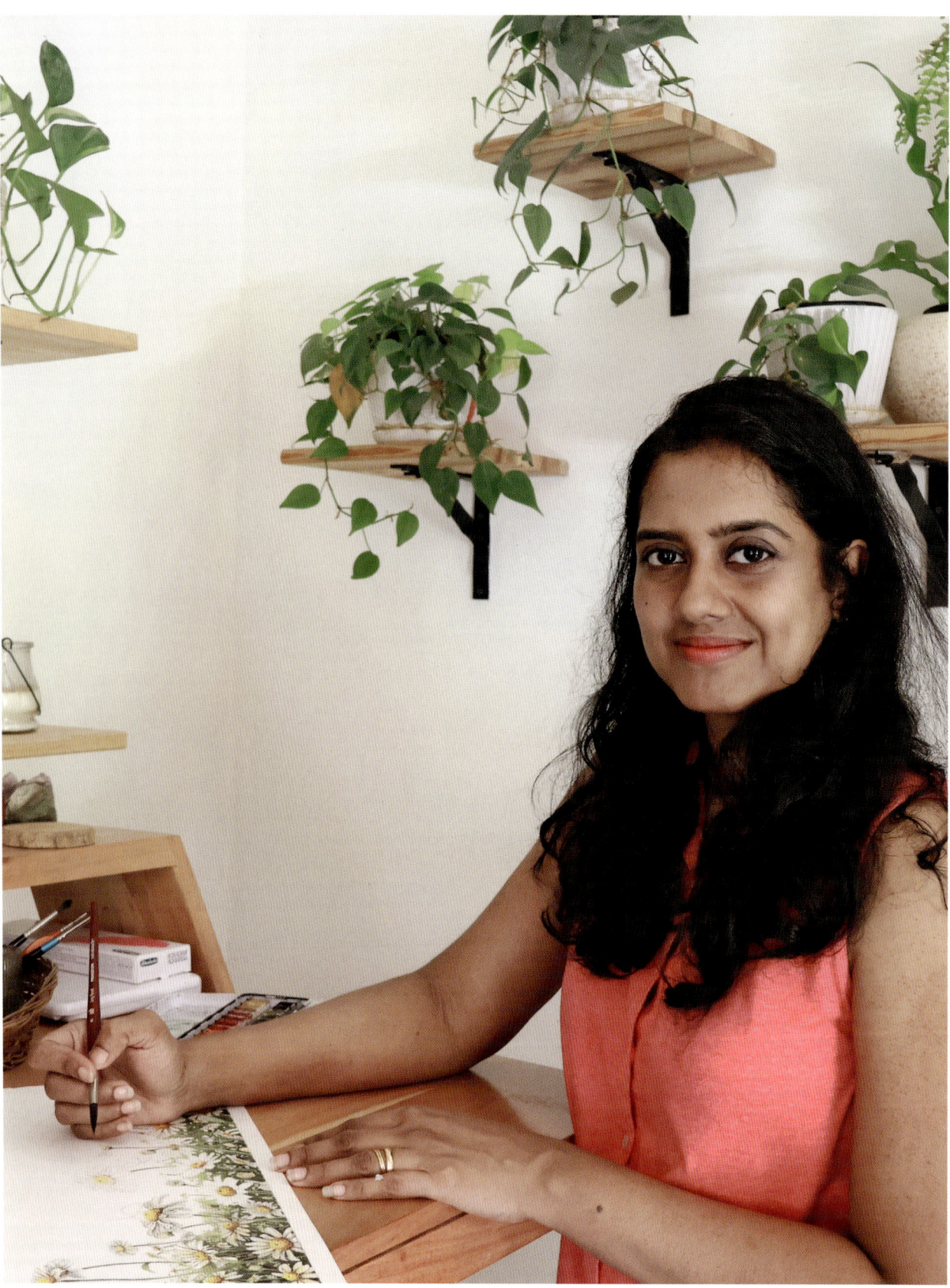

Introduction

HI, I AM CHITHRA, THE ARTIST BEHIND Littleheart-creates. I am a self-taught artist, and I started my Instagram channel (and now Pinterest, Facebook, and YouTube) @littleheartcreates during the COVID-19 pandemic as a stress reliever for myself and others. I started by drawing flowers to bring a smile to my lovely audience. I feel extremely happy when people tell me my art and art videos calm their souls. A year later I tried watercolor and fell in love with it. I am currently painting butterflies, flowers, and birds, but I also love to draw other animals, as well as portraits. I am also practicing oil painting and have completed a few of them.

I have loved to draw ever since I was a child and wanted to pursue art as a profession, which my parents always supported. After I graduated from my studies in Chemistry, I pursued a diploma cum certification course in 3D animation, after which I started working as a 3D lighting artist. I have had an amazing experience working with studios such as Technicolor and DreamWorks, on projects such as *All Hail King Julien*, *Puss in Boots*, and others. But I was missing my creative spark. I started sketching and painting as a hobby again and now here I am.

In the pages of this book, I feature twenty paintings of the shimmering butterflies and flowers I have become known for. I have broken down my painting techniques in an easy-to-replicate way so that you

can also fill your home with these beautiful works of art. To make this the easiest possible for those who are new to watercolor, I've included the sketch for you on a watercolor practice pad so all you have to do is start painting! I've also included the templates here so you can print or trace these onto your own watercolor paper and paint them again and again. I think they make great gifts for loved ones. I've also included videos for some of the paintings so be sure to scan the QR codes throughout this book.

For those who have already begun their watercolor painting journey, having the watercolor pad in the book makes it easy to pack your paints and brushes and bring them along anywhere you travel. I've done the sketching for you.

I hope to inspire you to create something beautiful. Now, let's begin!

Chithra

TOOLS & MATERIALS

THIS WATERCOLOR JOURNEY REQUIRES a few tools and materials. Let's make sure you use the right brush with the right color on the right paper. Let's start with watercolor paper.

Watercolor PAPER

I have included a watercolor practice pad in this book. The outlines of all the paintings have already

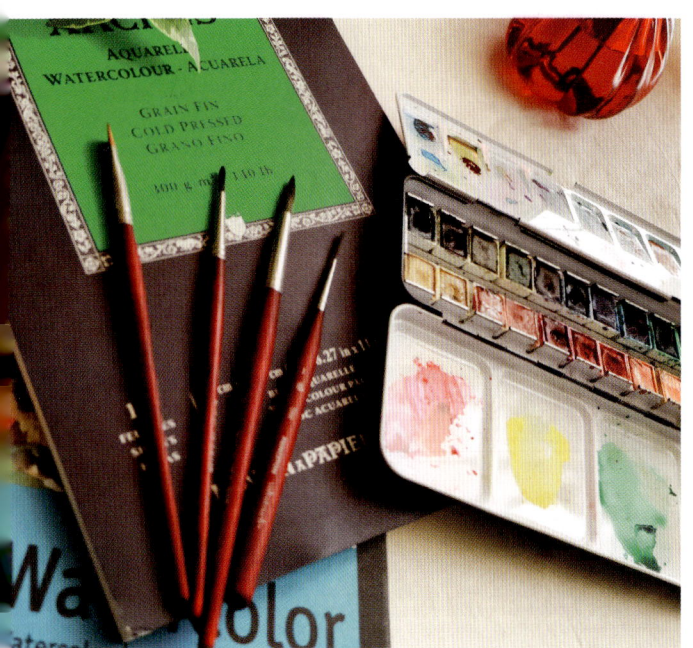

been printed for you, so there is no sketching or tracing required. It's a great idea to practice on this paper and then recreate the pieces on your own watercolor paper if you'd like. Or you can simply remove the painting from the pad and hang it up or gift it to someone. Whatever makes you happy!

When it comes to paper, the most important thing is the quality. Always use good-quality watercolor paper, and by this, I mean a trustworthy brand like Canson or Arches. Bad-quality papers soak in the water quickly and you won't have enough time to blend the paint. You may think you are a bad artist when the actual culprit was the bad-quality paper.

There are three factors when it comes to selecting watercolor paper: weight, material, and texture, which results from how it is made. I highly recommend a 300 gsm (140 lbs) (weight), 100% cotton (material), cold-pressed (texture) watercolor paper.

Choosing Watercolor Paper

- **PAPER WEIGHT:** I recommend paper of at least 250 gsm thickness. My favorite is the 300 gsm, or 140 lbs. Gsm or lbs refers to how much the paper weighs. Gsm is grams per square meter and lbs is the weight of the paper in pounds (generally found in the U.S.).

- **PAPER MATERIAL:** Cotton paper is more absorbent and stronger than those made with wood pulp. My favorite of all time is Canson watercolor paper, which is very good-quality, affordable paper and can handle so much abuse. Arches paper is also very good quality but a bit expensive.

- **PAPER TEXTURE:** Watercolor paper comes mostly in two options: hot-pressed and cold-pressed. Hot-pressed paper has a smooth surface due to the manufacturing process, where the pulp is pressed on hot rollers. Cold-pressed papers have a textured surface due to being pressed on cold rollers and are my favorite. They are typically more absorbent than hot-pressed paper.

Watercolor PAINT

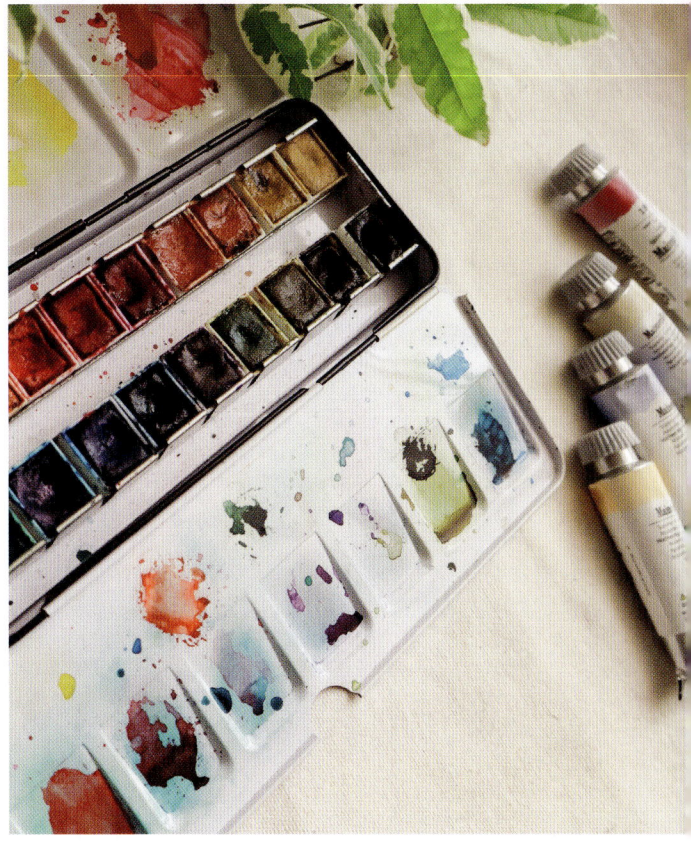

I strongly recommend buying high-quality watercolors, but rest assured I've recommended budget-friendly options. Low-quality watercolor dries with a chalky texture and the colors will fade out eventually. I recommend and use Daler-Rowney or Mungyo Korea watercolors. These are beginner-friendly watercolors with good pigments and come in sets for less than $30. Other high-quality watercolor brands include Schmincke, Daniel Smith, and Winsor & Newton. Don't feel that you need to buy new sets if you already have quality paints on hand.

I typically use watercolor pans rather than paint tubes because they are more affordable and I find them easy to work with. You can use the paint you already have or buy the colors in whatever brand is available to you and at your budget. If you don't have the same colors I use, don't worry; just do your best to approximate the color.

For this book, I used the following colors:

- Burnt Sienna
- Burnt Umber
- Black
- Cadmium Yellow
- Cobalt Blue
- Green
- Indian Yellow or Yellow
- Lemon Yellow
- Magenta
- Naples Yellow
- Olive Green
- Orange
- Permanent Rose
- Phthalo Blue
- Pink
- Prussian Blue
- Raw Sienna
- Red
- Sap Green
- Turquoise Blue
- Vermilion
- Violet
- Viridian
- Yellow Ochre

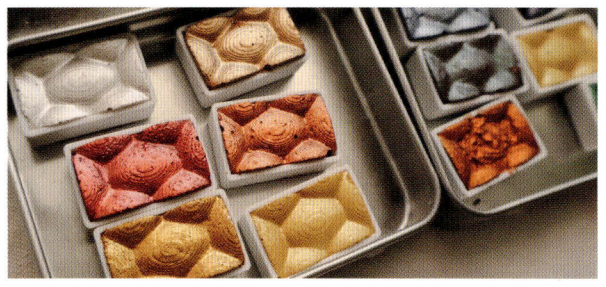

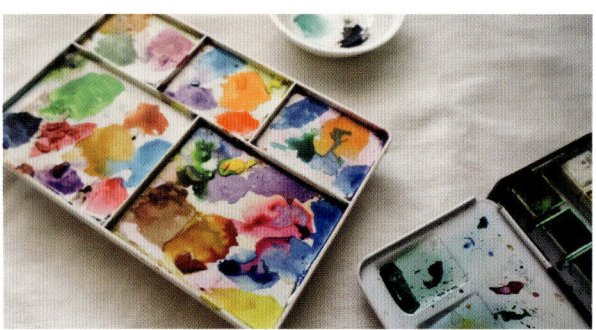

Mont Marte Taklon series and the number 1 Princeton Velvetouch series liner brush. To complete the projects in this book, you'll need the following brushes:

- Number 8 Round Brush
- Number 4 Round Brush
- Liner Brush

Other SUPPLIES

In addition to the main supplies, you'll want to ensure you have the following when you sit down to paint:

- **WATER CUPS:** Of course you'll need water as a medium to paint watercolors. You can keep a single cup of water for washing the brushes and mixing colors, or you may use two separate cups of water—one for washing and another for mixing.

- **PAPER TOWEL:** You will need a cotton towel or cotton paper towel throughout the process for cleaning brushes. If you accidentally add too much paint to your brush, you can wipe it with a cotton towel or paper towel.

- **HAIR DRYER:** Sometimes I use a hair dryer to speed up the drying process, or you can let the paint dry naturally.

- **TAPE:** I use masking tape or washi tape to tape down the paper onto the table or painting board.

- **MIXING WELL:** You can use a color mixing palette to mix the paint.

- **SPRAY BOTTLE:** A spray bottle is recommended for dry climates to moisten the paint before starting to paint. I personally live in a very humid climate so find I don't need to spray down my paints.

Metallic Watercolor PAINT

To put the finishing touches on the paintings in this book, you'll also need metallic watercolors. Metallics can be pricey, so I've only used three colors for the paintings in this book. I use Sapphire Shifters watercolor set from Skrim Watercolors, which costs about $40. You can either purchase this, or you can buy a light green and blue shade of any metallic watercolor brand. Additionally, you will also need a Gold Metallic watercolor. The metallics you'll need are:

- Light Green Metallic
- Blue Metallic
- Gold Metallic

PAINTBRUSHES

I recommend using high-quality brushes. I mostly use Princeton and Kum Germany round brushes. To paint the fine details, I use the 5/0 Detailer brush from the

WATERCOLOR PAINTING TECHNIQUES

BEFORE YOU GET STARTED on your painting journey, I'll be covering some basic watercolor techniques. These will help you to understand the instructions in the paintings that follow.

WET-ON-WET

Wet-on-wet in watercolor is a technique where wet paint is applied to a wet paper surface. This involves wetting the paper with water or another solvent before applying the paint, allowing the colors to blend and spread freely, creating soft edges and a fluid appearance. This technique is commonly used in watercolor painting to achieve various textures, gradients, and atmospheric effects. In wet-on-wet, the watercolor brush is consistently kept wet, emphasizing the wetness of the paper. This method, often employed in landscapes and vibrant flower paintings, results in natural-looking color blends with smooth transitions. It is typically used as the initial layer of a painting, providing artists with creative freedom. While the multitude of watercolor techniques might seem daunting for beginners, mastery comes with practice and experience in navigating these artistic choices.

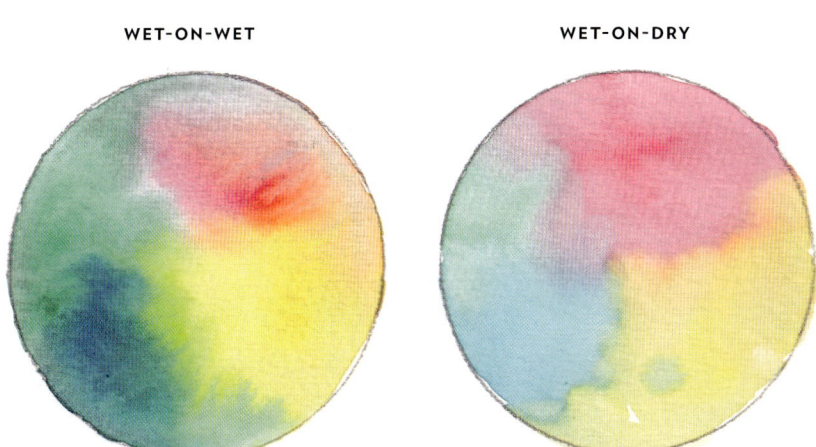

WET-ON-WET

WET-ON-DRY

I used the wet-on-wet technique in the circle on the left. This involves wetting the paper before applying the colors. In the circle on the right, I applied colors on a dry surface which is known as the wet-on-dry technique. See image 289. There are two color swatches below these circles that are missing from the book. If they cannot be added (looks like there isn't space) please delete the highlighted text.

WET-ON-DRY

In the wet-on-dry technique, the paper is dry, and colors are applied using a wet brush. This method is a personal favorite of mine due to the controlled and distinct look it imparts to the painting. It provides greater control over colors, making it ideal for layering to achieve more saturated hues. I will use this technique often in the paintings that follow to add layers of colors for richness. Artists commonly use wet-on-dry as a layer on top of wet-on-wet techniques. After the initial wet layer dries, applying colors without wetting the paper adds detail and saturation to the painting. This versatile approach allows for a dynamic interplay of techniques in watercolor art.

Types of
WASHES

Watercolor washes involve applying a thin, even layer of diluted paint over a large area to create a smooth and seamless color transition. This technique is achieved by wetting the paper first and then applying the paint, allowing it to flow and blend naturally.

Flat Wash

A flat wash involves painting a consistent and uniform color throughout a shape. As you progress, the color may lighten due to paintbrush bristle saturation. The speed of this effect depends on the space size and brush used. For smaller areas and larger brushes, one load may suffice, but for larger spaces and smaller brushes, frequent reloading is necessary. Watch for color weakening, and promptly reload to maintain a seamless wash before the paint dries.

Gradient Wash

A graded or gradient wash aims for a gradual change in color intensity, becoming lighter or darker as you move up or down the shape. Unlike a flat wash, you intentionally allow the color to weaken as you progress. Keep an eye on your paper, ensuring the color becomes more translucent. If not, dip your brush in water, remove excess water, and continue, repeating this to achieve maximum translucency by the end of the wash.

Variegated Wash

A variegated wash involves a gradual transition from one color to another within a shape. In this example, I have used Pink and Blue for a vibrant gradient. Paint one color in a section, clean your brush, remove excess water, load the brush with the next color, and continue painting the rest of the shape. Overlapping colors in the transitional area creates a smooth gradient. In the example, Pink and Blue transitions to Purple, with careful brush management for a seamless effect.

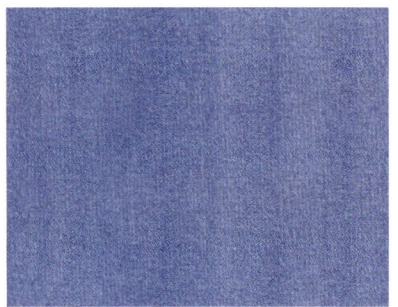

FLAT WASH

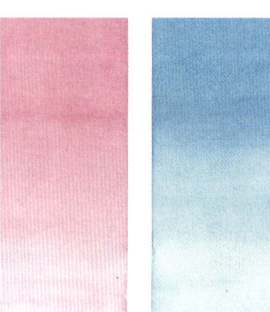

GRADIENT WASH

VARIEGATED WASH

Brush TECHNIQUES

Watercolor brushstrokes involve applying water-based paint to a surface, typically paper, using brushes. These strokes can vary in thickness, intensity, and direction, creating diverse textures and effects. Throughout the process I have used a number 8 round brush.

Thin Lines

For thin lines, lightly touch the brush tip to the paper and drag it consistently from one edge to the other. Maintain a consistent thickness throughout the stroke by ensuring only the brush's tip contacts the paper from start to finish.

Thick Lines

For thick lines, apply pressure with the brush's belly to the paper. Maintain consistent pressure and thickness from start to finish, noting potential dry brushing effects as paint and water reduce near the ends of the lines.

Thin-to-Thick Lines

To create thin-to-thick lines, vary the pressure as you move laterally from one edge to the other. Simultaneously lift and press the brush, generating thickness variations throughout the line. The challenge is to maintain some contact with the paper from start to finish.

C-strokes

These are short, curved brushstrokes that begin wider and taper at their ends. Start by pressing down the brush's belly at the top, gradually releasing pressure as you move towards the stroke's end, creating a curved or "c" shape.

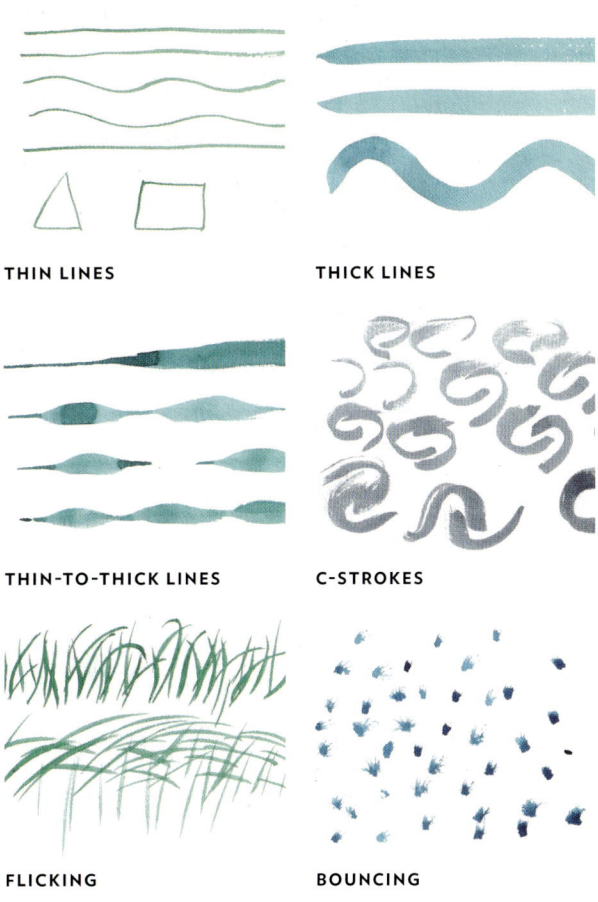

THIN LINES

THICK LINES

THIN-TO-THICK LINES

C-STROKES

FLICKING

BOUNCING

Flicking

Flicking involves a quick, short stroke by flicking your wrist in any direction. There's minimal pressure on the brush bristles on the paper, and at the end of the motion, lift the bristles for a tapered appearance. The base or root of the stroke should appear slightly thicker than the end. This technique is useful for creating the illusion of grass in landscapes.

Bouncing

Bouncing is akin to stamping with your loaded paintbrush, pressing down the bristles entirely on the paper and then lifting repeatedly. There is no dragging or lateral movement; it's a simple press-and-lift motion. The choice of brush shape, such as round versus flat,

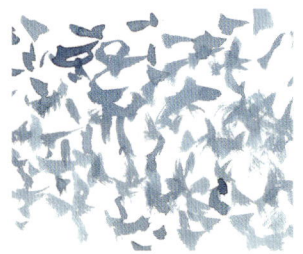

SCRIBBLING

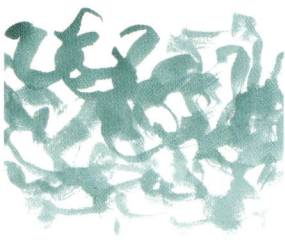

SCRIBBLING & BOUNCING

Blending Color Wet-on-Wet

STEP 1: Wet the area with water using a number 8 round brush.

STEP 2: Apply red color on one side of the wet area.

STEP 3: Before the water and the red color dry, swiftly clean your brush to remove the red paint. Then, switch to yellow and begin applying it from the right side of the wet area. Stop when the yellow color is close to the red.

STEP 4: Using a clean, wet brush (a "nude brush" with no paint), gently move the yellow color towards the red in an up-and-down motion. Avoid going from right to left; instead, stick to the up-and-down motion. Also, be careful not to add more water or use too much water when blending. This helps keep the blending area just right for a smooth transition of colors.

significantly affects the appearance of the "stamped" shapes. Bouncing is particularly useful for creating the illusion of leaves when painting trees and plants.

Scribbling

This style involves loosening your wrist and experimenting with various brush movements. Aim for irregularity, avoiding organized patterns or perfect shapes. Achieve this by changing pressure and direction, moving the brush up and down laterally and incorporating curves and loops.

Scribbling and Bouncing

This style combines the techniques of scribbling and bouncing. This dynamic approach involves varied brush movements with irregular patterns and the stamping motion of bouncing. It is particularly effective for creating the organic shapes and textures found in leaves of plants and trees.

Blending Color Over Wet Color

STEP 1: Use a number 8 round brush to apply yellow color on dry paper.

BLENDING COLOR WET-ON-WET

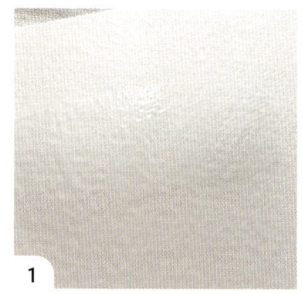

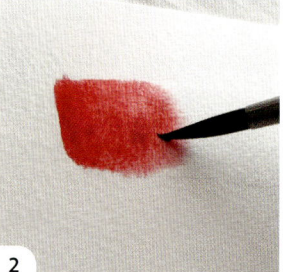

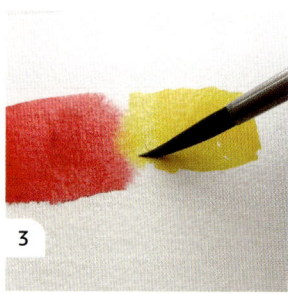

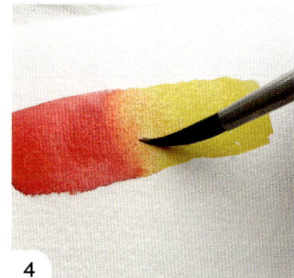

Color BLENDING

Mastering color blending in watercolor painting might seem challenging, but with practice, you'll get the hang of it. Try these techniques to improve, keep practicing, and you'll become skilled at blending colors seamlessly.

step 2: After cleaning the brush to remove the yellow pigment, switch to red and apply it on top of the yellow color which is still wet. It's important to control the amount of water—too much makes blending tricky, and too little causes the color to dry fast. Don't worry if it's challenging initially; practice will help you gain mastery over it.

step 3: Clean your brush and, using the wet brush, gently soften the edges of the color. Avoid adding more water to your brush now, as it may make blending the colors challenging.

Blending Color Over Dry Color

When the first layer is dry, you can blend in two ways.

WET THE FIRST LAYER AGAIN and then blend the colors together. In this technique, you dampen the existing color before adding another color for blending.

step 1: Apply yellow color on the paper and make sure it is completely dry.

step 2: Using a number 8 round brush, moisten the surface of the yellow color. Remember not to use too much water during this process.

step 3: Apply red color onto the wet surface of the yellow color.

step 4: Using a wet brush, gently blend and soften the edges of the color.

BLENDING IN DRY COLOR. This is a crucial technique that I've frequently employed in this book.

step 1: Apply yellow color on the paper and make sure it is completely dry.

step 2: Apply red color over the dried yellow color.

step 3: Take a wet number 8 round brush and gently blend and soften the edges of the color.

BLENDING COLOR OVER WET COLOR

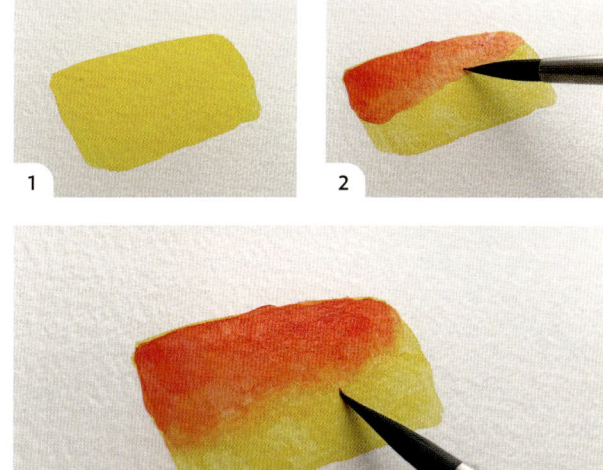

BLENDING COLOR OVER DRY COLOR

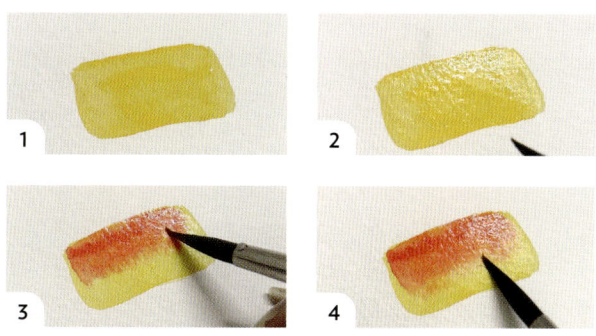

BLENDING IN DRY COLOR

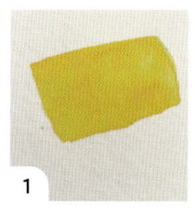
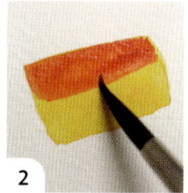
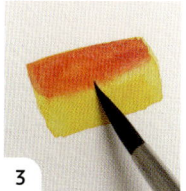

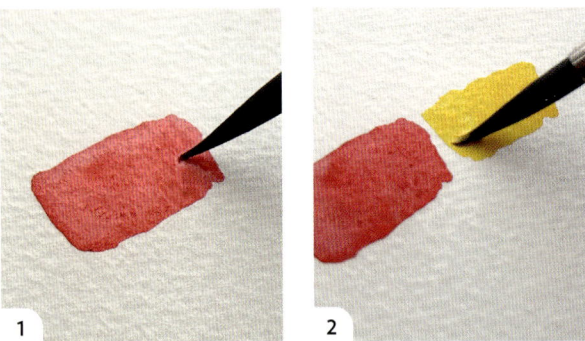
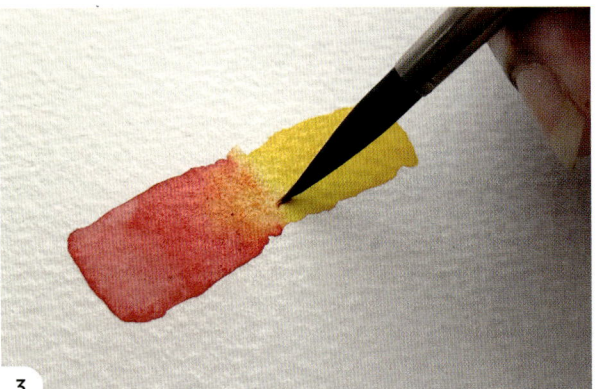
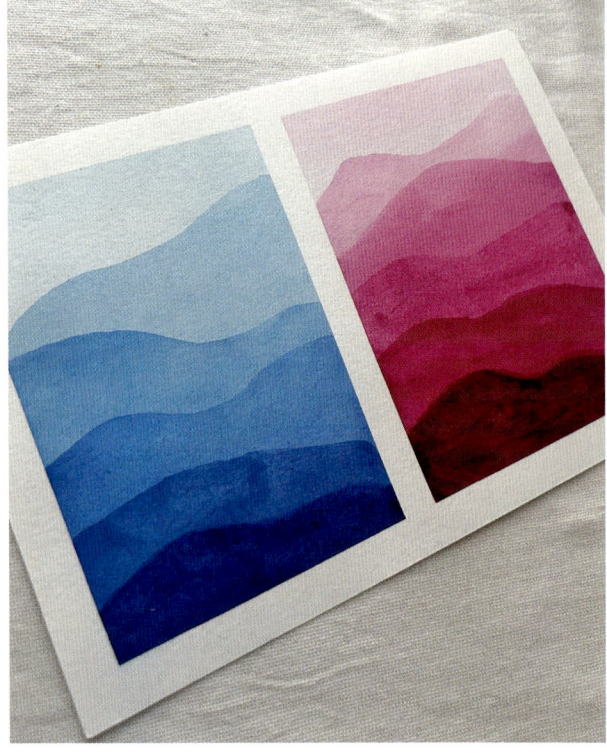

BLENDING ON DRY PAPER

Blending on Dry Paper

For this technique, make sure the paper is dry before you start applying colors.

STEP 1: Use a number 8 round brush to apply red color on one side.

STEP 2: Clean the brush, then pick up yellow color on the other side. Gently bring it towards the red color.

STEP 3: Using a wet brush, blend the colors in the middle with gentle upward and downward strokes.

LAYERING

We've already explored the wet-on-dry technique. Layering involves painting one color over another, but here's the key: each layer must be completely dry before you apply the next one. This technique, also known as glazing, allows you to enhance the intensity or change the temperature of a color.

In watercolor, you can use an infinite number of layers, but it's crucial to ensure that the previous layer is fully dry before adding the next. Failure to wait for the paint to dry may lead to unintentional blending of colors. In my example, I've crafted curvy mountains using pink and blue colors, showcasing how the intensity of colors escalates with each layer. I frequently employ layering in my paintings to boost the saturation and intensity of colors. As you progress through this book, you'll naturally become adept at layering, particularly when painting butterflies and flowers. Enjoy the learning journey!

COLOR THEORY

THE FASCINATING WORLD OF COLOR THEORY
explores how colors work and evoke feelings. In this
section I explain the simplicity of Primary, Secondary, and Tertiary colors; complementary hues; and
analogous blends. Let's make learning about colors a
vibrant adventure together!

COLOR WHEEL

The color wheel is the heart of color theory, where
all the secrets of colors come to life in a single wheel.
It's the basics of color theory creativity.

Primary Colors

Red, blue, and yellow are the Primary colors, and you
can spot them on the color wheel where I've placed them.

Secondary Colors

Secondary colors are created by mixing Primary colors.
When you combine red and yellow, you get orange.
Yellow and blue make green. Red and blue make violet.
See the spots on the color wheel in the picture.

Tertiary Colors

Tertiary colors come to life when Primary colors
mix with Secondary ones. Red and orange create

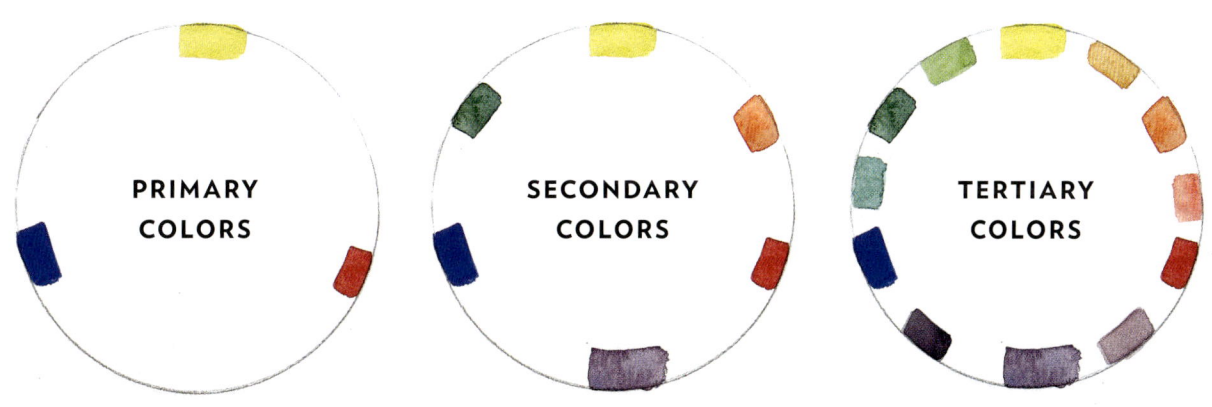

red-orange or vermillion. Yellow and orange make amber or gold. Red and violet produce magenta or maroon. Blue and violet make indigo or purple. Blue and green result in teal, turquoise, or aqua. Yellow and green yield lime or chartreuse.

Complementary Colors

Complementary colors are the ones opposite each other on the color wheel that have the strongest contrast and harmony:

- Blue complements orange
- Indigo complements amber
- Violet complements yellow
- Red complements green
- Magenta complements lime
- Vermilion complements teal

Analogous Colors

The term analogous suggests a close correspondence or similarity between colors. Analogous colors are groups of colors that sit next to each other on the color wheel, such as:

- Green, yellow, and orange
- Red, orange, and vermilion

Color TEMPERATURE

Color temperature in art helps determine whether a color appears warmer or cooler. Cool colors, like blues and bluish shades, are often used for painting cooler objects, such as the sea or the sky. On the other hand, warm colors, like yellows and reds, are ideal for painting light, fire, and warm objects. Placing warm and cool colors next to each other can draw attention to specific objects in a painting, and they complement

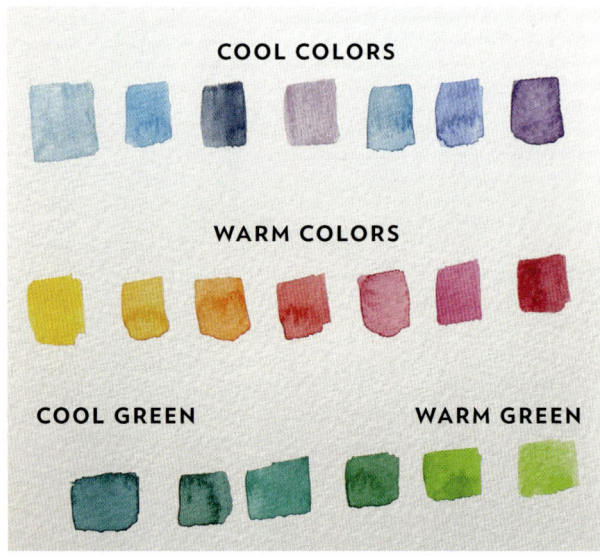

COLOR TEMPERATURE

each other well in larger artworks. Green is unique because it comes in both warm and cool tones; warm greens are used for painting fruits with a yellowish mix, while cool greens are used for painting water or grass. Understanding color temperature adds depth and nuance to the artist's palette.

Color INTENSITY

Color intensity, also known as color value, refers to the brightness or dullness of a color. In watercolor, it is influenced by the amount of water mixed with the pigment or color. A lower intensity is achieved by using a larger amount of water, while a higher intensity is attained with a smaller amount of water in the pigment mix. Understanding color intensity is crucial in this book, as it plays a significant role in painting transparently and is particularly useful for darkening specific areas during flower paintings. This knowledge will enhance our ability to control and manipulate colors for desired effects.

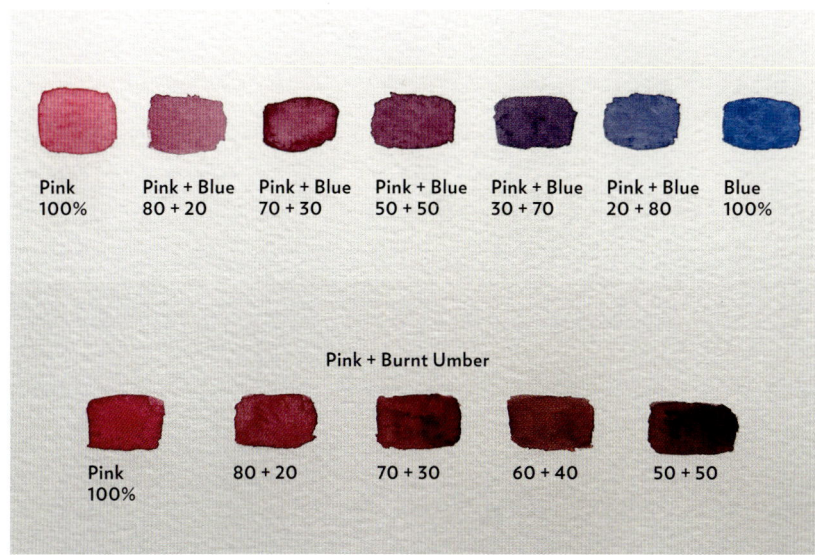

COLOR MIXING

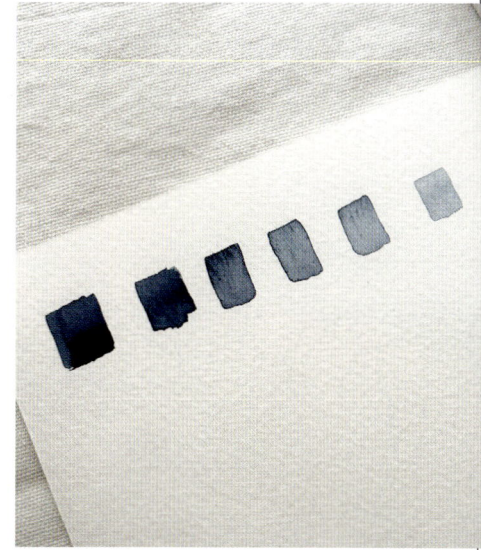

AMOUNT OF WATER WHEN MIXING COLORS

Color
MIXING

Color mixing involves combining two or more colors to create a brand-new hue. Throughout this book, I've emphasized the importance of understanding color proportions. When we alter the percentage of mixed colors, we can expect to witness the birth of entirely different colors.

You are free to mix the amount of colors as you wish. Here I have referred to the amount of colors in percentages. If you look at the example, you can see when you mix 20% Pink with 80% Blue you get a dusty blue color, whereas when you mix 20% Blue and 80% Pink, you get purplish pink color.

In the example, I demonstrated the transformation of colors by blending pink and blue, showcasing how different percentages yield diverse results. Additionally, I illustrated how incorporating burnt umber can intensify the color, creating a darker shade.

A helpful tip when using dark colors: when you mix any color with burnt umber, the warmth of burnt umber subtly influences the hue. However, once

applied to the painting, it seamlessly integrates with the underlying layers, resulting in a stunning and rich dark value.

Amount of Water When Mixing Colors

The amount of water used in watercolor mixing depends on the desired consistency. When picking up more color multiple times while mixing on a palette, the resulting mixture tends to be less watery, offering a higher-intensity pigment. Conversely, using only a tiny amount of color and mixing it with more water yields very watery and transparent colors. The water-to-color ratio is key to changing the value of the color, and this can be illustrated with an example using Prussian Blue. On the left side, the color has the darkest or highest intensity, and as more water is added, the intensity decreases. On the right side, the color has the lowest intensity or the lightest value. Understanding and experimenting with watercolor consistency contributes to achieving the desired effects in painting.

BUTTERFLY & FLOWER ANATOMY

I FIND BUTTERFLIES AND FLOWERS fascinating. In this section, I'll break down the different parts of each. It can be helpful to understand a bit about how butterflies and flowers are put together so that you can create your own beautiful paintings.

Butterfly ANATOMY

The anatomy details are intended for artistic purposes and may not adhere strictly to zoological accuracy.

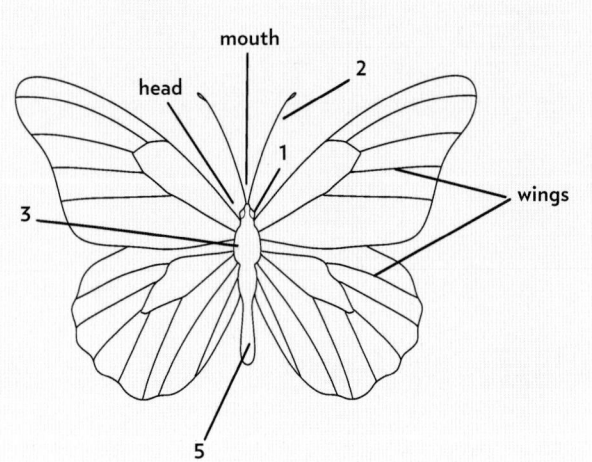

1 **EYES:** Butterflies have compound eyes made up of tiny units called ommatidia, each with a lens and light-sensitive cells. This allows them to create a full picture of their surroundings by combining inputs from each ommatidium.

2 **ANTENNAE:** The head also contains a pair of segmented antennae that act as sensors for a variety of purposes.

3 **THORAX:** The thorax is like a butterfly's engine, with muscles that make its wings move. It has three parts, and each part has legs. The second and third parts also have wings.

4 **LEGS:** A butterfly has three pairs of legs—forelegs, midlegs, and hindlegs. Each leg has three main sections.

5 **ABDOMEN:** The butterfly's abdomen has ten segments and is important for adult functions such as mating, laying eggs, etc. It can bend because the segments are connected by tissues.

Learn More about Wing Structure

Butterflies have two pairs of wings: the front ones (forewings) and the back ones (hindwings). These wings are delicate but have a strong network of tiny veins inside the wings that give them structure and keep them in shape. This vein pattern is the same for all butterfly species.

1 BASE AND APEX:

a BASE: The wing's base is where it connects to the body (thorax), at the inner end of the wing.

b APEX: The apex is the farthest point from the body, found at the outer edge of the wing.

2 COASTAL MARGIN: The wing's outer edge, meeting the butterfly's body. It's the shortest wing margin, closest to the body, and tends to be smoother and less detailed than the outer margin.

3 OUTER MARGIN: The wing's edge farthest from the body, displaying intricate patterns and designs. Shapes like scalloped edges or pointed tips vary among butterfly species.

4 INNER MARGIN: The wing's edge closest to the body, linking the coastal margin to the butterfly's body. It often features patterns or colors seamlessly connecting with those on the rest of the wing.

5 VEINS AND CELLS: The wings have a network of veins for support, with main thicker veins and smaller branching ones. The spaces between the veins are called cells, which can be filled with color to create the wing's pattern.

6 CELL AND DISCAL CELL: The spaces enclosed by veins are called cells. The discal cell is a specific cell in the center of the wing, surrounded by veins, and its shape can vary between species.

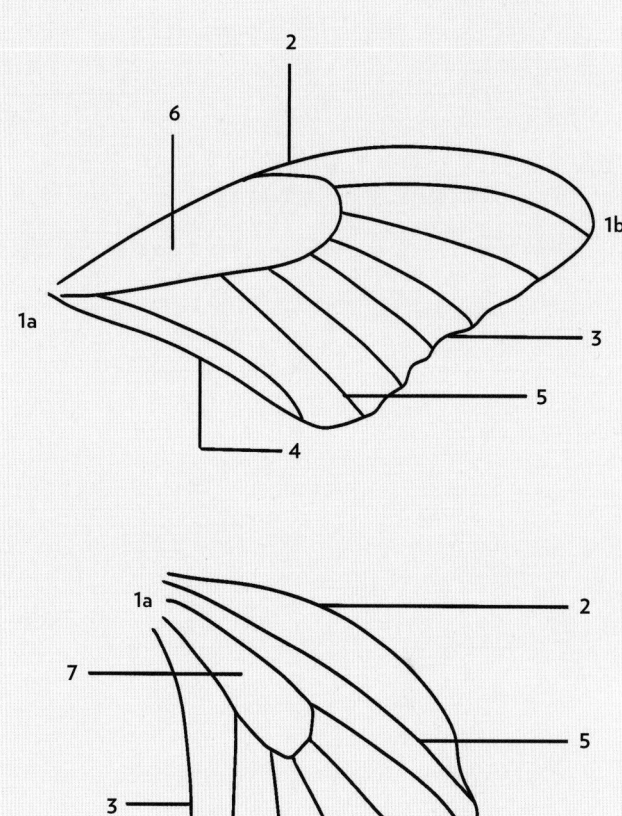

7 WING SHAPE: Butterfly species display various wing shapes, ranging from elongated and pointed to rounded.

8 WING TAILS: The extensions at the end of their hindwings, contributing to their distinctive appearance. These tails vary in shape and size among species.

Types of BUTTERFLIES

There are thousands of butterfly species, each having distinctive beauty and characteristics. Below are a few examples of different types of butterflies that represent just a fraction of the vast diversity within the world of butterflies. Their captivating colors and intricate patterns render them a truly fascinating group of creatures, highlighting the rich tapestry of nature's creations. In this book, I have created my own fantasy butterflies based in part on real butterflies but according to my imagination.

1 SWALLOWTAILS: Diverse family with tails, like the Eastern Tiger Swallowtail.

2 ADMIRALS AND EMPERORS: Includes Red-spotted Admiral, Hackberry Emperor.

3 WHITES AND SULPHURS: White or yellow species, such as the Cabbage White.

4 BRUSH-FOOTED BUTTERFLIES: Varied group like Painted Lady, often with reduced front legs.

5 MONARCHS: Known for orange and black wings, famous for long migrations.

6 HAIRSTREAKS: Named for hair-like extensions, like the Gray Hairstreak.

7 METALMARKS: Have metallic markings, like the Crimson Patch.

8 SKIPPERS: Known for rapid, darting flight, e.g., Silver-spotted Skipper.

9 BLUES: Small, vibrant blue butterflies like the Eastern Tailed-Blue.

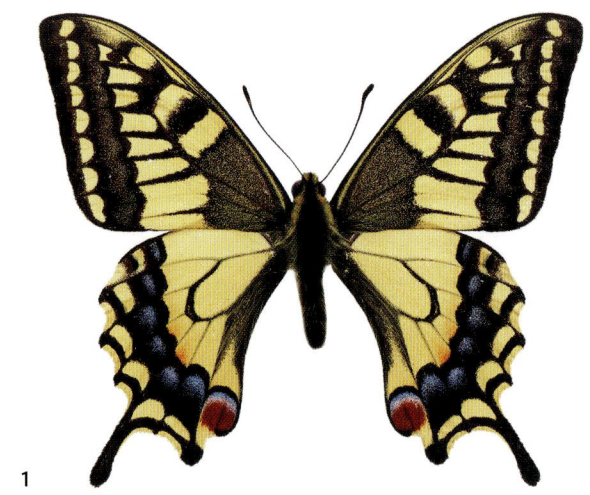

1

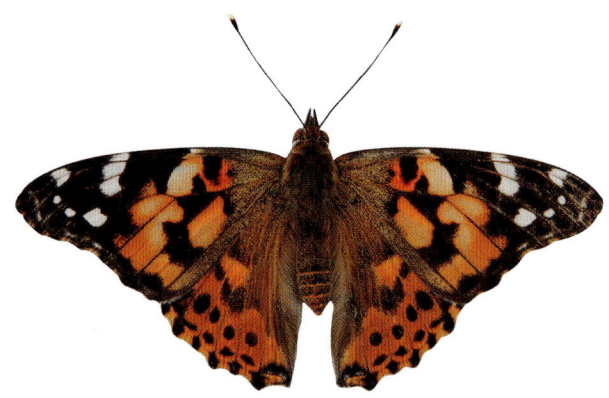

4

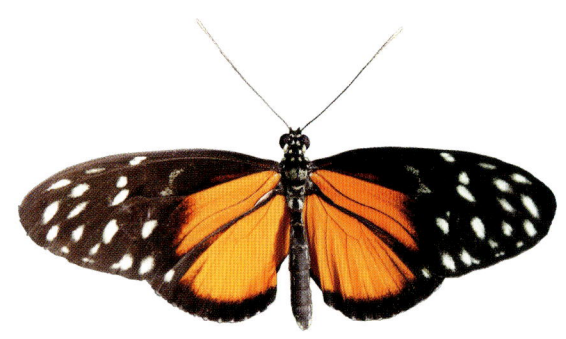

7

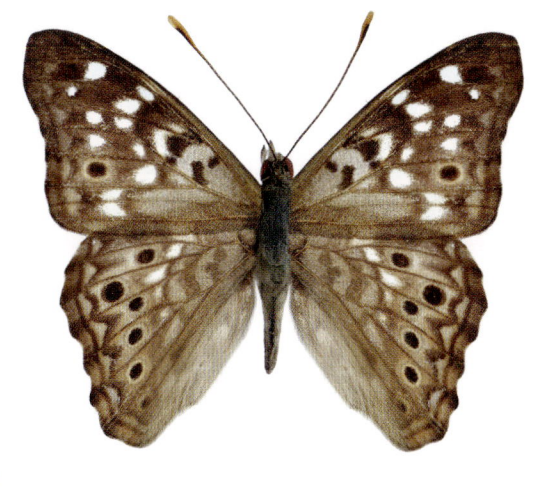

2

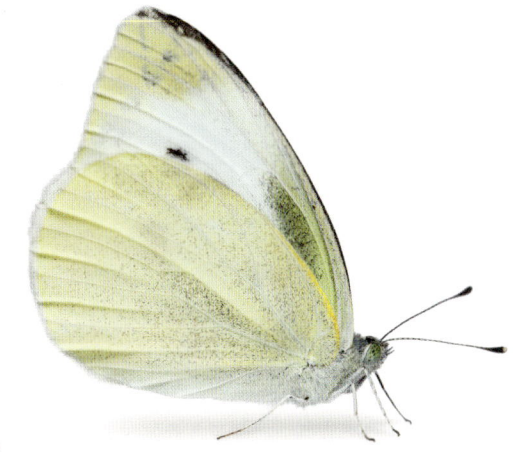

3

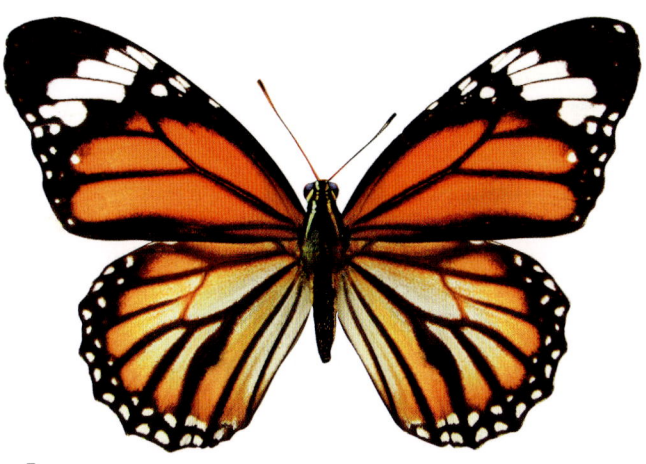

5

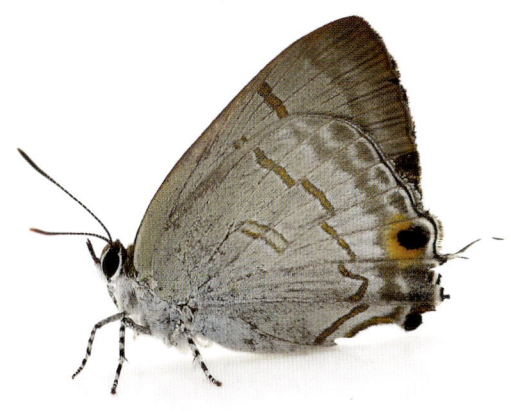

6

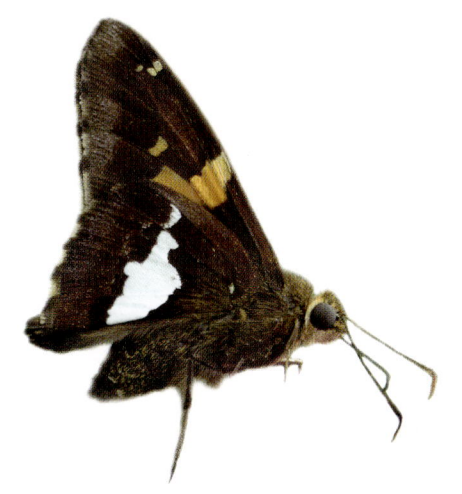

8

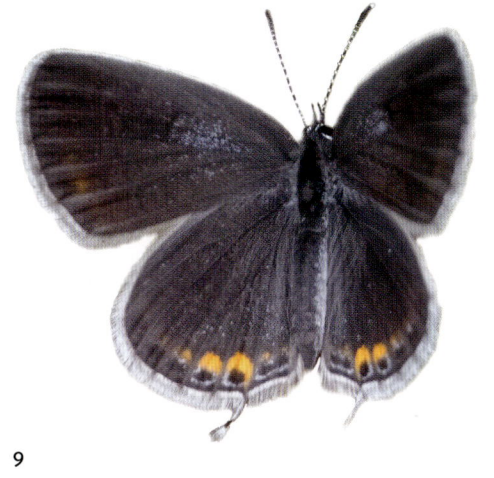

9

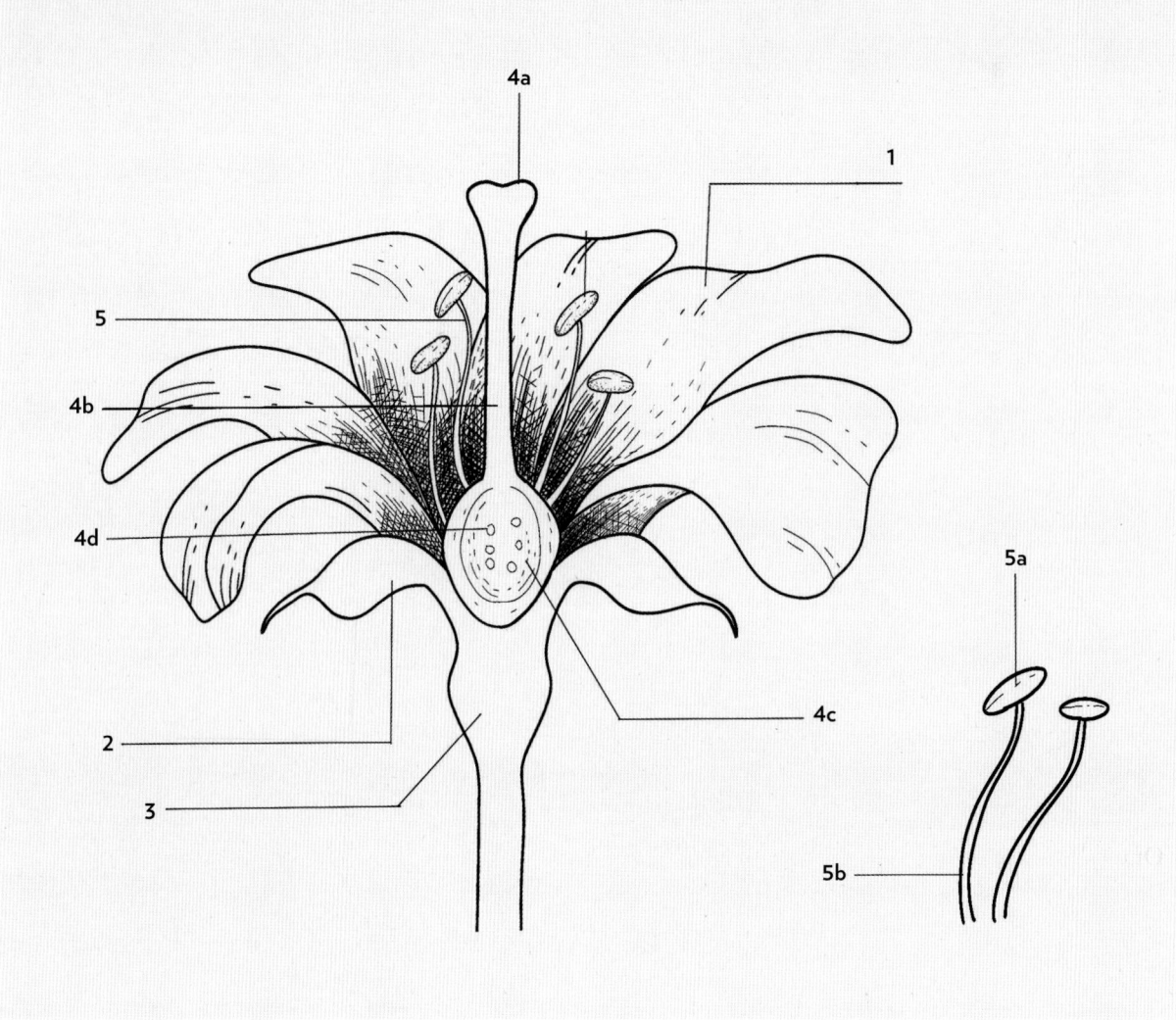

Flower
ANATOMY

Flower anatomy refers to the structure and arrangement of the essential parts within a flower.

1 PETALS: The colorful, often vibrant, outermost part of a flower that contributes to its distinctive appearance.

2 SEPALS: The small, leaf-like structures located at the base of petals in a flower. Their primary function is to protect the flower during its bud stage, offering a shield before it fully blossoms

3 RECEPTACLE: The thickened part at the base of a flower, providing support for and holding the major reproductive organs such as the stamen, pistil, and other floral structures.

4 PISTIL: The female reproductive organ of a flower, comprising four major parts:
  a STIGMA: The pistil's head that receives pollen.
  b STYLE: A slender, tube-like structure connecting the stigma to the ovary.
  c OVARY: The base of the pistil containing ovules.
  d OVULES: Flower's eggs housed in the ovary; upon pollen fertilization, they develop into seeds.

5 STAMEN: The stamen is the male reproductive organ in a flower, comprising two main parts:

a ANTHER: The top part that produces and releases pollen.

b FILAMENT: The slender stalk that supports the anther.

How to Paint
REALISTIC PETALS

Here is a quick how-to to create realistic looking petals. We'll be using this technique throughout the book.

Brushes

- Number 4 round brush
- Liner brush

Color Palette

- Cadmium Yellow
- Orange
- Red

STEP 1 Wet the petal area with water.

STEP 2 Use a number 4 round brush to apply Cadmium Yellow to the petal. Stroke from the bottom to the top for a smooth color application.

STEP 3 Apply bold and intense Cadmium Yellow strokes using the same round brush, following the previous bottom-to-top technique.

STEP 4 Apply Orange to create veins on the petal. Blend the colors smoothly to avoid sharp edges.

STEP 5 Use a liner brush to paint Red veins on the petal, allowing sharp edges for a higher contrast.

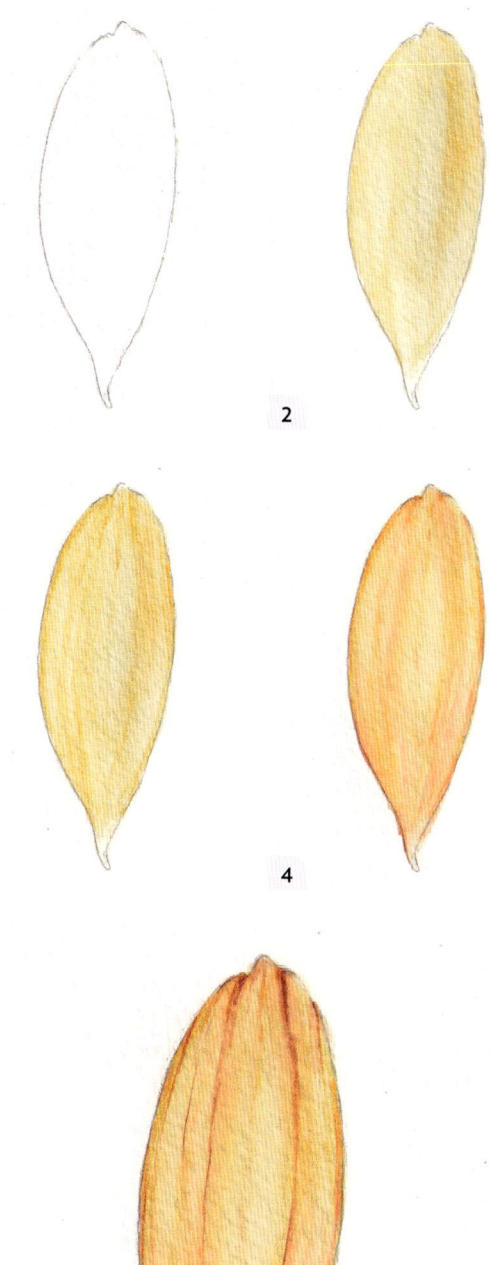

1

2

3

4

5

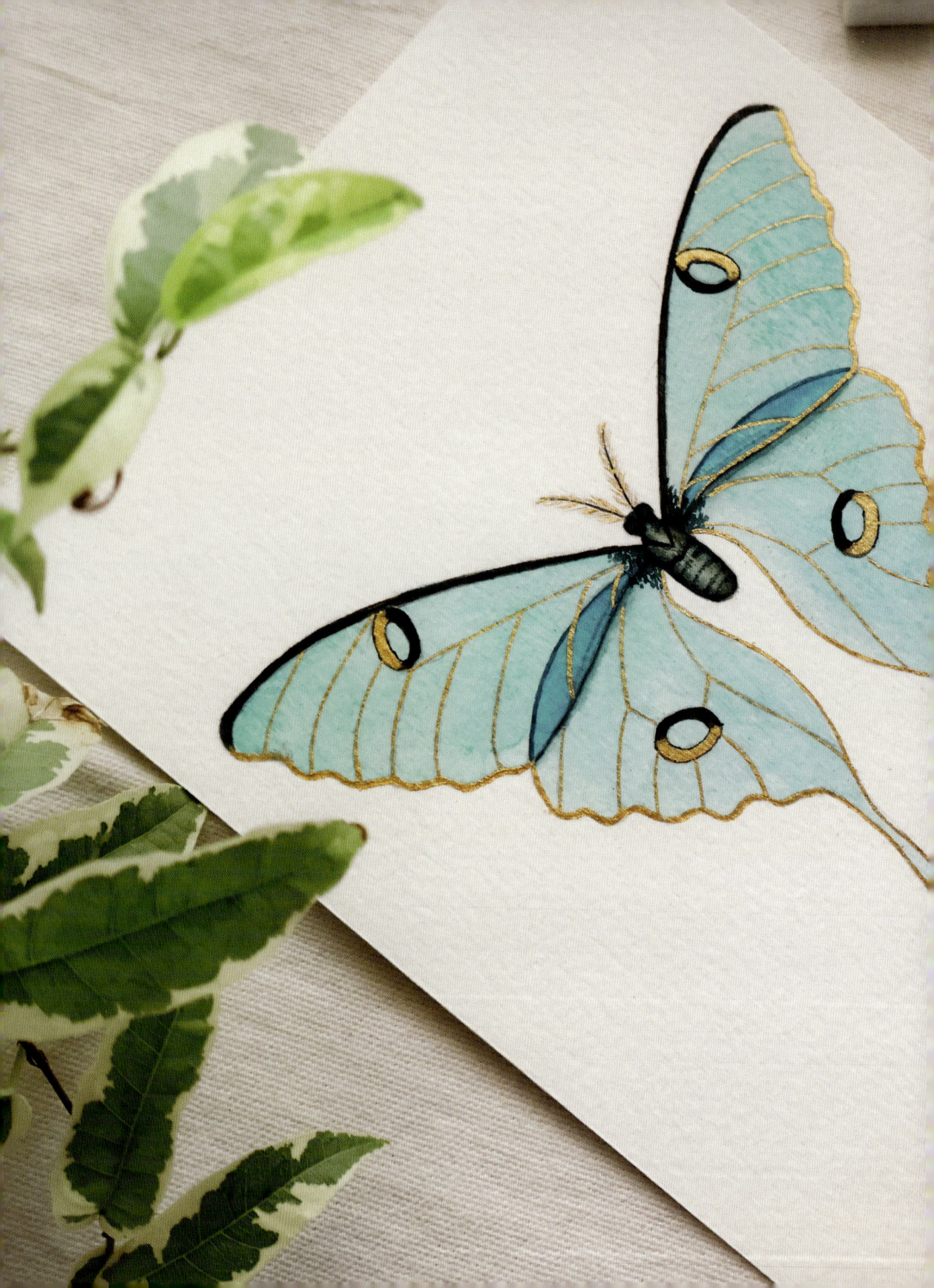

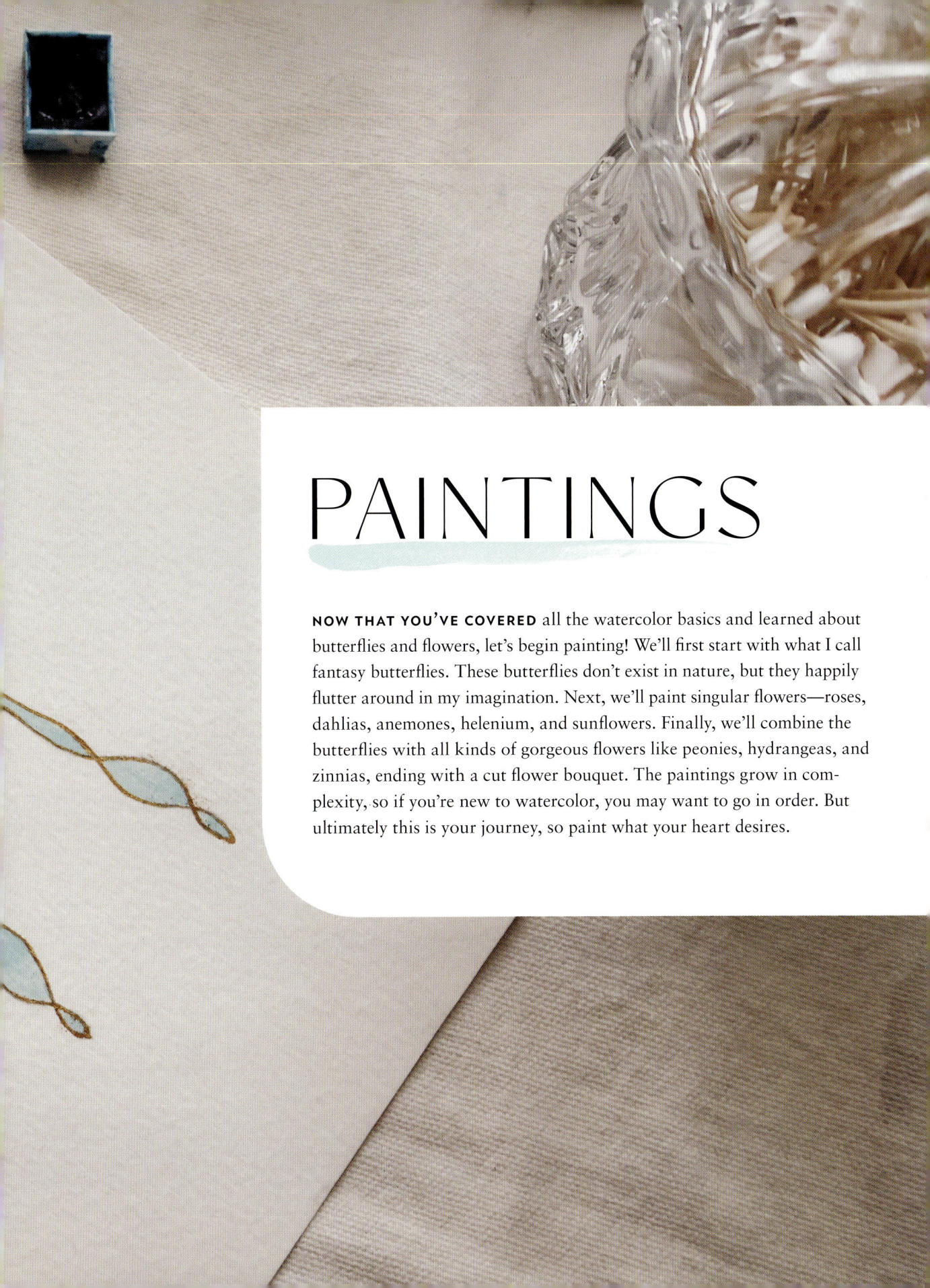

PAINTINGS

NOW THAT YOU'VE COVERED all the watercolor basics and learned about butterflies and flowers, let's begin painting! We'll first start with what I call fantasy butterflies. These butterflies don't exist in nature, but they happily flutter around in my imagination. Next, we'll paint singular flowers—roses, dahlias, anemones, helenium, and sunflowers. Finally, we'll combine the butterflies with all kinds of gorgeous flowers like peonies, hydrangeas, and zinnias, ending with a cut flower bouquet. The paintings grow in complexity, so if you're new to watercolor, you may want to go in order. But ultimately this is your journey, so paint what your heart desires.

THE YELLOW SUNSHINE

For this first paining, we'll be starting with simple techniques, with the only challenging aspects being layering and blending. By following these six steps, you can create a beautiful and detailed painting of a butterfly with realistic shading and vibrant colors. Remember to take your time and practice to achieve the desired level of detail and precision in your artwork. Let's embark on this easy yet visually delightful project! The three custom color combinations will help you achieve the desired shades for your artwork, particularly for creating the warm and vibrant hues of "The Yellow Sunshine!"

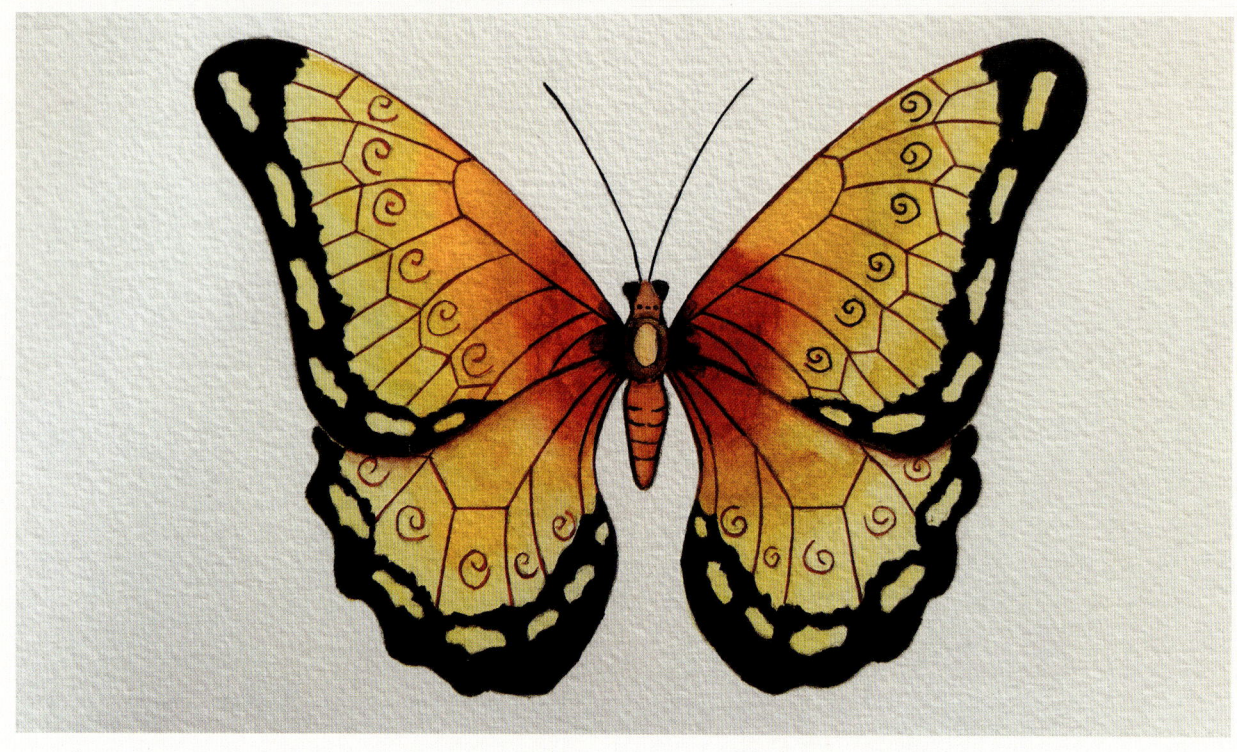

Brushes

Number 8 round brush
Number 4 round brush
Liner brush

Color Palette

Indian Yellow or Yellow

Red

Burnt Sienna

Burnt Umber

Black

Color Recipes

ORANGE: 50% Yellow +50% Red

DARK RED: 60% Red + 40% Burnt Sienna

DARK BROWN: 40% Red + 30% Burnt Sienna + 30% Burnt Umber

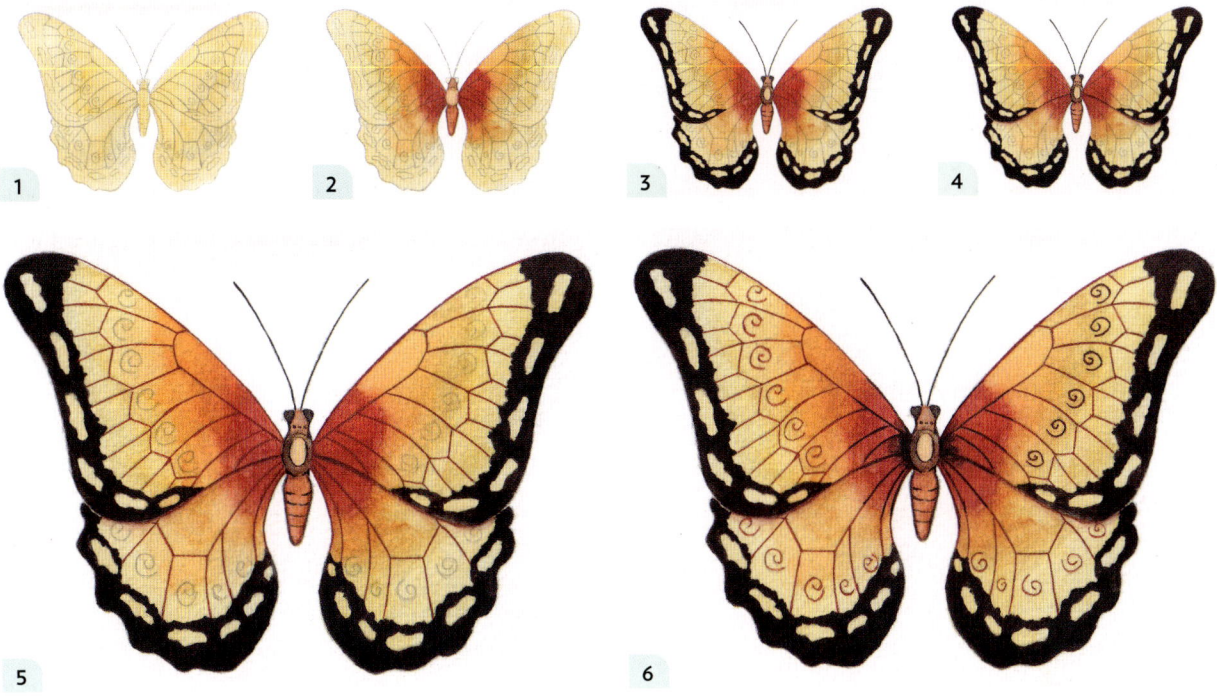

STEP 1: Base Coat with Yellow Color

Using the wet-on-dry technique, start applying a base coat of Yellow paint to the wings and body of the butterfly. This serves as the foundational color for your butterfly. After every step in this painting, allow the previous layer to dry.

STEP 2: Applying Variegated Wash

Use the variegated wash technique to create a gradient effect. Begin by applying the custom Dark Red paint near the body of the butterfly. Gradually transition into the custom Orange as you move outward towards the wings. Continue to apply Dark Red to the body to enhance its contrast with the wings.

STEP 3: Adding Black to Edges and Details

Using a number 4 round brush, add a thick layer of Black paint to the edges of the wings and use a liner brush to paint the butterfly's antennae and any intricate details on the body. This step helps define the butterfly's outline and gives it a more realistic appearance.

STEP 4: Creating Shadows with Dark Brown

To give depth and dimension to the butterfly, apply the custom Dark Brown paint to the areas where the top wings cast a shadow onto the second set of wings. This step adds a three-dimensional quality to your painting.

STEP 5: Painting Veins with Dark Red

Using a liner brush, carefully paint the veins on the wings with the custom Dark Red. These veins are essential for replicating the delicate and intricate patterns found on a butterfly's wings. Take your time to create fine, branching lines.

STEP 6: Darkening the Body and Final Touches

In the final step, darken the area of the wings near the body using the custom Dark Brown. This adds more contrast and depth to the butterfly's body and its immediate surroundings. Add the swirls on the wings to complete your butterfly painting.

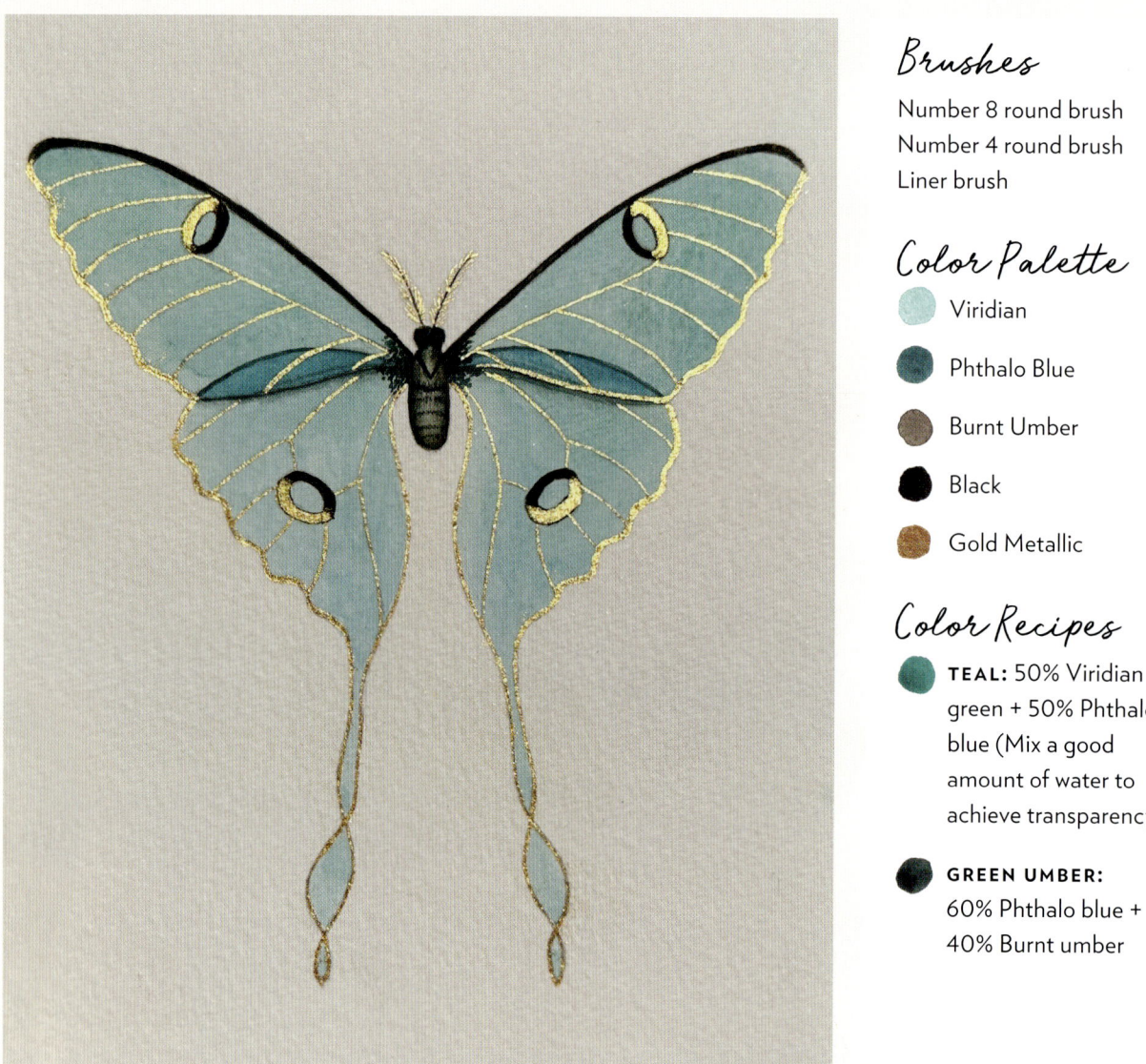

Brushes

Number 8 round brush
Number 4 round brush
Liner brush

Color Palette

- Viridian
- Phthalo Blue
- Burnt Umber
- Black
- Gold Metallic

Color Recipes

TEAL: 50% Viridian green + 50% Phthalo blue (Mix a good amount of water to achieve transparency)

GREEN UMBER: 60% Phthalo blue + 40% Burnt umber

THE GOLDEN TEAL

Creating art with transparency is like solving a delightful puzzle using colors. It's a challenge that stimulates the mind and promises an enjoyable journey. I hope you relish every moment of this creative process. These color combinations will enable you to capture the beauty of "The Golden Teal" while playing with the magic of transparency in your artwork.

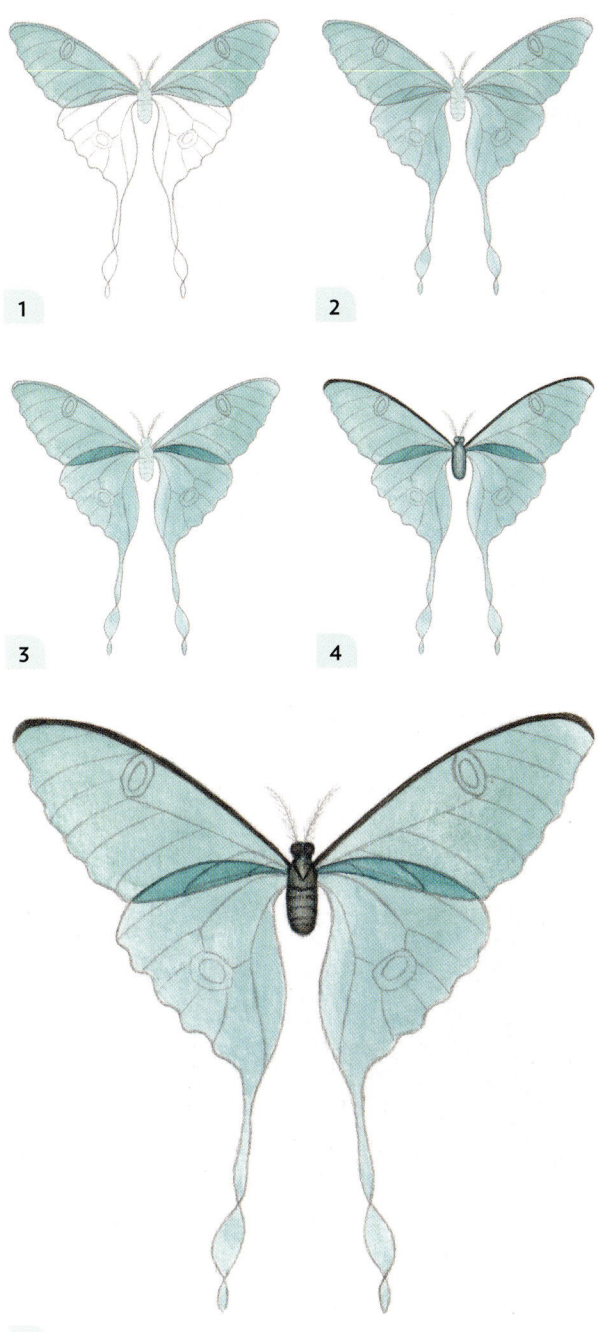

STEP 1: Top Wing Base Color

Use the wet-on-dry technique. To paint a see-through butterfly, follow the bold outline of each wing to make sure you don't miss any overlapping parts when filling in colors. Fill the top wings and the body with the transparent Teal color you've prepared, which is a mix of Viridian and Phthalo Blue. Allow the paint to dry naturally or speed up the drying process using a hair dryer. After every step in this painting, allow the previous layer to dry.

STEP 2: Bottom Wing and Tail

Once the top wing is dry, move on to the bottom wings and the tail. Pay attention to transparency by ensuring that each layer dries properly.

STEP 3: Overlapping Area

Fill the area where the top and bottom wings overlap using a mixture of Viridian and Phthalo Blue with less water. Create a gradient effect from the center of the body to the edges of the wings, enhancing the transparency of the butterfly.

STEP 4: Darker Shade on Top Portion

Apply the custom Green Umber shade, which is a mix of Phthalo Blue and Burnt Umber, to the top portion of the upper wings. Add dark shades to the body as well to bring depth and life to your artwork.

STEP 5: Body Details

Paint a small layer of the custom Green Umber with more water onto the body. When dry, add the details to the body. Paint the Green Umber on the edge of the body and blend it using a layering method. Darken tiny details and create a black or darker eye.

STEP 6: Black Color on Eye Shapes

Add a Black color to the eye-shaped details on the wings. Ensure that only half of the circle is painted, providing a distinct look.

STEP 7: Adding Shadows

Create shadows where the upper wings lie on top of the lower wings. Use Black color and blend it carefully to achieve a visually pleasing effect. Add Gold Metallic to the eye details on the wings to enhance their appearance.

STEP 8: Details at the Body-Wing Junction

Add detailed elements to the area where the wings meet the body using the dark shade. This step adds realism to the connection point of the wings.

STEP 9: Paint Gold Veins

Carefully use a liner brush to paint the gold colors onto the veins of the wings. This step imparts a magical and intricate effect to your butterfly.

STEP 10: Paint Gold Edges

Lastly, paint the edge of the wings with a thicker line of gold color. This final touch adds a touch of elegance to your transparent-winged butterfly.

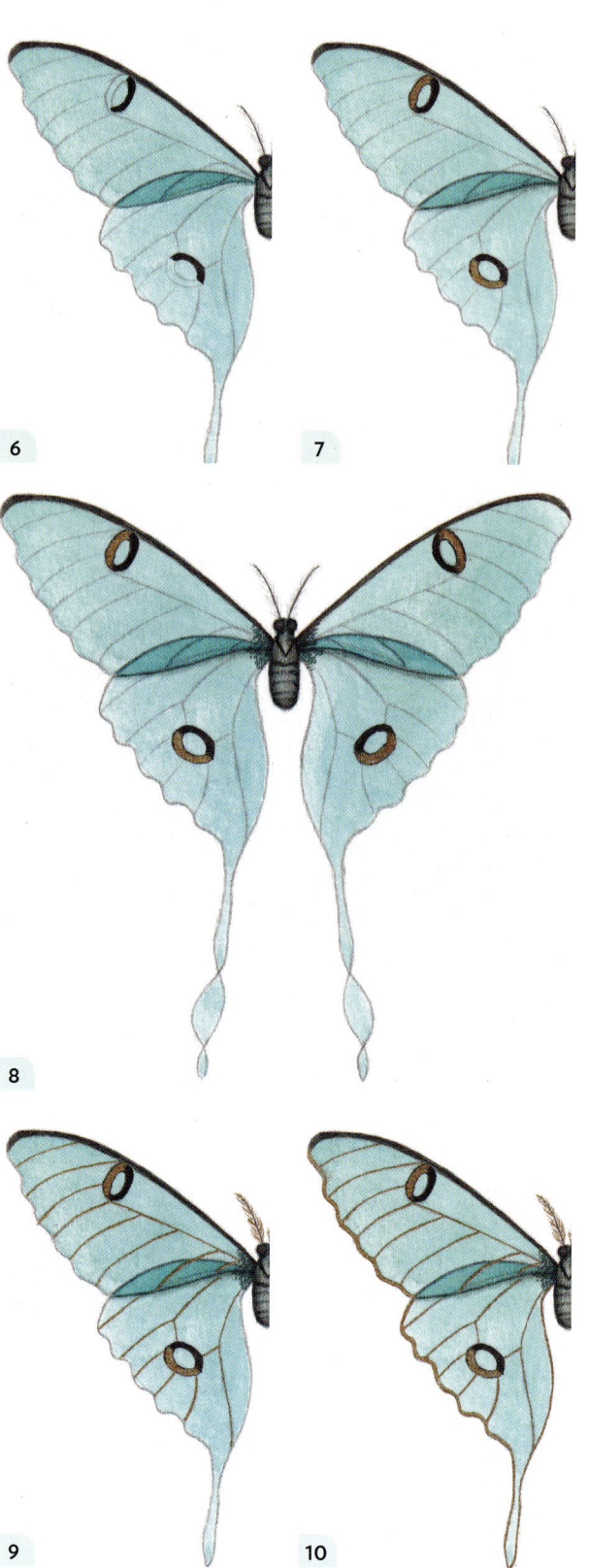

Brushes

Number 8 round brush
Number 4 round brush
Liner brush

Color Palette

- Cobalt Blue
- Green
- Prussian Blue
- Gold Metallic

Color Recipes

- **TURQUOISE BLUE:**
  95% Cobalt Blue +
  5% Green

- **DARK GREEN:**
  80% Turquoise Blue
  + 20% Burnt Umber

LONG-TAILED BUTTERFLY

This butterfly is similar to the Golden Teal butterfly but features three wings on each side, giving it a distinctive and elegant appearance. These color combinations will help you bring the Long-Tailed Butterfly to life, with its beautiful hues and shimmering metallic accents. By following these ten steps, you can create a stunning and intricate painting, showcasing its layered wings and the play of color and light.

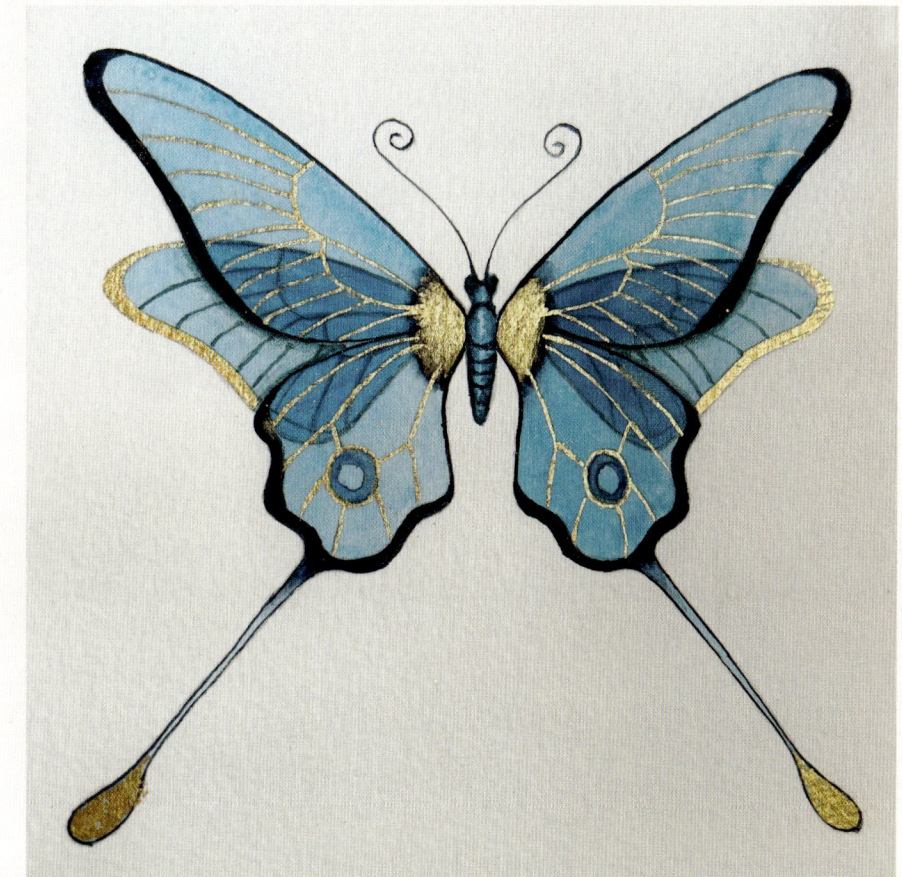

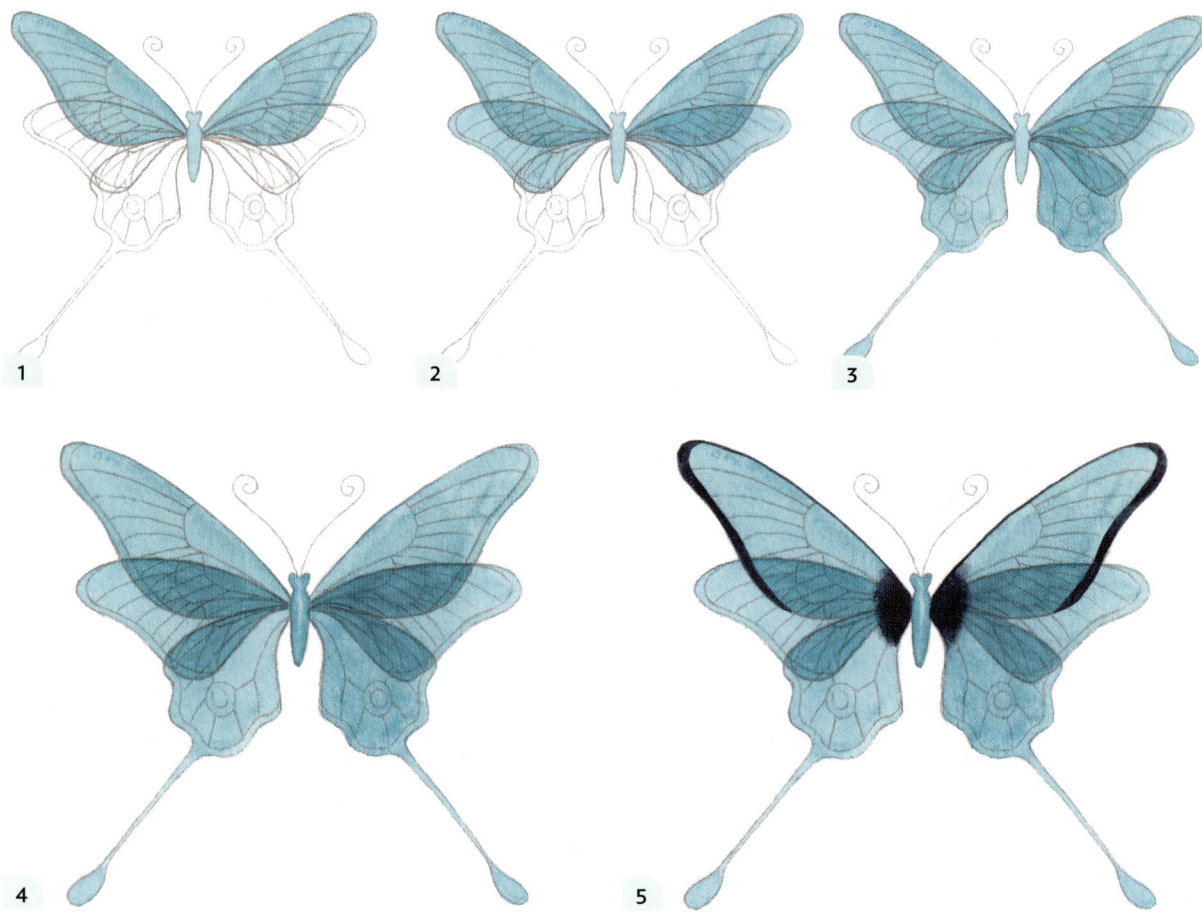

STEP 1: Top Wing Base Color

Use the wet-on-dry technique. Begin by painting the top wings of the butterfly with a beautiful custom Turquoise Blue using the number 8 round brush. These will be the uppermost wings. After every step in this painting, allow the previous layer to dry.

STEP 2: Middle Wing Coloring

Ensure that the top wings are completely dry, and then apply the same Turquoise Blue color to the middle wings using the same brush.

STEP 3: Bottom Wing Coloring

Once the middle wings are dry, again use the same brush to paint the bottom wings with Turquoise Blue.

STEP 4: Adding Overlapping Areas

Now use the number 4 round brush to darken the areas where the wings overlap to create a perfect transparency effect with Turquoise Blue (use less water and more pigment to get high intensity and darker value). This step adds depth and realism to the butterfly.

STEP 5: Prussian Blue Details

Apply Prussian Blue to the wings with the liner brush where the body of the butterfly meets the edges of the upper wings for added contrast. Add Prussian Blue to the edges of the top wings.

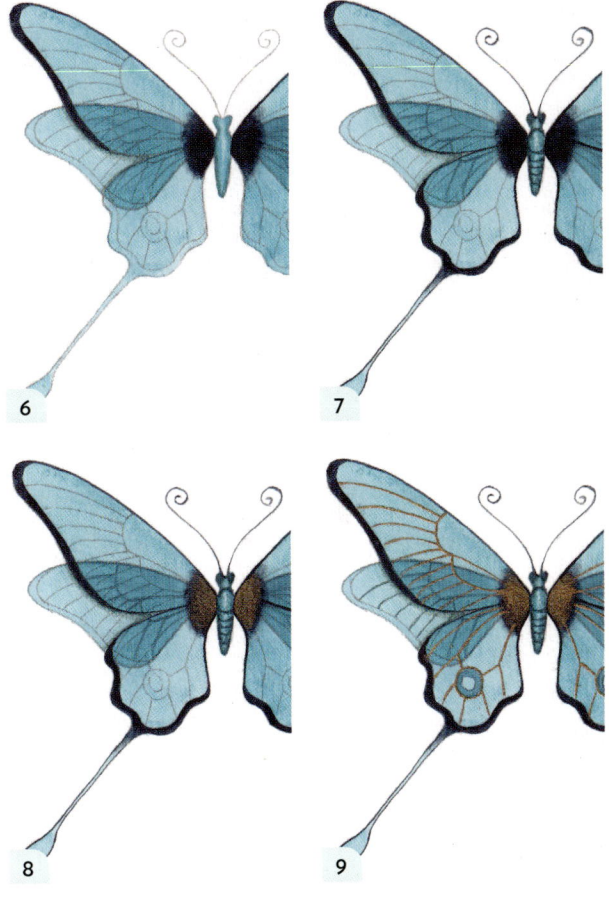

STEP 6: Creating Shadows

In this step, think of the upper and lower wings as layers on the middle wings. Using the liner brush with Dark Green, paint shadows of the top and bottom wings on the middle wings to add depth and dimension to the butterfly.

STEP 7: Adding Intensity and Details

Using a liner brush, apply a beautiful, thick layer of Prussian Blue to the edge of the top and bottom wing. Use Prussian Blue for adding details to the body of the butterfly, including the antennae.

STEP 8: Gold Metallic Accent

Using the number 4 round brush, introduce the Gold Metallic color to the darker areas near the body, creating a shimmering effect.

STEP 9: Painting Veins with Gold

Using the liner brush, paint the veins of the upper and lower wings with the Gold Metallic. This adds a touch of elegance and draws attention to the intricate details.

STEP 10: Final Touches

For the middle wings, paint the veins with Prussian Blue and add Gold Metallic accents to the edges using a liner brush. Highlight the tail of the wings with the Gold. With these finishing touches, you've completed your gorgeous fantasy butterfly.

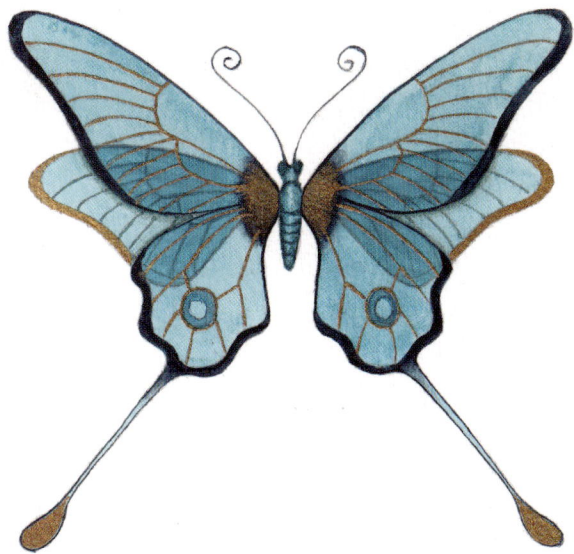

THE PINK BEAUTY

The Pink Beauty is an intricate and captivating subject, resembling a puzzle.
However, this artistic puzzle can be elegantly solved using colors to unveil its
charm. I find it beautiful and festive, perfect to gift during the holidays.

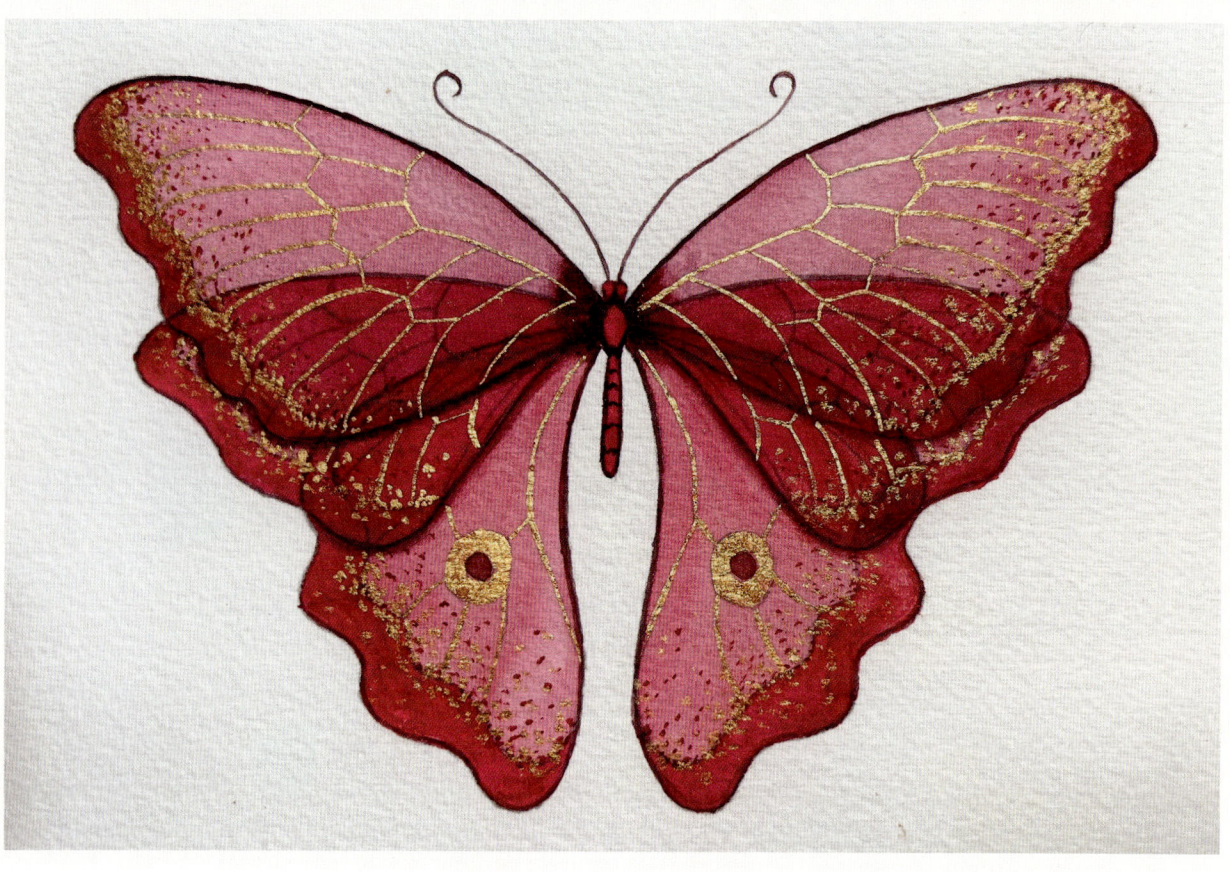

Brushes

Number 8 round brush
Number 4 round brush
Liner brush

Color Palette

Pink

Burnt Sienna

Burnt Umber

Gold Metallic

Color Recipes

DARK PINK: 80% Pink +
20% Burnt Sienna

DARK BURGUNDY: 50% Pink
+ 50% Burnt Umber

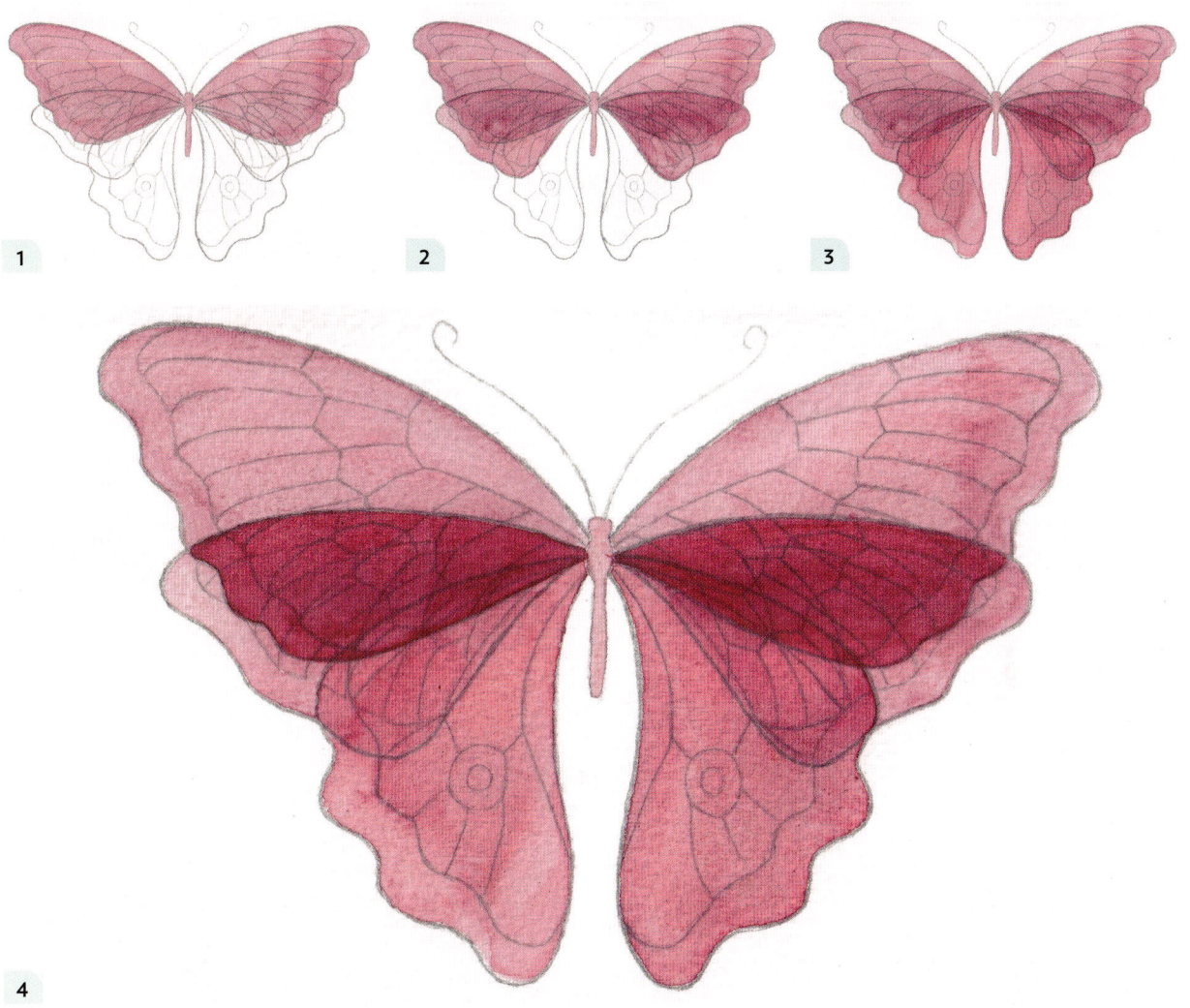

STEP 1: Top Wing Base Color

Use the wet-on-dry technique. Start by painting the top wings of the butterfly with Pink using your number 8 round brush. After every step in this painting, allow the previous layer to dry.

STEP 2: Middle Wing Color

Once the top wings are completely dry, proceed to paint the middle wings with Pink using the number 8 round brush. You need the top wings to be dry to create the layered paint effect.

STEP 3: Bottom Wing Color

After the middle wings dry, apply Pink to the bottom wings, carefully following the design. Use the same number 8 round brush.

STEP 4: Overlapping Areas—Upper Wings

Enhance the areas where the upper wings overlap with high-intensity Pink color with your number 4 round brush. This step requires more pigment and less water for a vibrant effect.

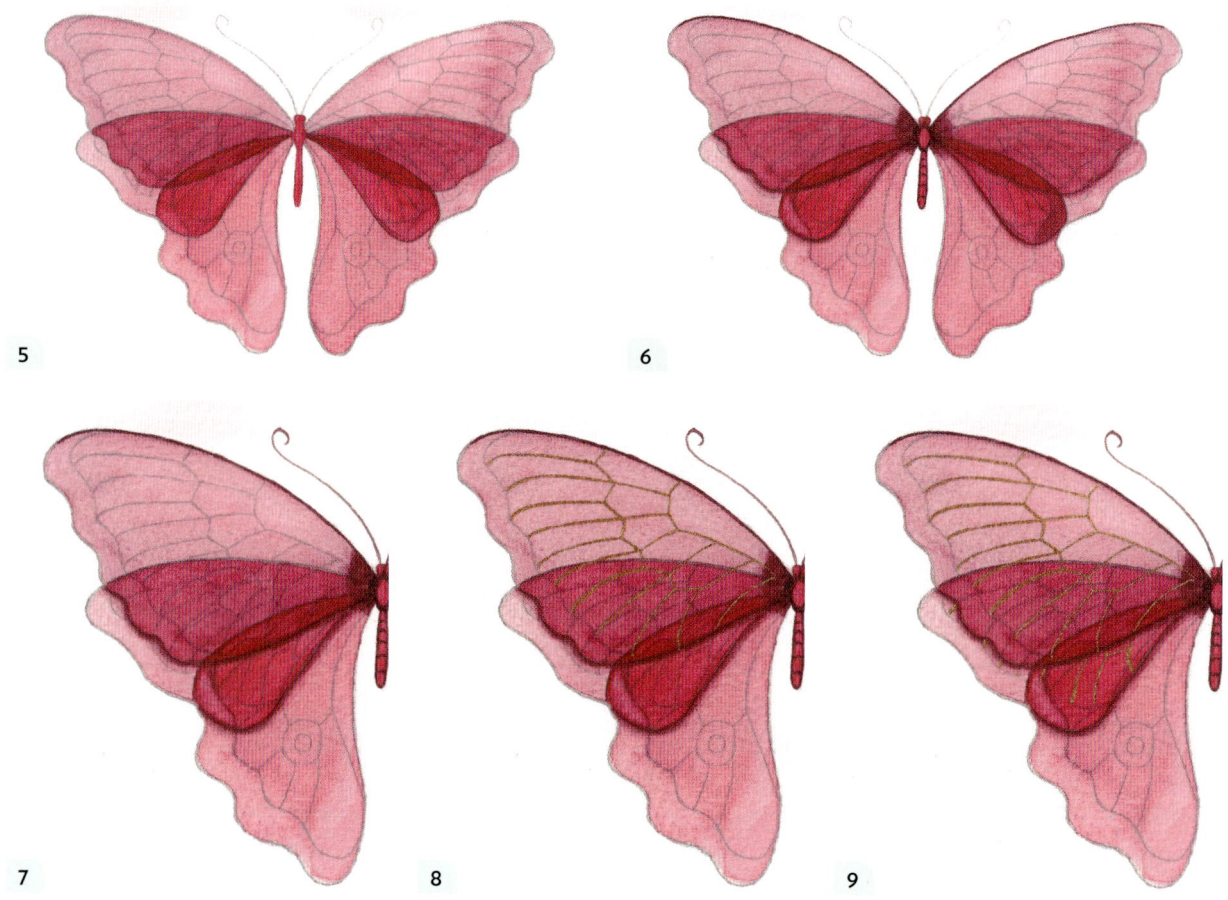

5

6

7

8

9

STEP 5: Overlapping Areas—Bottom Wings

Similarly, add high-intensity Pink color to the overlapping areas of the bottom wings, maintaining the vibrant effect.

STEP 6: Adding Dark Burgundy Details

Apply your custom Dark Burgundy color to the top section of the top wings with a liner brush. Additionally, add this color to the body to create intricate details and definition.

STEP 7: Antennae Detailing

Paint the antennae using a liner brush in the custom Dark Pink color to make them stand out and add a touch of elegance.

STEP 8: Golden Veins on Upper Wings

Paint the veins on the upper wings with Gold Metallic using a liner brush. This adds a beautiful, luxurious detail to the butterfly.

STEP 9: Golden Details on Second Wings

Using a liner brush, apply Gold Metallic details to the veins of the middle wings to complement the overall design.

STEP 10: Golden Details on Bottom Wings

Continue by painting the Gold Metallic details to the veins of the bottom wings, maintaining consistency in the artwork.

STEP 11: Edges with High-Intensity Pink

Using a number 4 round brush, apply high-intensity Pink (more pigment and less water) to the edges of each wing, emphasizing the contours of the butterfly.

STEP 12: Bounce Techniques for Gold and Pink Dots

To create a festive and dynamic appearance, use the bounce technique (see page 11) to fill the edges of the butterfly wings with Gold and Pink dots using a number 4 round brush. This step adds a sense of celebration and joy to your artwork.

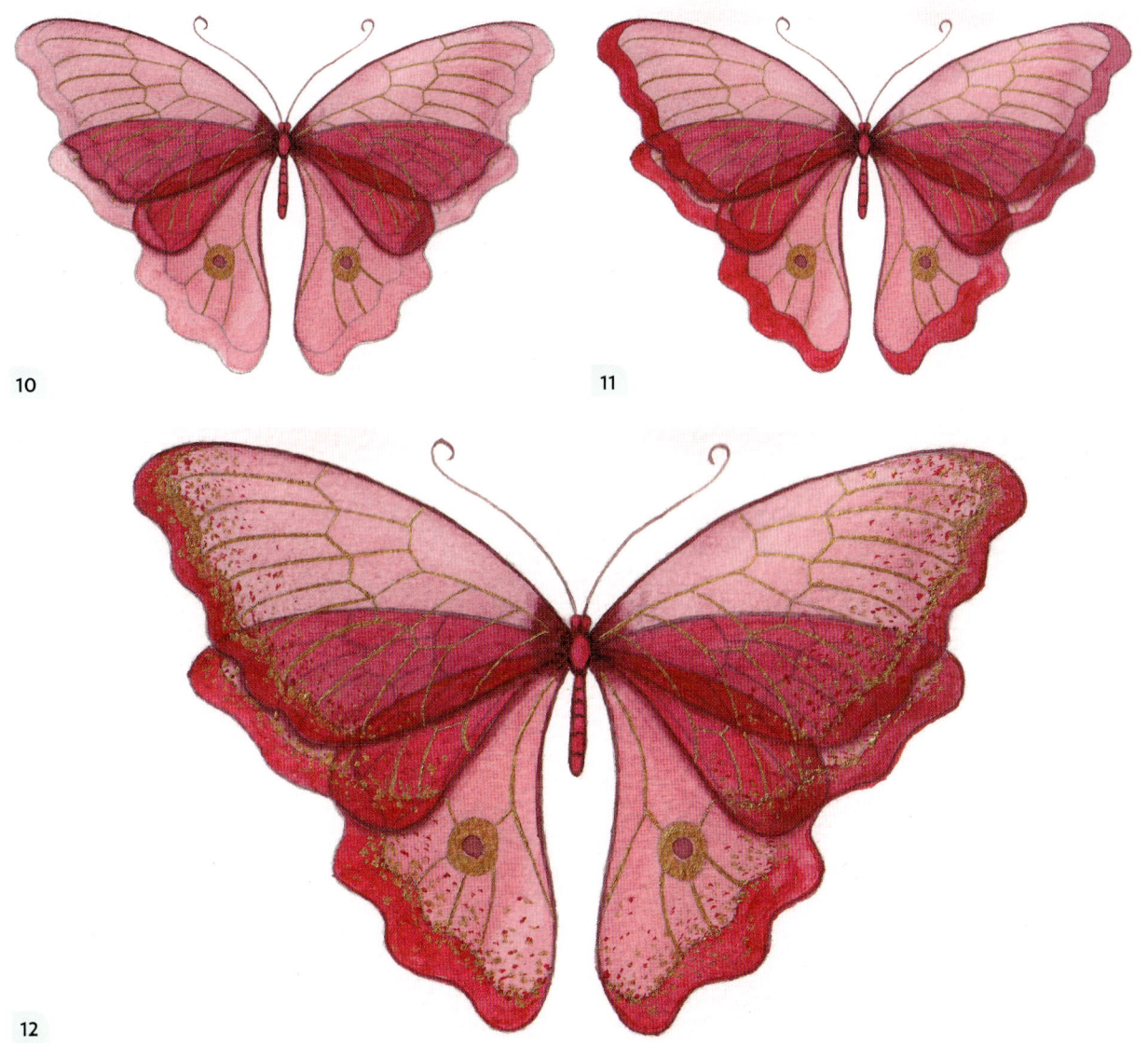

10

11

12

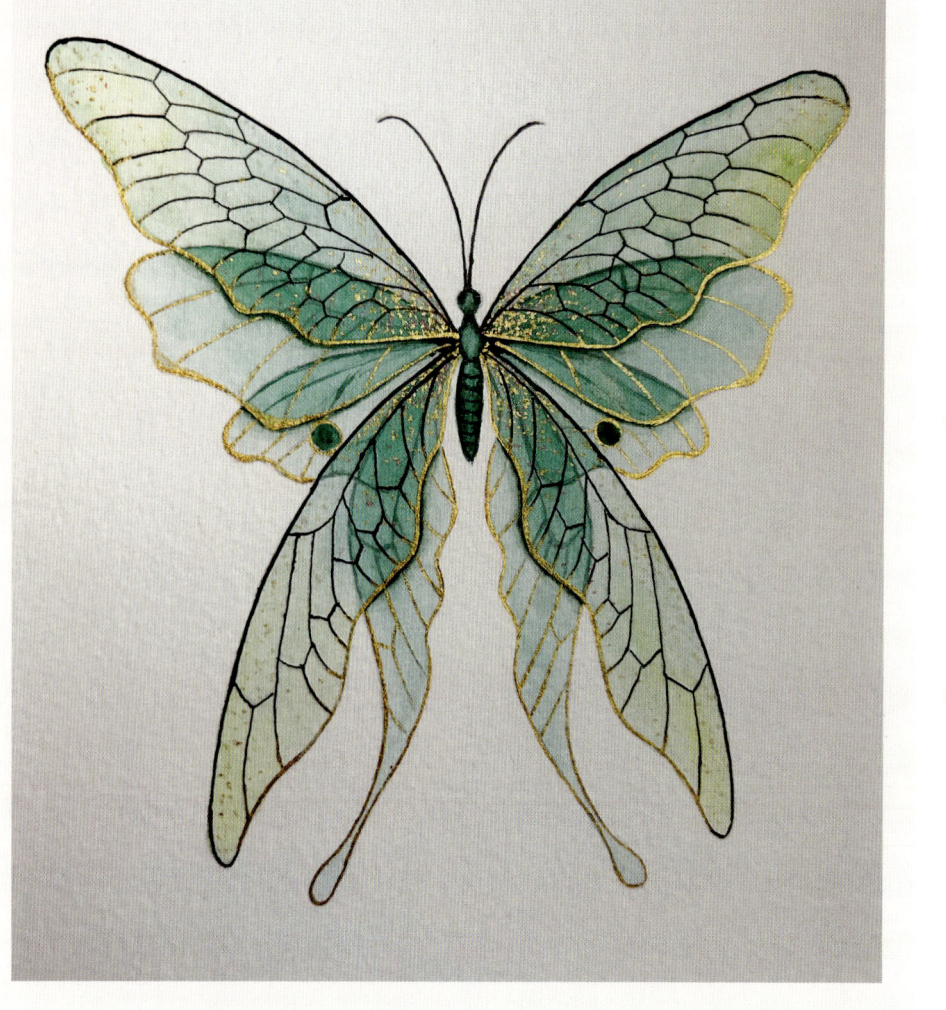

Brushes

Number 8 round brush
Number 4 round brush
Liner brush

Color Palette

- Viridian
- Cobalt Blue
- Cadmium Yellow
- Burnt Umber
- Black
- Gold Metallic

Color Recipes

MALACHITE GREEN: 95% Viridian + 5% Cobalt Blue

DARK GREEN: 80% Malachite Green + 20% Burnt Umber

THE MAGICAL FANTASY

This magical butterfly has five delicate wings on each side, giving off a transparent and enchanting vibe. There are more steps involved in this final, stand-alone butterfly than the previous projects, but you'll practice the same layering and blending techniques as before. Let the magical fantasy unfold on your canvas.

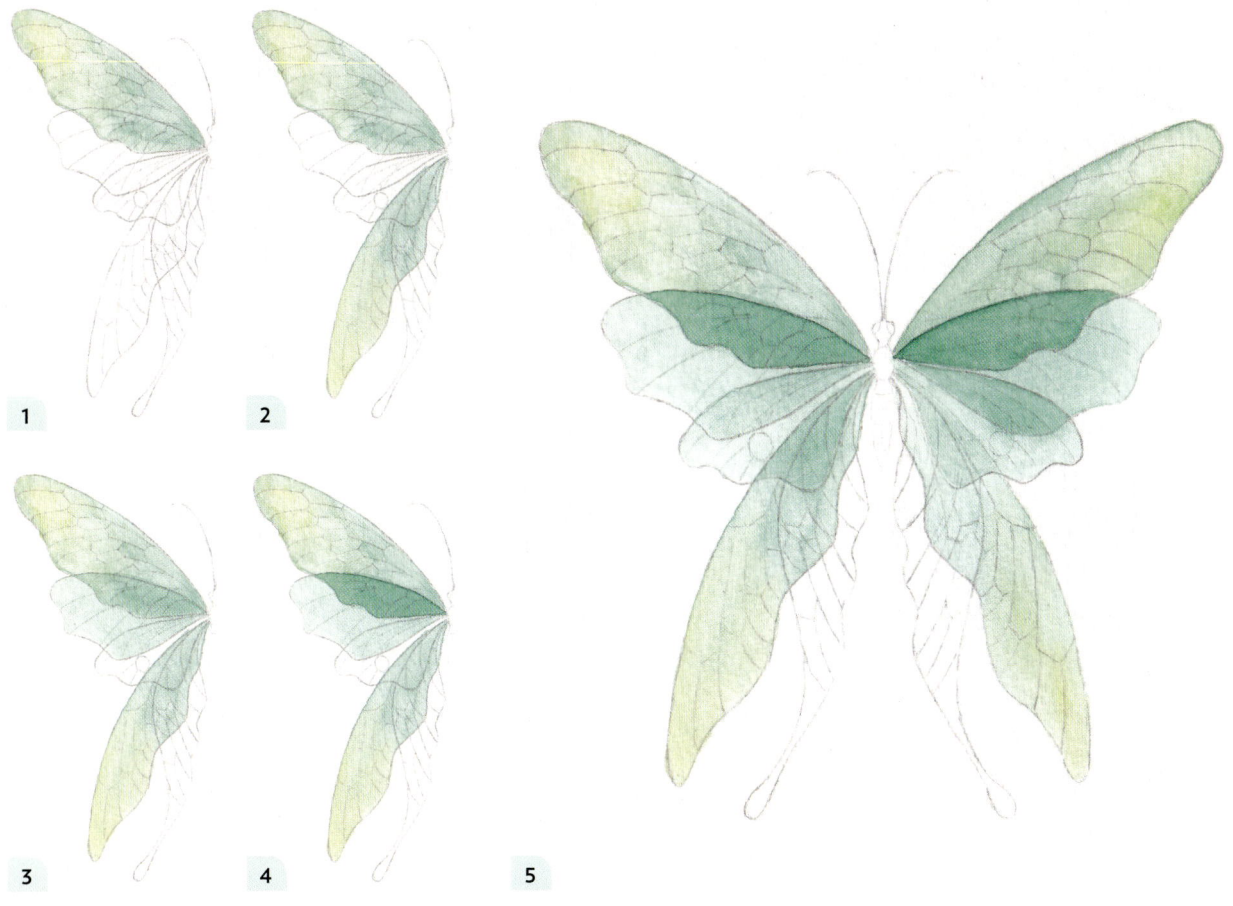

STEP 1: Base Colors for Top Two Wings

Using the wet-on-dry technique, apply highly diluted custom Malachite Green on the top two wings, transitioning to Cadmium Yellow towards the ends. Gently blend both colors using a number 8 round brush for Malachite Green and number 4 for Cadmium Yellow. After every step in this painting, allow the previous layer to dry.

STEP 2: Colors for Fourth Wing

Repeat the wet-on-dry technique, applying highly diluted Malachite Green on the fourth wing and Cadmium Yellow on the edges. Blend the colors gently using the round brushes.

STEP 3: Detailing the Second Wings

Apply highly diluted Malachite Green to the entire second set of wings, using the smaller number 4 round brush.

STEP 4: Intensifying Overlapping Areas

Apply high-intensity Malachite Green to the overlapping area between the first and second wings, using a number 4 round brush.

STEP 5: Delicate Touch for Third Wings

Paint highly diluted Malachite Green to the third set of wings using a number 8 round brush.

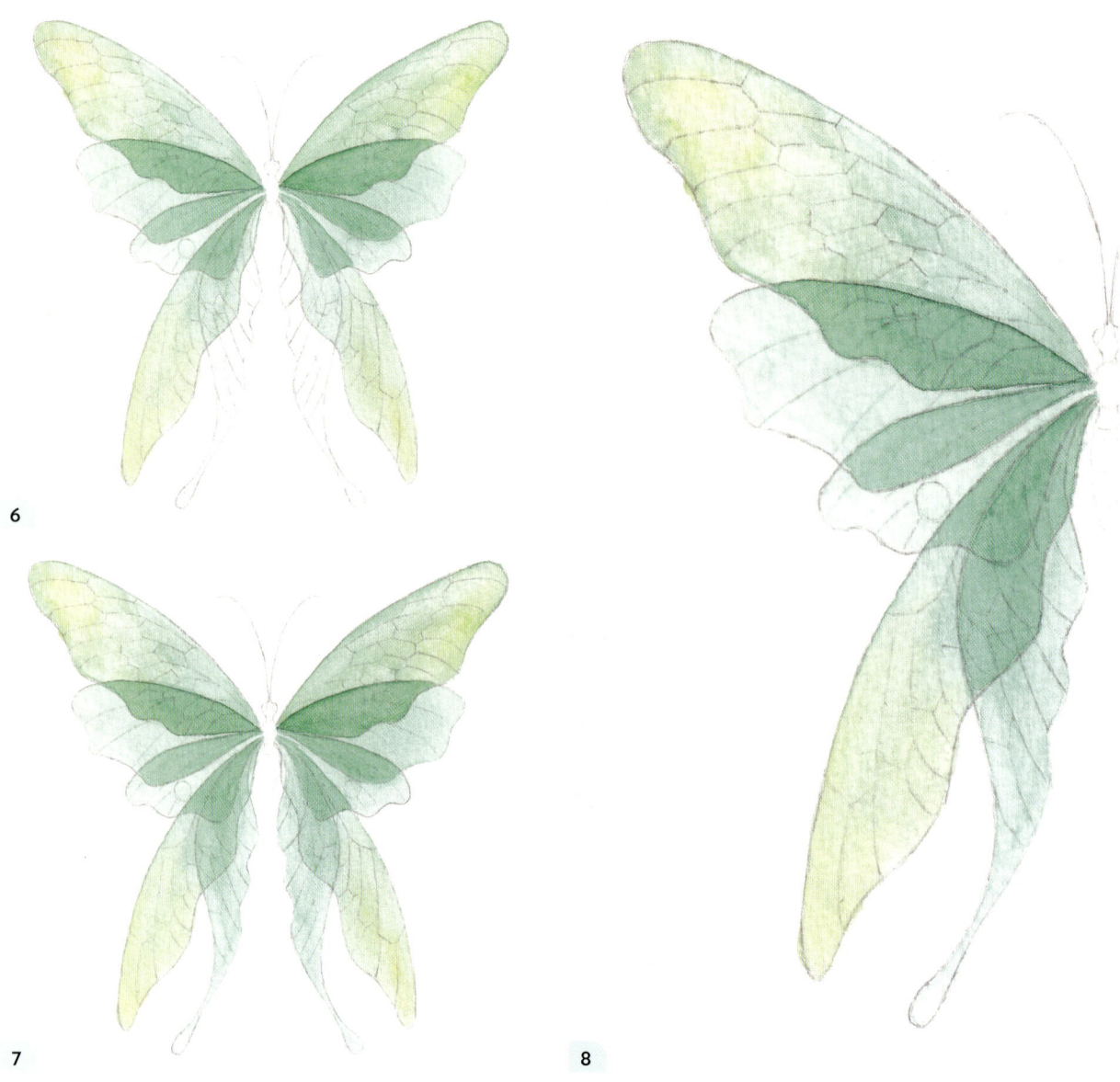

STEP 6: Adding Dark Values to Overlapping Areas
Apply a darker shade of Malachite Green to the overlapping areas between wings two and three, and between the third and fourth wings, using the small number 4 round brush.

STEP 7: Detailing the Fifth Wings
Apply highly diluted Malachite Green to the fifth set of wings, using a number 8 round brush.

STEP 8: Enhancing Overlapping Areas
Apply high-intensity Malachite Green to the overlapping areas between the fourth and fifth wings, using a number 4 round brush.

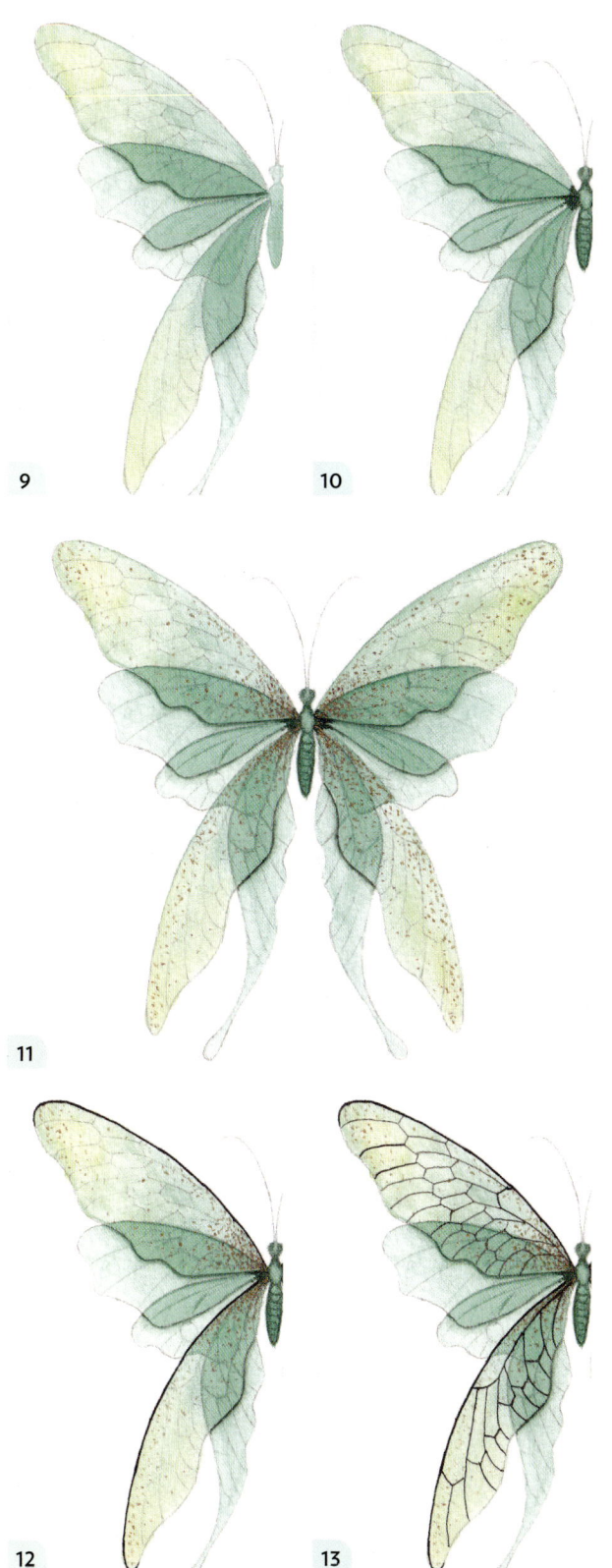

STEP 9: Adding Shadows and Body Details

Use Dark Green under each wing to create shadows and apply Malachite Green to the body of the butterfly. Use a liner brush for precision.

STEP 10: Vein Details

Paint lines with a liner brush using high-intensity Malachite Green to add details to the veins of the butterfly. Use Dark Green for details around the body.

STEP 11: Add Metallic Dots

Using a liner brush, apply Gold Metallic and Metallic Pink dots to the first and fourth set of wings. If you only have Gold Metallic, use that color for this step.

STEP 12: Outline with Black

With a liner brush, draw black lines along the top edge of the first and fourth set of wings, adding definition.

STEP 13: Paint Veins in Black

Using a liner brush, carefully paint all the veins of the first and fourth set of wings with black, enhancing the intricate details.

STEP 14: Apply Gold Metallic on the Bottom

Using a liner brush, apply Gold Metallic on the bottom side of the first and fourth set of wings, providing a touch of shine to these areas.

STEP 15: Add Golden Lines to Second Wings

Using a liner brush, apply golden lines to the veins and the outer line of the second set of wings, enhancing their elegance and detail.

STEP 16: Apply Golden Lines to Third Wings

With a liner brush, add golden lines to the veins and the outer line of the third set of wings, bringing a touch of brilliance to this set.

STEP 17: Enhance Fifth Wings with Golden Lines

Using a liner brush, give golden lines to the veins and the outer line of the fifth set of wings, adding a final layer of radiance and intricacy to complete the butterfly's enchanting appearance.

STEP 18: Final Touches

Complete the masterpiece by giving the antennae a black color with a liner brush and filling the eye of the third wing with high-intensity Malachite Green.

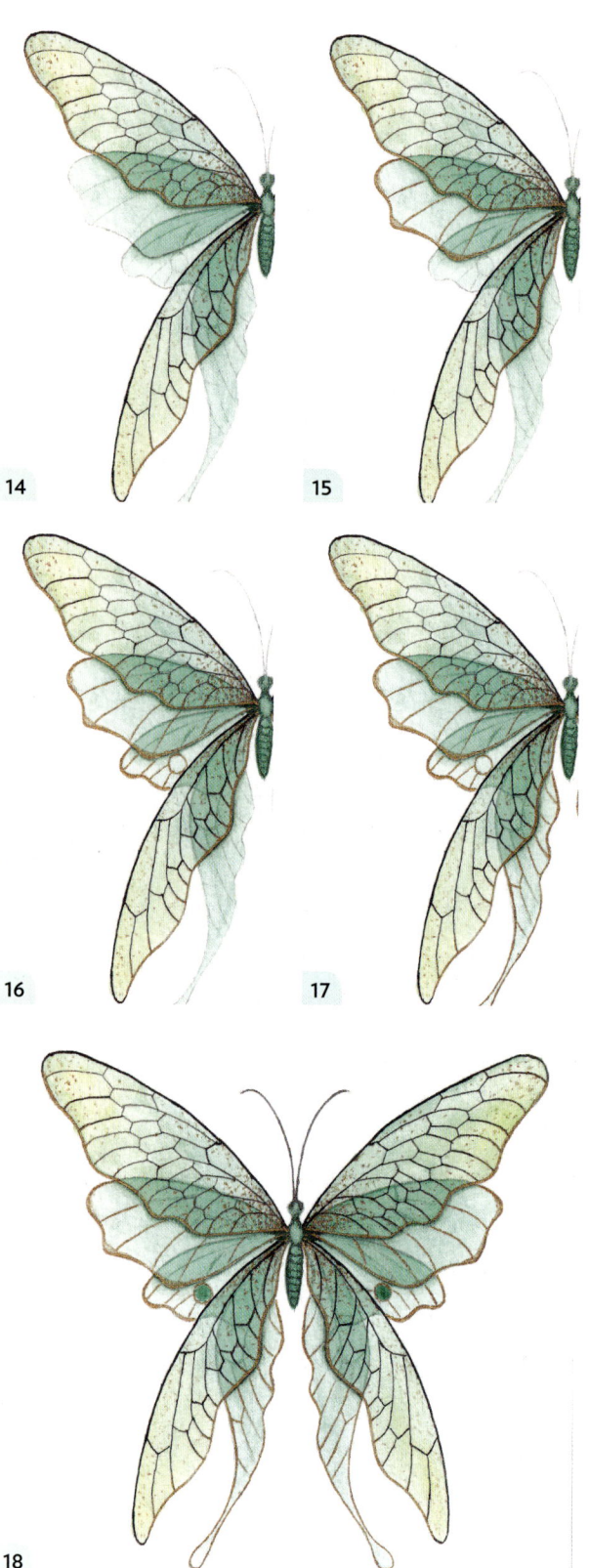

Brushes

Number 8 round brush
Number 4 round brush
Liner brush

Color Palette

Magenta or
Cold Pink

Cadmium Yellow

Indian Yellow

Vermilion

Burnt Sienna

Color Recipes

PEACHY PINK:
80% Magenta (Cold
Pink) + 20% Cad-
mium Yellow

DARK PINK:
60% Magenta +
40% Burnt Sienna

DAHLIA

Dahlias hold a special place as one of my favorite flowers, known for their tight and elegant petals. Here, I've crafted easy steps using a mix of wet-on-dry and wet-on-wet techniques to bring the soft beauty of Dahlia petals to life. Celebrate the beauty of Dahlias with this step-by-step watercolor painting guide.

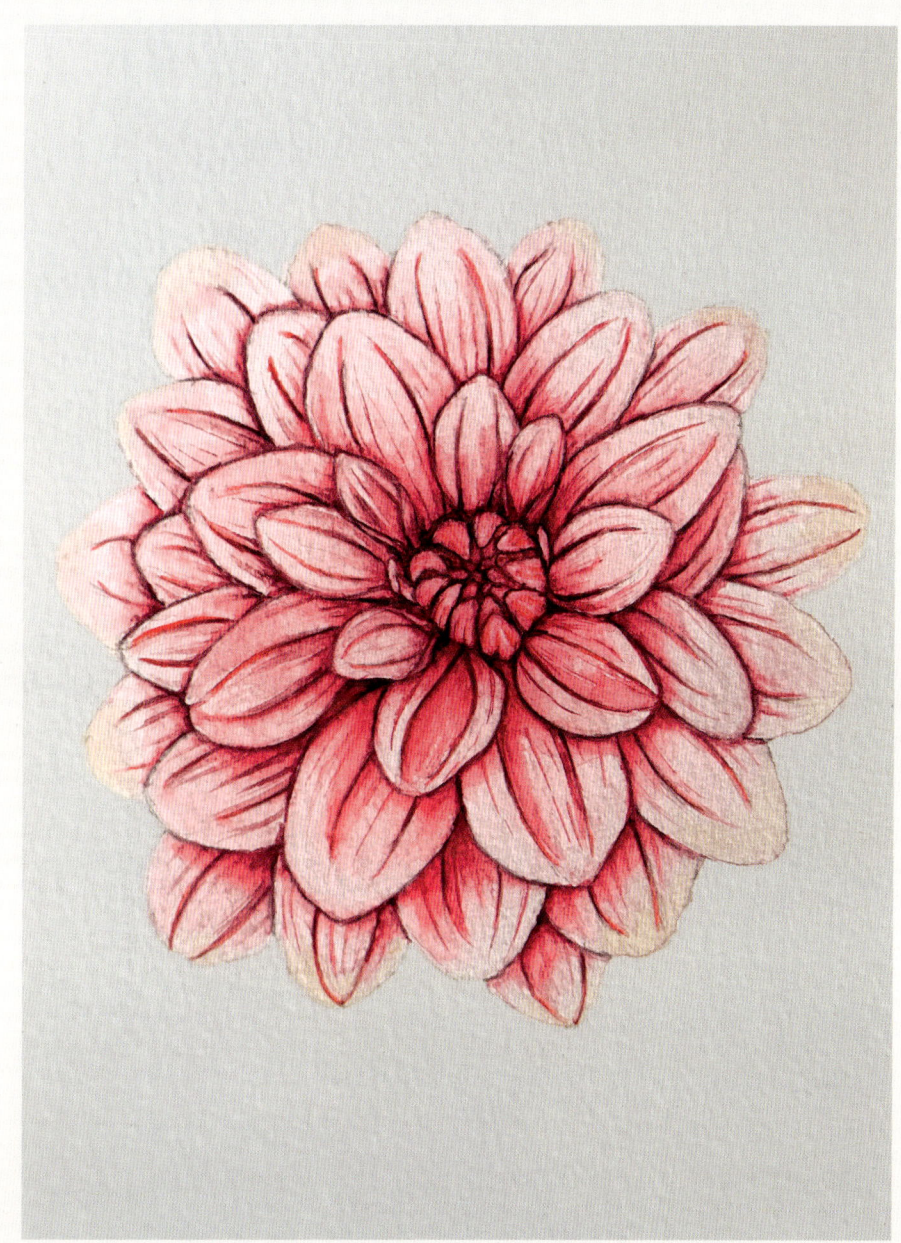

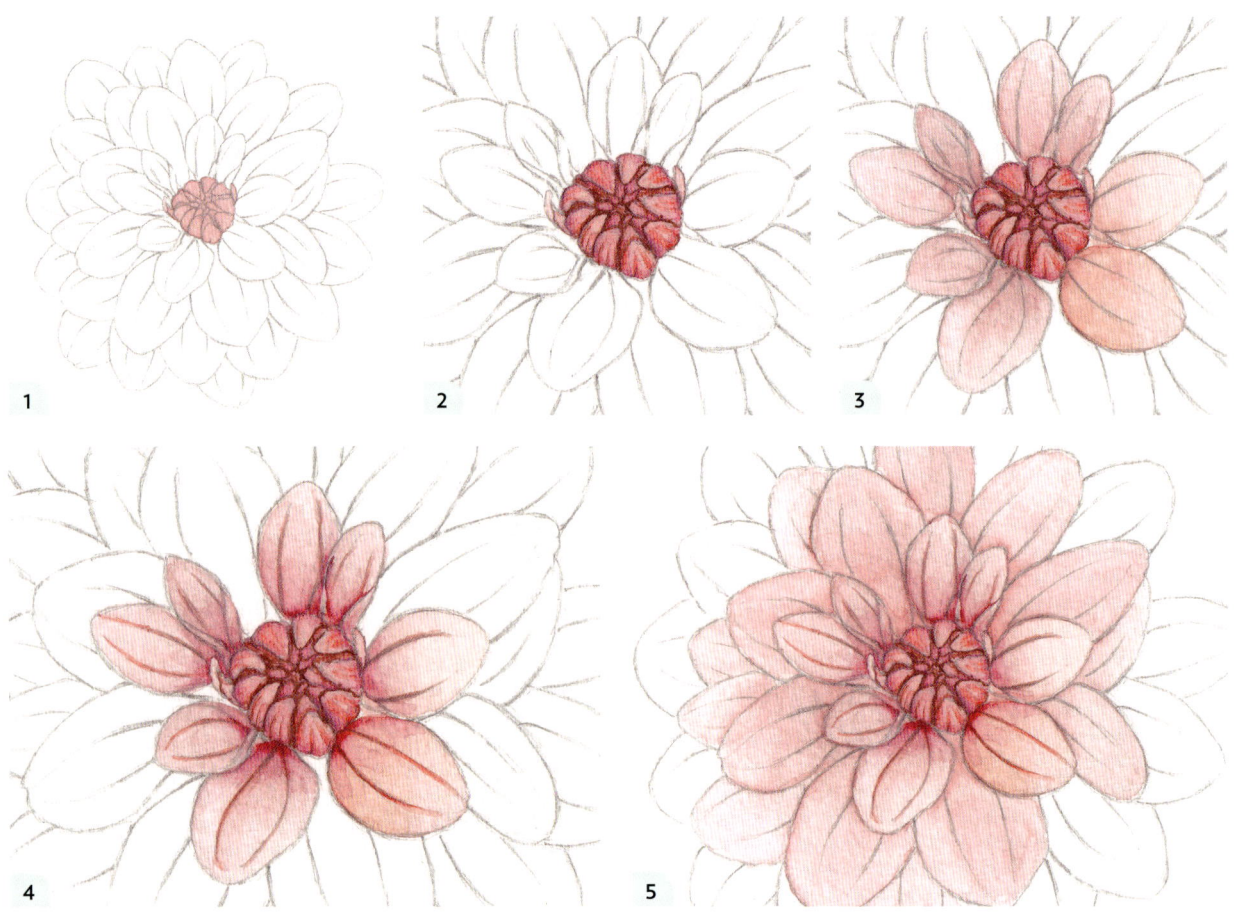

STEP 1: Painting the Center

Using a wet-on-wet technique, wet the center of the flower with water. With a number 8 round brush, apply custom Peachy Pink evenly to the center. Let it dry naturally or use a hair dryer.

STEP 2: Adding Depth to Petals

Once the center is completely dry, apply Magenta (high intensity) in between the petals with a liner brush to provide depth. Apply Vermilion to the lines on the petal and blend it slightly for a natural look.

STEP 3: Painting Inner Petals

Wet the petals near the center with water and apply Peachy Pink with a number 8 round brush. Ensure even application and let the colors dry.

STEP 4: Detailing Inner Petals

After drying, apply Vermilion to the lines of the petals with a liner brush. Use custom Dark Pink with a number 4 round brush on the areas where the petals attach to the flower in high intensity. Blend with an empty brush for a natural look.

STEP 5: Painting Next Set of Petals

Wet the next set of petals with water, apply custom Peachy Pink with a number 8 round brush, and let it dry.

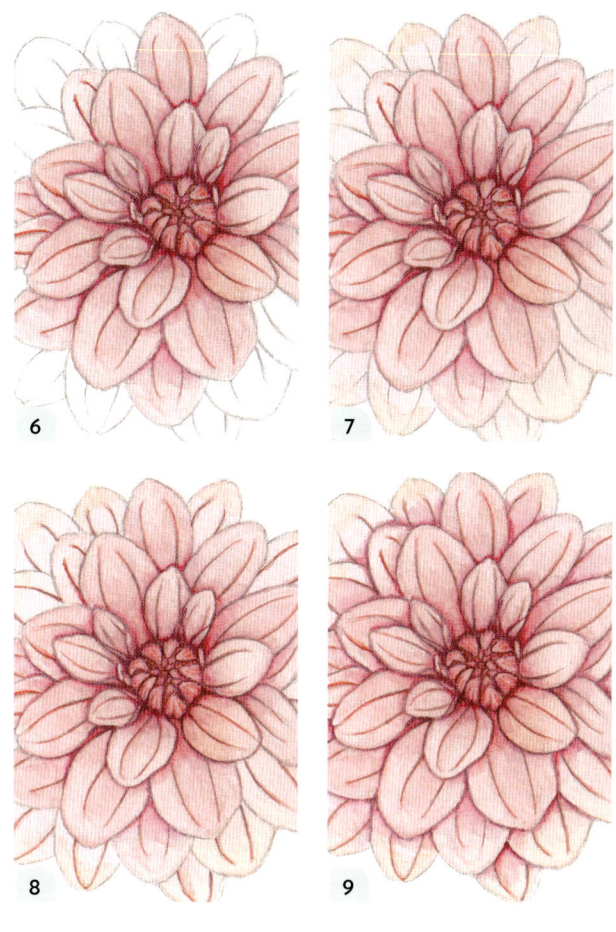

STEP 6: Adding Details to Second Set of Petals

Apply Vermilion to the lines of the petals using a liner brush. Blend slightly and apply Dark Pink between the petals and at the base of the petal. Blend again with an empty brush while ensuring the Dark Pink is still wet.

STEP 7: Adding Aging Effect

Wet the paper, apply Peachy Pink to the inner side of the petal, and use a number 4 round brush to apply Indian Yellow to the outer part. Colors will naturally blend due to the wet paper. Use less intense pigments to depict the aging of outer petals.

STEP 8: Adding Detail Lines

After the first layer dries, apply Vermilion to the lines of the petals with a liner brush and blend naturally.

STEP 9: Enhancing Depth

Apply Dark Pink between the petals with a number 4 round brush and blend slightly.

STEP 10: Adding Final Details

Ensure the paper is completely dry before using a liner brush for details. Darken some areas of the petals with Dark Pink for shadows and depth. Add thin lines to provide a natural look to the petals.

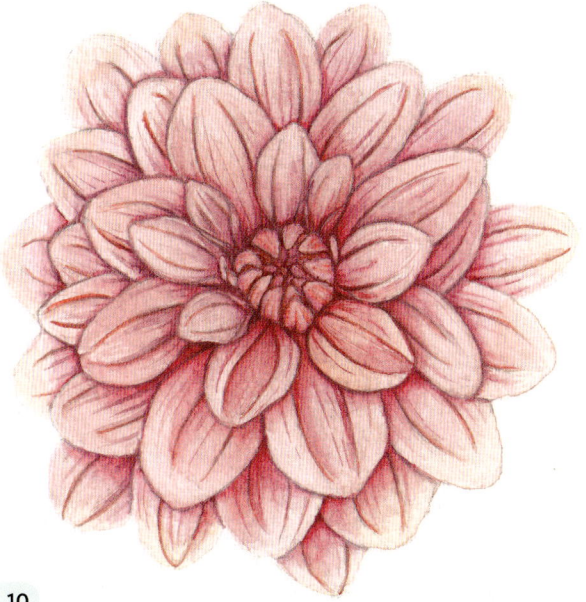

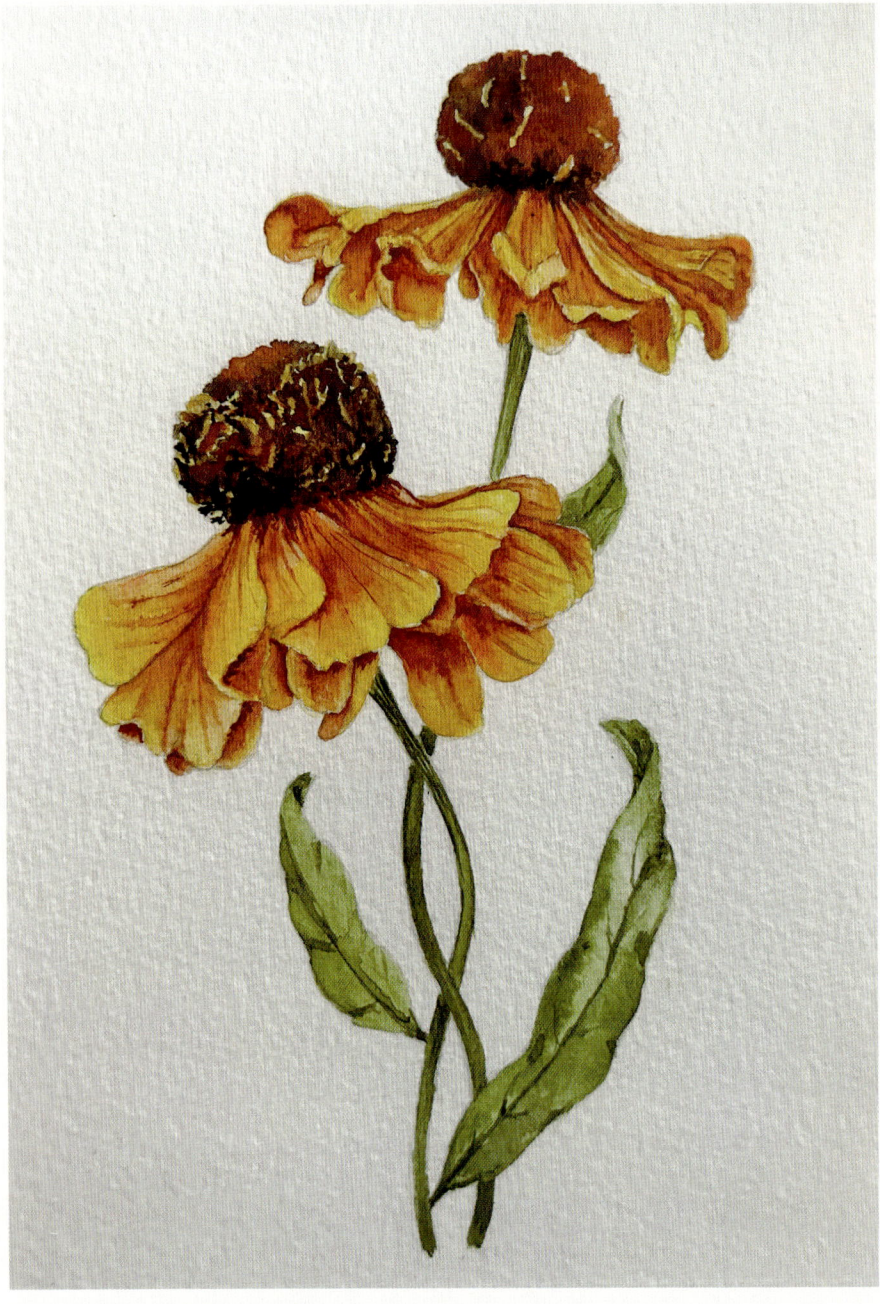

Brushes

Number 8 round brush
Number 4 round brush
Liner brush

Color Palette

Cadmium Yellow

Orange

Red

Burnt Sienna

Burnt Umber

Color Recipes

DARK RED: 60% Red + 40% Burnt Sienna

ORANGE: 50% Red + 50% Yellow

OLIVE GREEN: 60% Sap Green + 40% Burnt Umber

DARK OLIVE GREEN: 80% Olive Green + 20% Burnt Umber

HELENIUM

I always imagine Helenium flowers as ballet dancers, with their unique and gorgeous petal structure resembling the skirt of a beautiful girl. Using a mix of wet-on-dry and wet-on-wet techniques, let's paint these exquisite flowers together. Enjoy the process of painting these graceful Helenium flowers.

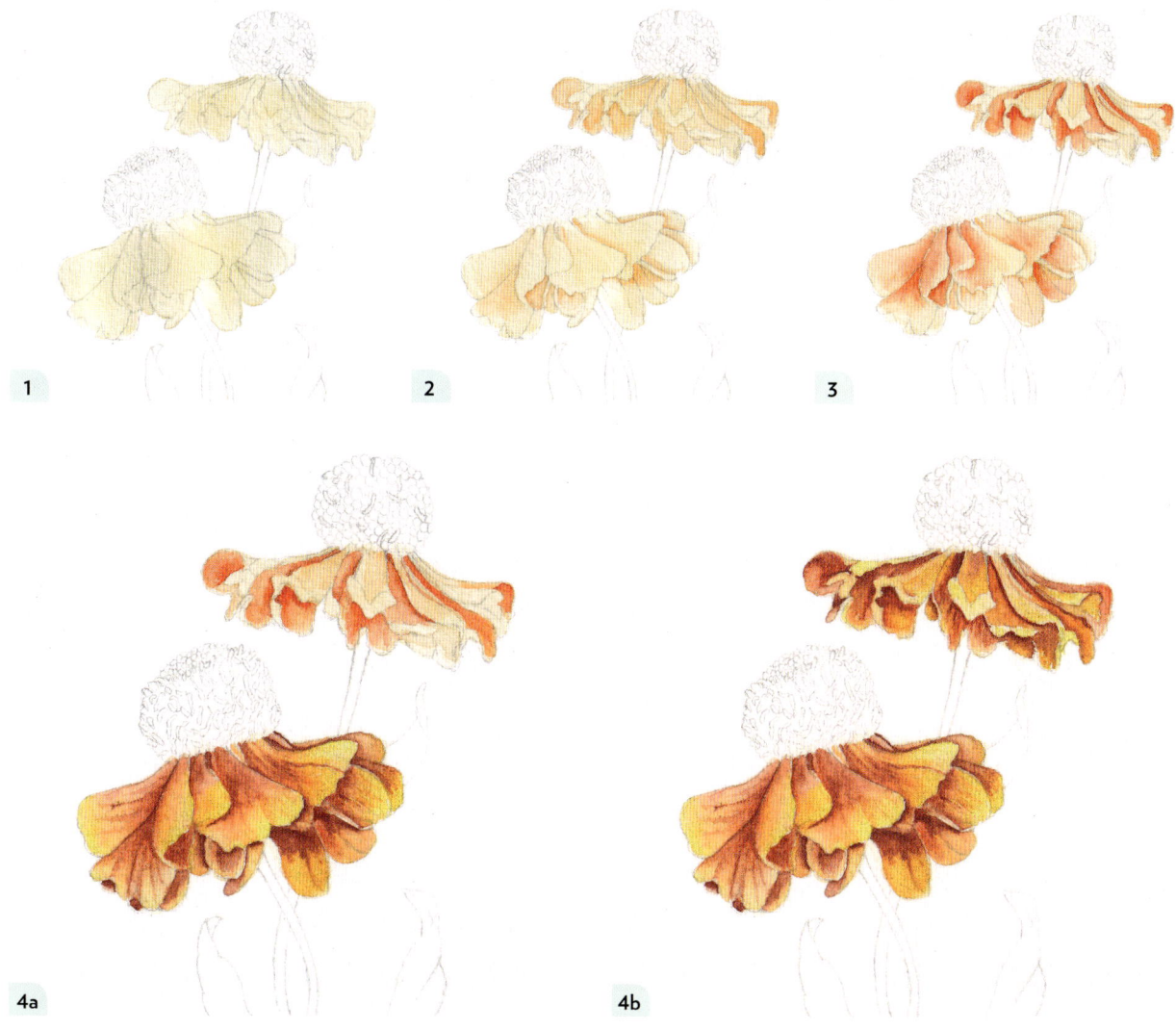

1

2

3

4a

4b

STEP 1: Base Coat with Cadmium Yellow

Wet the paper on the petal area with water and apply a less intense Cadmium Yellow with a number 8 round brush. Allow the colors to dry

STEP 2: Adding Orange Shadows

Once the first layer is completely dry, use a number 4 round brush to apply Orange in the shadow areas between and under the petals.

STEP 3: Introducing Dark Red

With a number 4 round brush, apply Dark Red in the shadow areas. Let the colors dry.

STEP 4: Dual Brush Technique

Use two round brushes simultaneously—number 8 for Dark Red and number 4 for Cadmium Yellow. Apply Dark Red from the base of the petal towards the center, and Cadmium Yellow from the tip of the petal towards the center. Paint one petal at a time, ensuring a smooth blend between the colors.

STEP 5: Center Highlights with Cadmium Yellow

Wet the center of the flower with water and apply a less intense Cadmium Yellow with a number 8 round brush. This Cadmium Yellow represents the color for the tiny flowers inside the center of the flower.

STEP 6: Adding Depth to Center

Using Dark Red and Burnt Umber, apply Dark Red with a bouncing brush technique, leaving the tiny flowers in the center. Before it dries, apply Burnt Umber towards the bottom side of the flower center, also with a bouncing brush technique.

STEP 7: Second Layer for Center and Bottom

When the last layer is completely dry, apply Burnt Umber to the bottom part of the flower center with a bouncing brush technique with a number 4 round brush. Also, apply the same colors to the tiny flowers in the center.

STEP 8: Stem and Leaves

Apply Olive Green to the stem and leaves using the wet-on-wet technique, which will give the leaves texture and variation when they dry. Use a liner brush for the stems and a number 4 round brush for the leaves.

STEP 9: Detailing with Dark Olive Green

Apply Dark Olive Green to the leaves and stems to add veins and details.

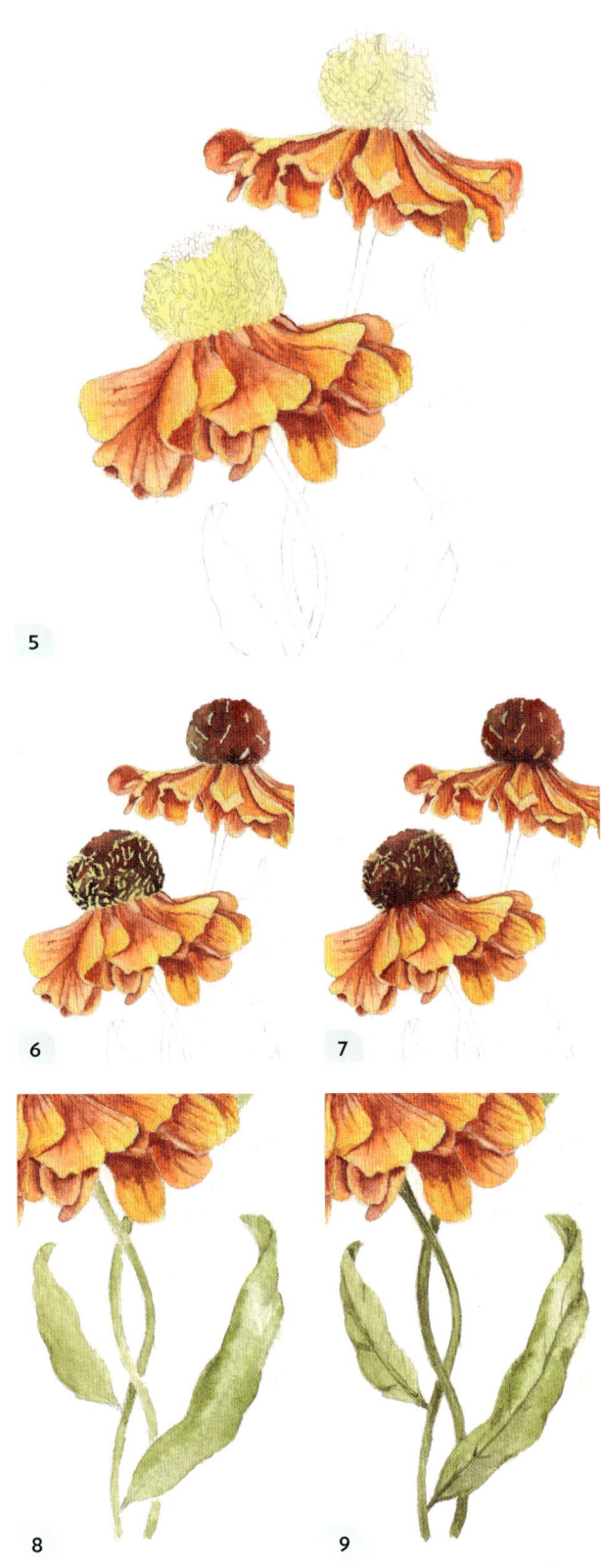

5

6

7

8

9

SUNFLOWER

Sunflowers, beloved globally, evoke the vibrant spirit of summer. Here are some simple steps using a mix of wet-on-dry and wet-on-wet techniques to achieve a realistic-looking sunflower in watercolor. Enjoy your vibrant sunflower creation.

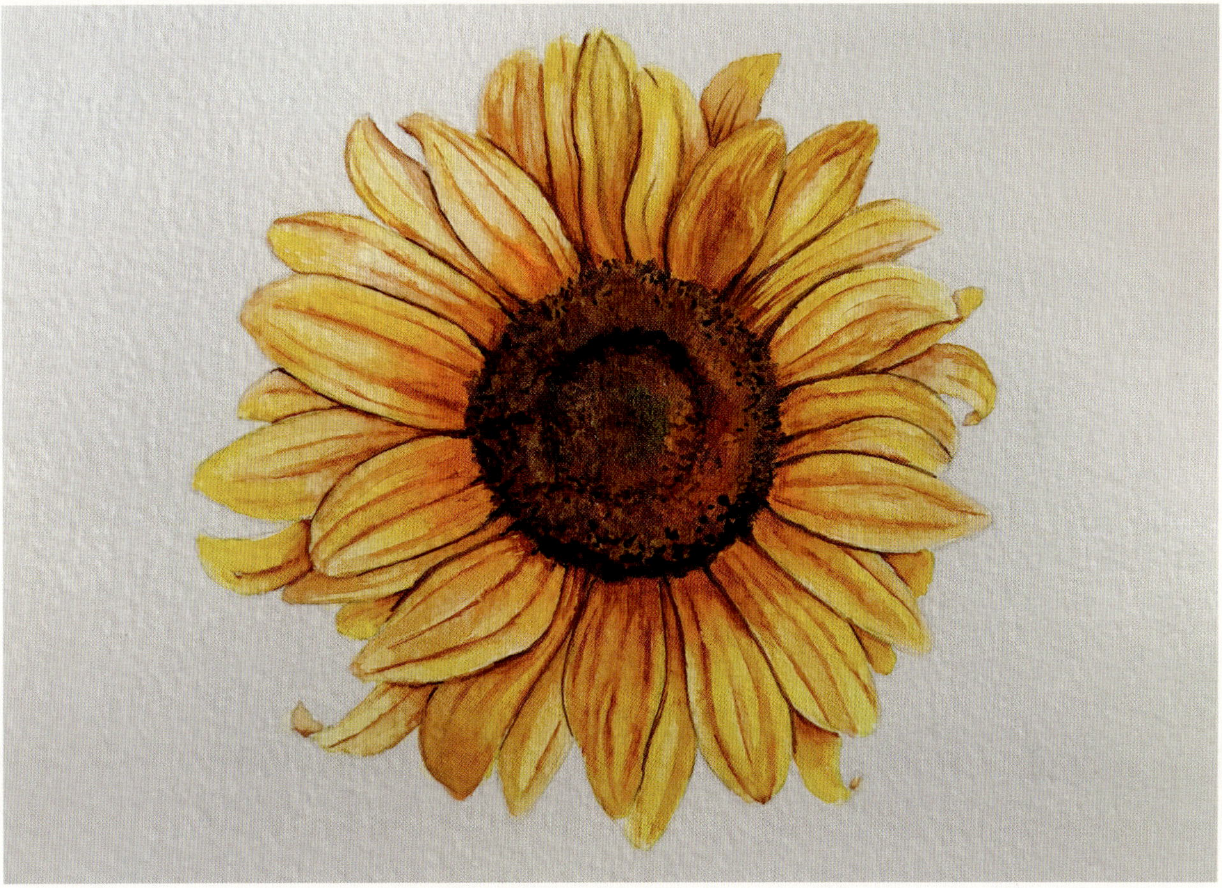

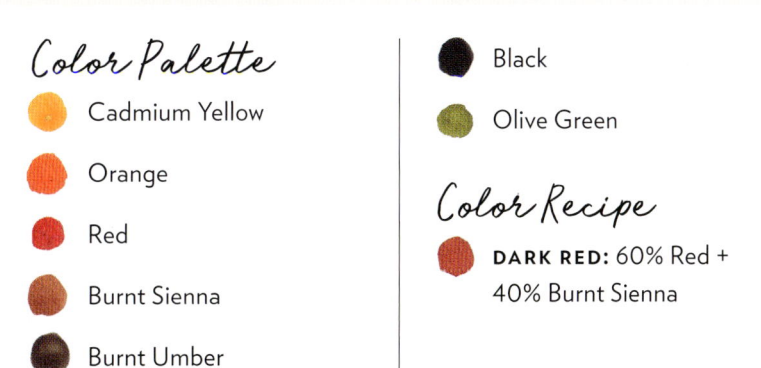

Brushes

Number 8 round brush
Number 4 round brush
Liner brush

Color Palette

🟠 Cadmium Yellow

🔴 Orange

🔴 Red

🟤 Burnt Sienna

⚫ Burnt Umber

⚫ Black

🟢 Olive Green

Color Recipe

🔴 **DARK RED:** 60% Red + 40% Burnt Sienna

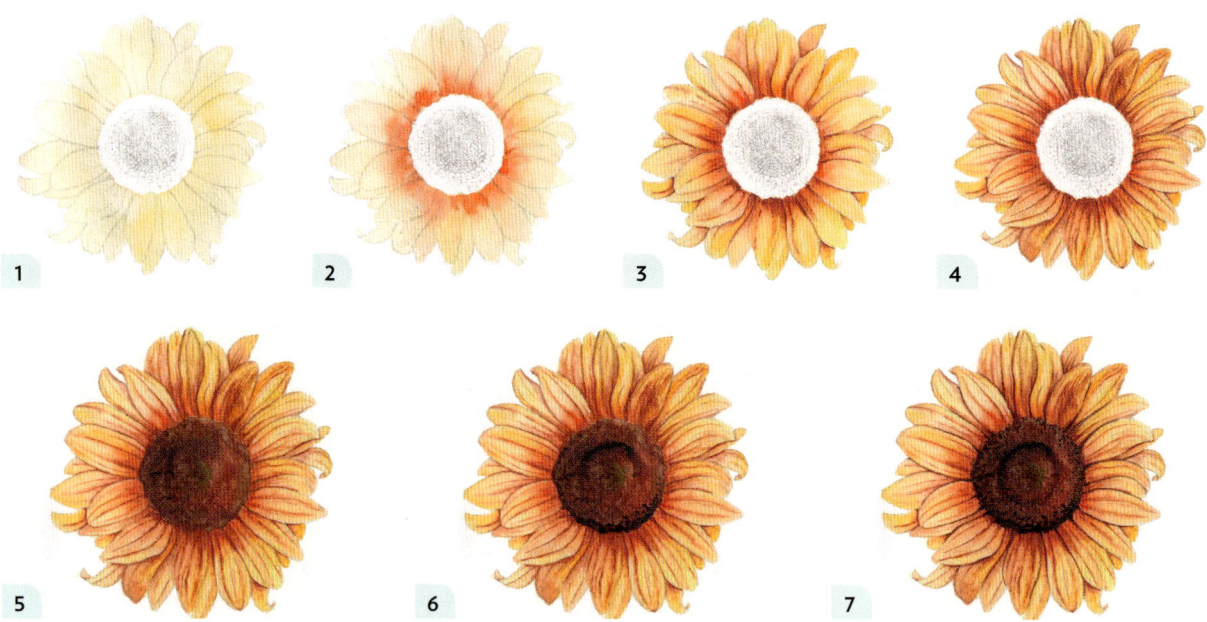

STEP 1: Base Coat with Cadmium Yellow

Wet only the petal area with a number 8 round brush. Apply light-intensity Cadmium Yellow all over the petals. Allow the paper to dry naturally or use a hair dryer.

STEP 2: Adding Orange to the Center

Apply Orange towards the center of the flower using a number 4 round brush. Ensure to blend the colors as you progress.

STEP 3: Two-Color Blend for Petals

Using two brushes, a number 8 round brush with Dark Red and number 4 round brush with Cadmium Yellow, apply Dark Red towards the center from the base and also in between the petals. Apply Cadmium Yellow from the edges to the center, and blend both colors in the center. Let the colors dry completely.

STEP 4: Detailing Petals with Dark Red

Using a liner brush, apply Dark Red to the edges and lines on the petals. Blend the colors, ensuring the pigments have a high intensity.

STEP 5: Painting the Sunflower Center

Wet the center. Apply Olive Green to the center's most central area with a number 4 brush, creating the smallest circle in the middle. The pigment should be highly intense. Wash the brush and apply Dark Red, using a bouncing brush technique all over the center, avoiding the Olive Green area. Wash the brush again and pick up Burnt Umber, applying it among the edges of the center, covering one side to show shadow areas. Let the colors dry.

STEP 6: Adding Black to the Center

When the colors are completely dry, pick up Black with a number 4 round brush and apply it using the bouncing brush technique, covering similar areas as in the reference.

STEP 7: Final Details with Burnt Umber

Let the paints dry completely. Pick up Burnt Umber with a liner brush in very high intensity. Apply it to the edges of the center and create a small inner circle for more details. Apply Burnt Umber to the edges of each petal, providing more depth to the painting. Do not blend the colors.

Brushes

Number 8 round brush
Number 4 round brush
Liner brush

Color Palette

Permanent Rose

Pink

Indian Yellow

Burnt Sienna

Raw Sienna

Burnt Umber

Olive Green

Viridian

Color Recipes

DARK ROSE:
60% Permanent Rose
+ 40% Burnt Sienna

GREEN MUD:
80% Raw Sienna +
20% Olive Green

DARK PINK:
70% Pink + 30%
Burnt Umber

DARK VIRIDIAN:
60% Viridian +
40% Burnt Umber

ROSE

Roses symbolize romance, being the most beloved flowers of all time. Painting them is a delicate process, and here we'll capture the beauty of a gorgeous pink rose.

Using a mix of wet-on-wet and wet-on dry techniques, enjoy the process of bringing this beautiful pink Rose to life on your canvas.

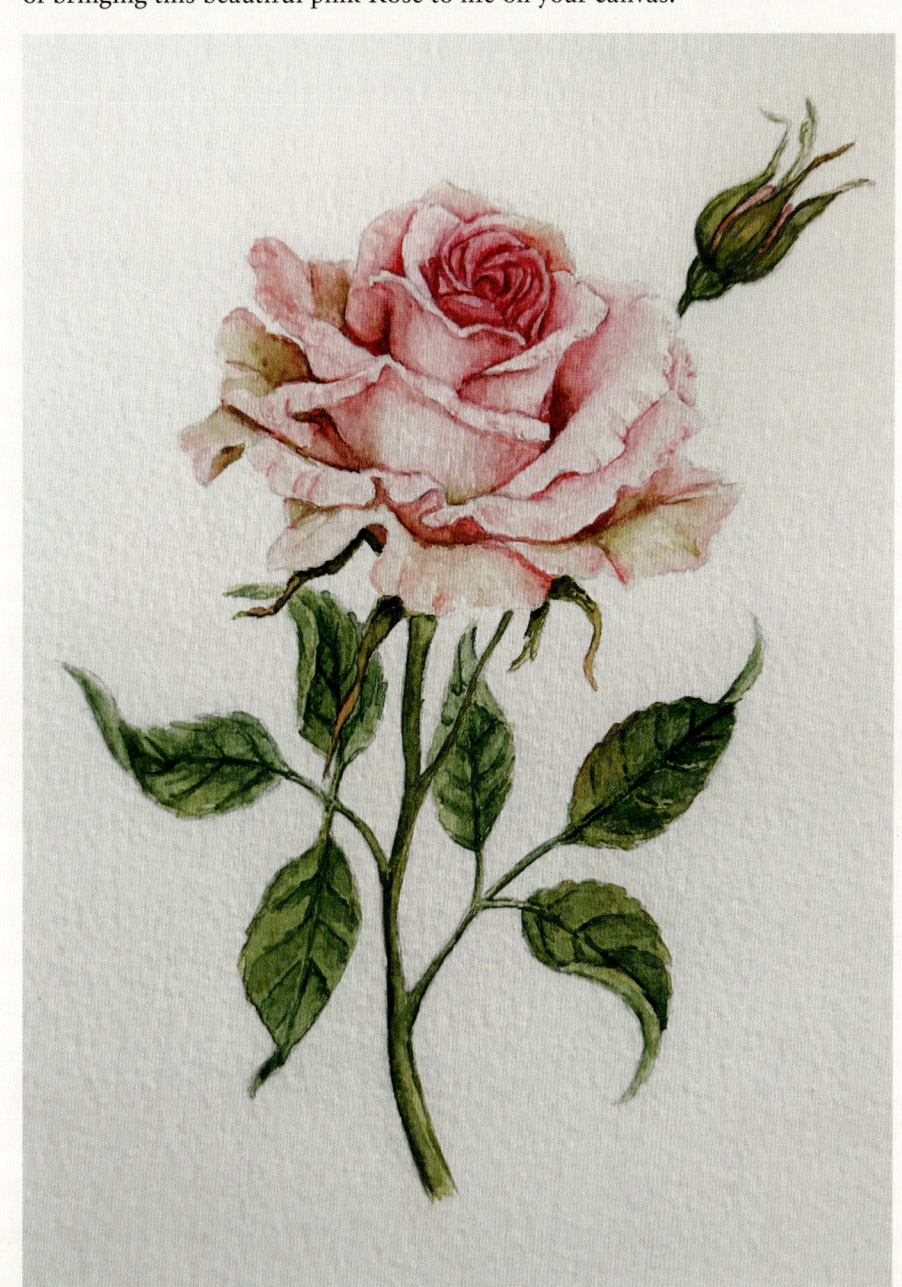

STEP 1: Base Coat with Permanent Rose

Apply Permanent Rose with a number 8 round brush all over the flower, concentrating more pigments towards the center. Ensure the area of the flower is wet before applying the colors.

STEP 2: Shadows with Permanent Rose

Once the previous layer is completely dry, paint the shadow areas of the flower with a high-intensity Permanent Rose, using a number 4 round brush.

STEP 3: Adding Dark Rose and Details

When the colors are dry, apply Dark Rose to the shadow areas and the center of the flower. Add Permanent Rose to the petals and buds using a number 4 round brush for the flower and a liner brush for the bud.

STEP 4: Green Mud and Dark Pink

Apply Green Mud with low intensity to the bottom of the outer petals. While the paint is still wet, add Dark Pink to the bottom part of the petals using a number 4 round brush.

STEP 5: Details with Permanent Rose

Give more depth to the flower by detailing the petals with Permanent Rose using a liner brush. Blend before the paint dries for a natural look.

STEP 6: Painting Stems and Leaves

Using the wet-on-dry technique, with a number 4 round brush, apply Olive Green to stems, leaves, and buds. Add a touch of Burnt Sienna to the tip of the bud sepals and flower sepals. Let dry.

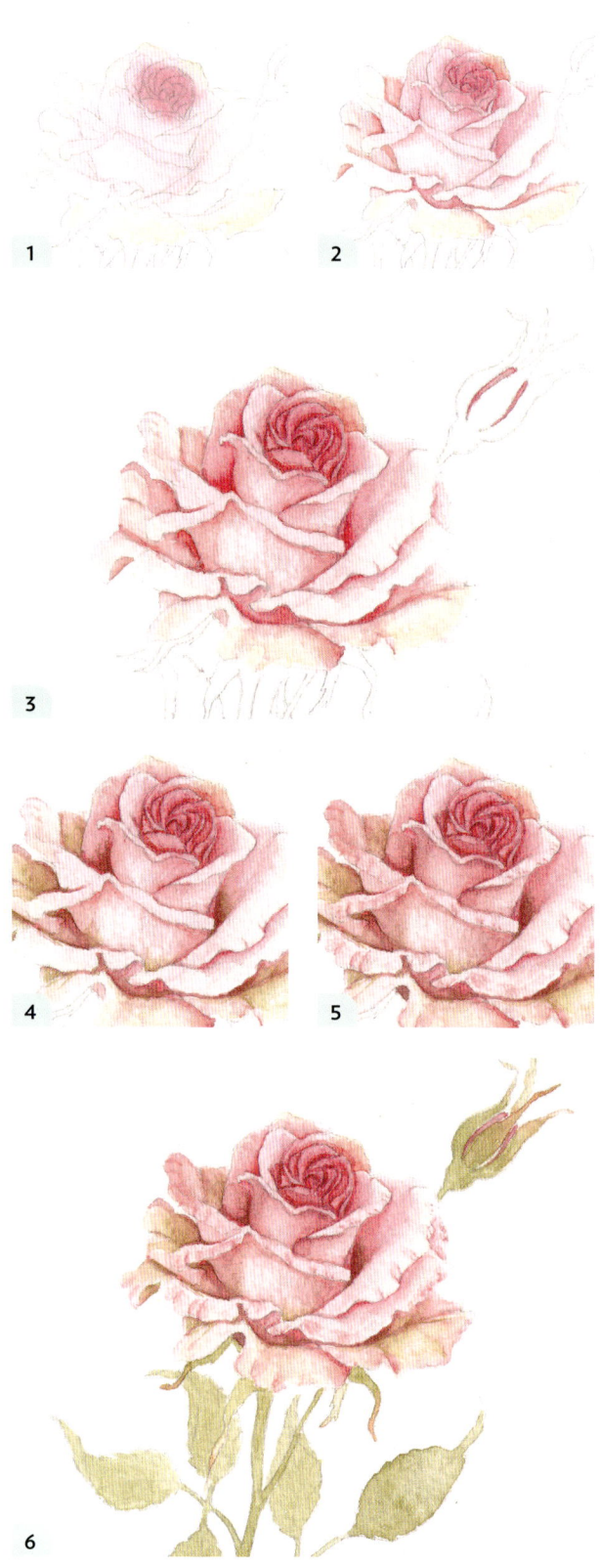

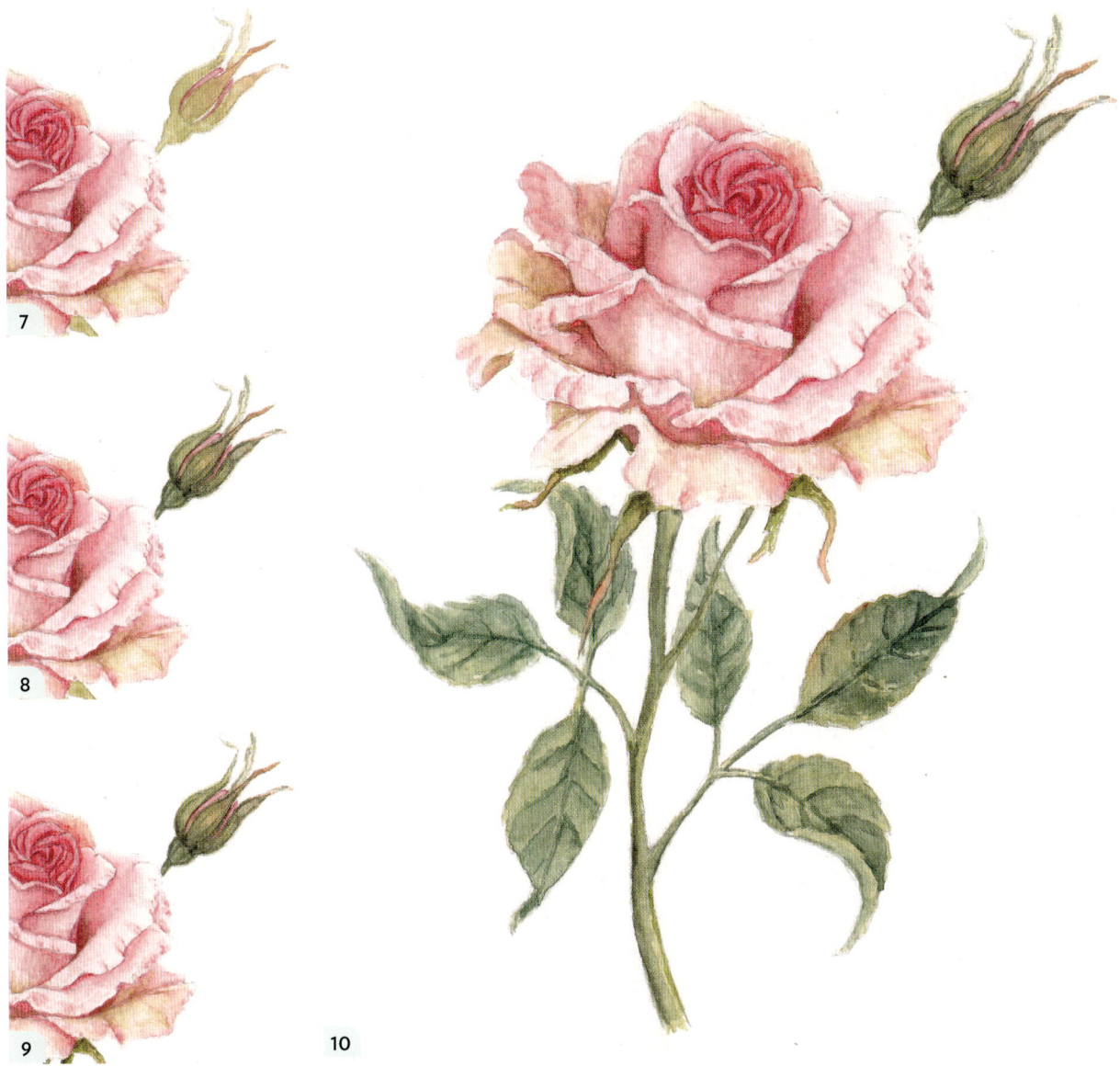

STEP 7: Dark Viridian to Stems and Sepals

Apply Dark Viridian to stems and bud sepals for variation. Also, add Burnt Sienna with high intensity to the tip of the sepals using a liner brush. Allow to dry.

STEP 8: Further Details to Sepals

Apply Dark Viridian with a liner brush to the flower sepals. Add Burnt Sienna to the tips of the sepals for additional detail.

STEP 9: Detailing Leaves

After the colors dry, give details to the leaves by adding Viridian color with a number 4 round brush.

STEP 10: Veins on Leaves

Create veins on the leaves by applying Dark Viridian color with a liner brush, enhancing the realism of the foliage.

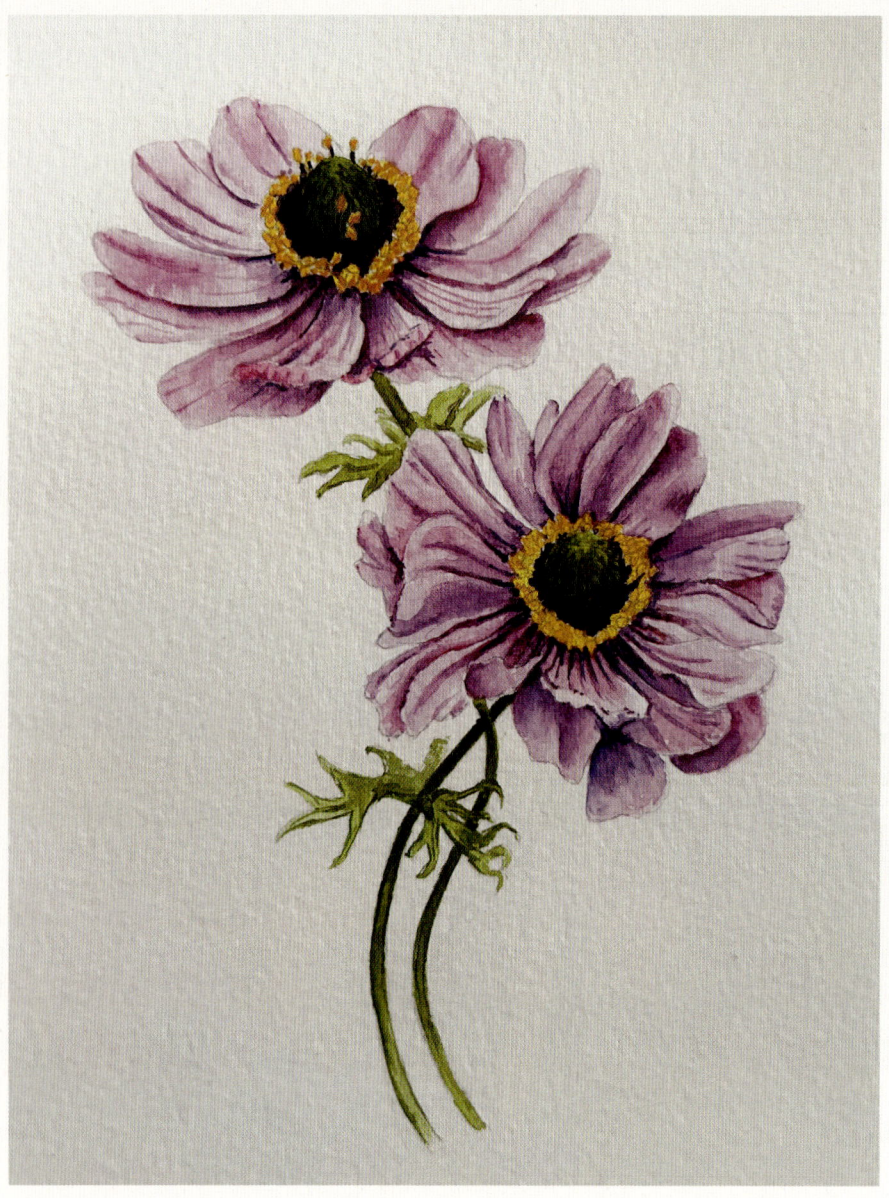

Number 8 round brush
Number 4 round brush
Liner brush

Color Palette

- Pink
- Violet
- Vermilion
- Cadmium Yellow
- Yellow Ochre
- Black
- Sap Green
- Burnt Sienna

Color Recipes

PURPLE: 50% Pink + 50% Violet

RED PURPLE: 60% Purple + 40% Vermilion

OLIVE GREEN: 60% Sap Green + 40% Burnt Umber

ANEMONE

Anemones are beloved by artists for their exquisite beauty in drawings and paintings. Here, I've painted purple Anemone flowers, and you can easily recreate them using a mix of wet-on-wet and wet-on-dry techniques and these step-by-step instructions. In this painting, the focus is on the flowers, but feel free to add more details to the leaves if desired. Enjoy creating your beautiful Anemone masterpiece!

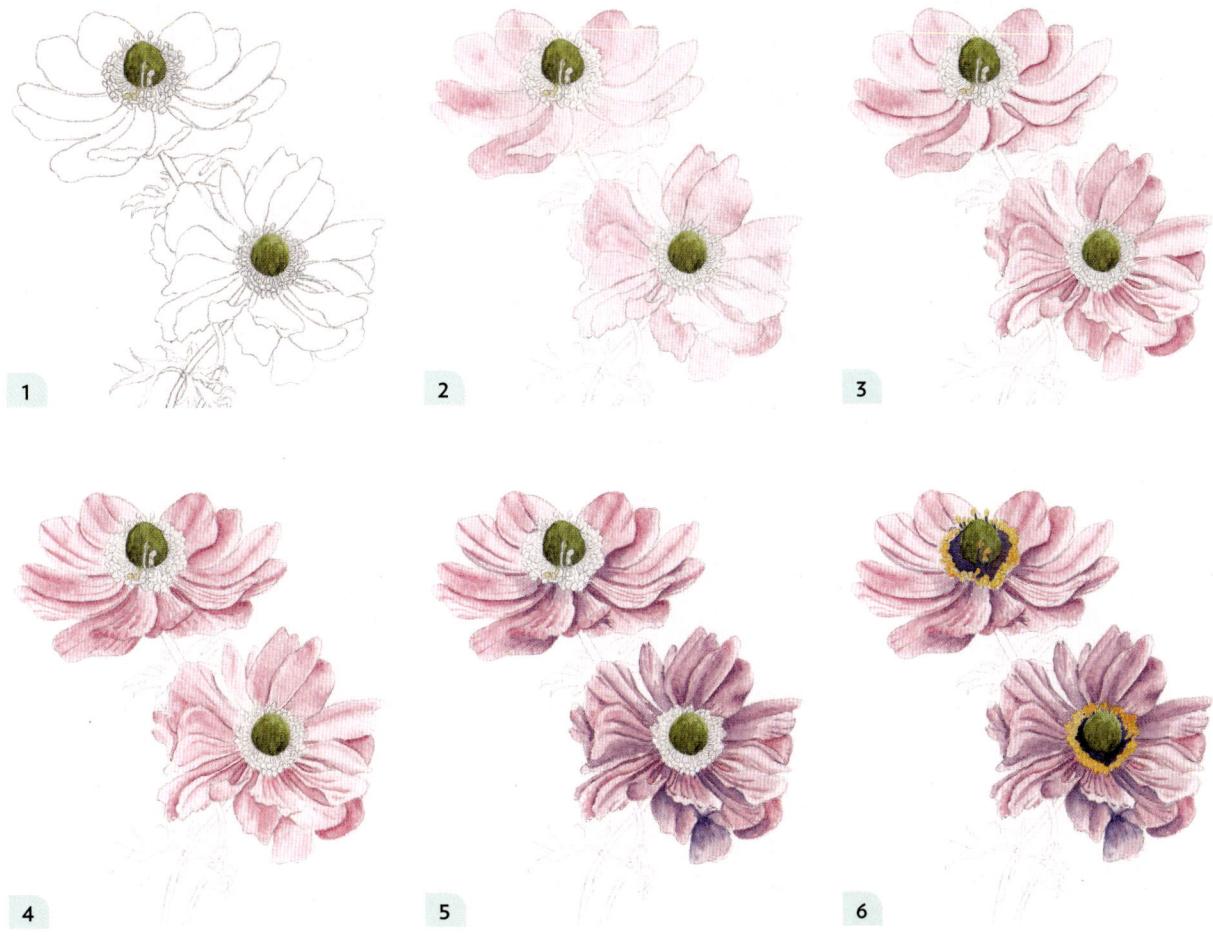

STEP 1: Center of the Flower

Apply Olive Green to the center of the flower using a number 4 round brush with the wet-on-dry technique.

STEP 2: Base Coat for Petals

Wet the entire petals with water and apply Purple in low intensity using a number 8 round brush. Allow the colors to dry completely.

STEP 3: Define Petals

Using a liner brush, apply high-intensity Purple between the petals, smoothly blending the colors to differentiate the petals.

STEP 4: Petal Details

Once all the paints are dry, use a liner brush to apply Red Purple for details on the petals. Add lines and blend them for a simple yet intricate look. Let dry.

STEP 5: Adding Shadows

Apply Violet with medium intensity using a liner brush under the flower center and petals to create shadows and depth. Allow to dry.

STEP 6: Stamens and Lines

Apply Cadmium Yellow to the stamens and Violet to the lines around the flower center using a liner brush.

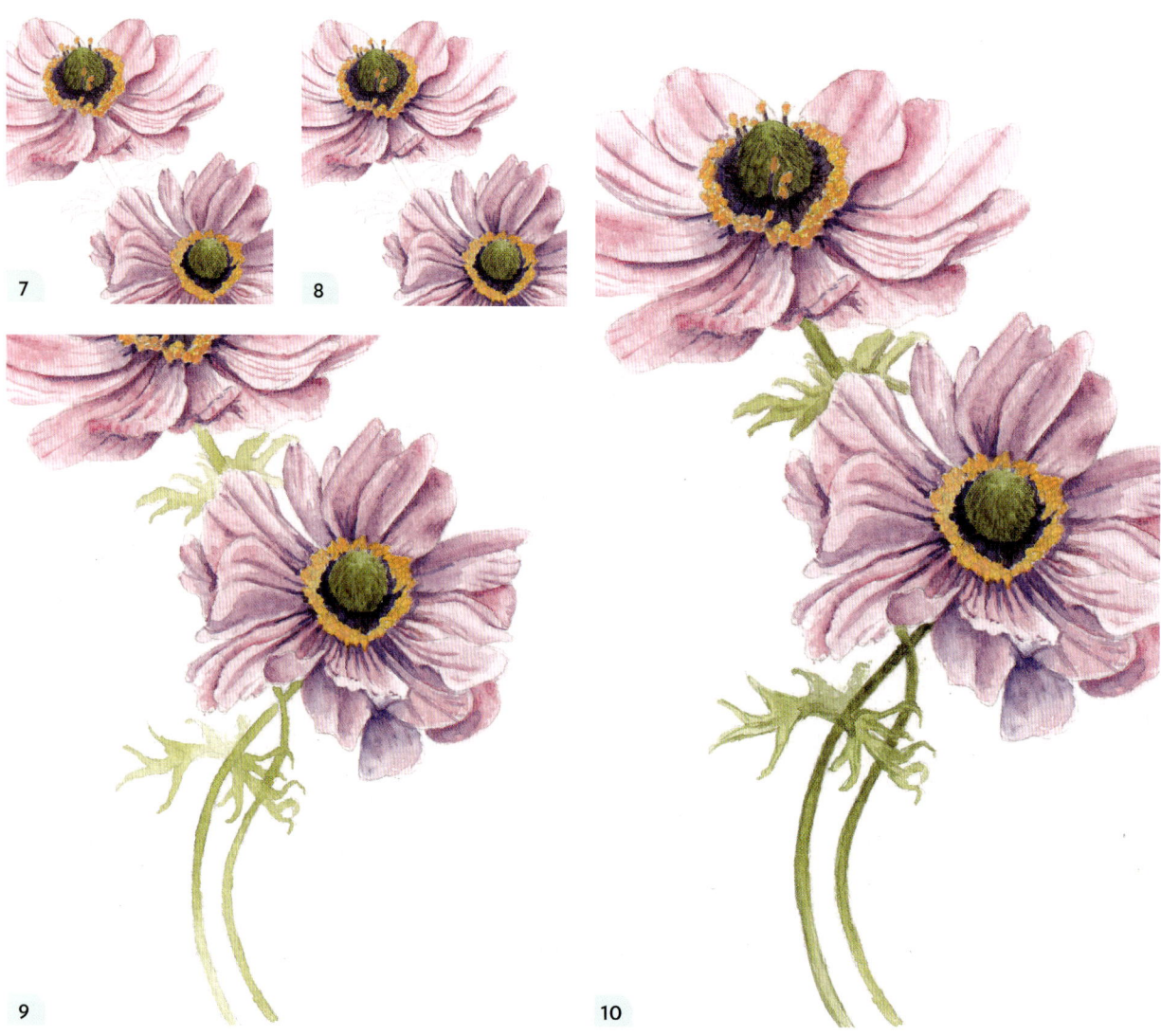

STEP 7: Depth to Center

When the colors are dry, add Black to the lines where they touch the center and Yellow Ochre to the stamens using a liner brush for added depth. Let dry.

STEP 8: Center Shadows

Apply high-intensity Violet under the center of the flowers with a liner brush. This serves as a shadow for the center on the petals.

STEP 9: Stem and Leaves

When dry, apply Sap Green color to the stem and leaves using the wet-on-dry technique and a number 4 round brush.

STEP 10: Enhancing Depth

For added depth, use Olive Green with high intensity under the flowers, along the edges of the leaves, and on the stem using a liner brush.

Brushes

Number 8 round brush
Number 4 round brush
Liner brush

Color Palette

- Prussian Blue
- Black
- Raw Sienna
- Yellow Ochre
- Cadmium Yellow
- Orange
- Burnt Sienna
- Burnt Umber
- Sap Green
- Cobalt Blue
- Red
- Gold Metallic

Color Recipes

DARK PRUSSIAN BLUE: 60% Prussian Blue + 40% Black (highly diluted)

DARK YELLOW OCHRE: 60% Yellow Ochre + 40% Raw Sienna

DARK SAP GREEN: 80% Sap Green + 20% Burnt Umber

DAISY AND A BUTTERFLY

Daisies, the flowers that sparked my love for drawing, are easy to paint with these simple steps. Elevate the vibrancy of the painting by adding a charming butterfly. Enjoy the beauty of daisies and butterflies with this step-by-step watercolor painting guide, which uses a mix of wet-on-wet and wet-on-dry techniques.

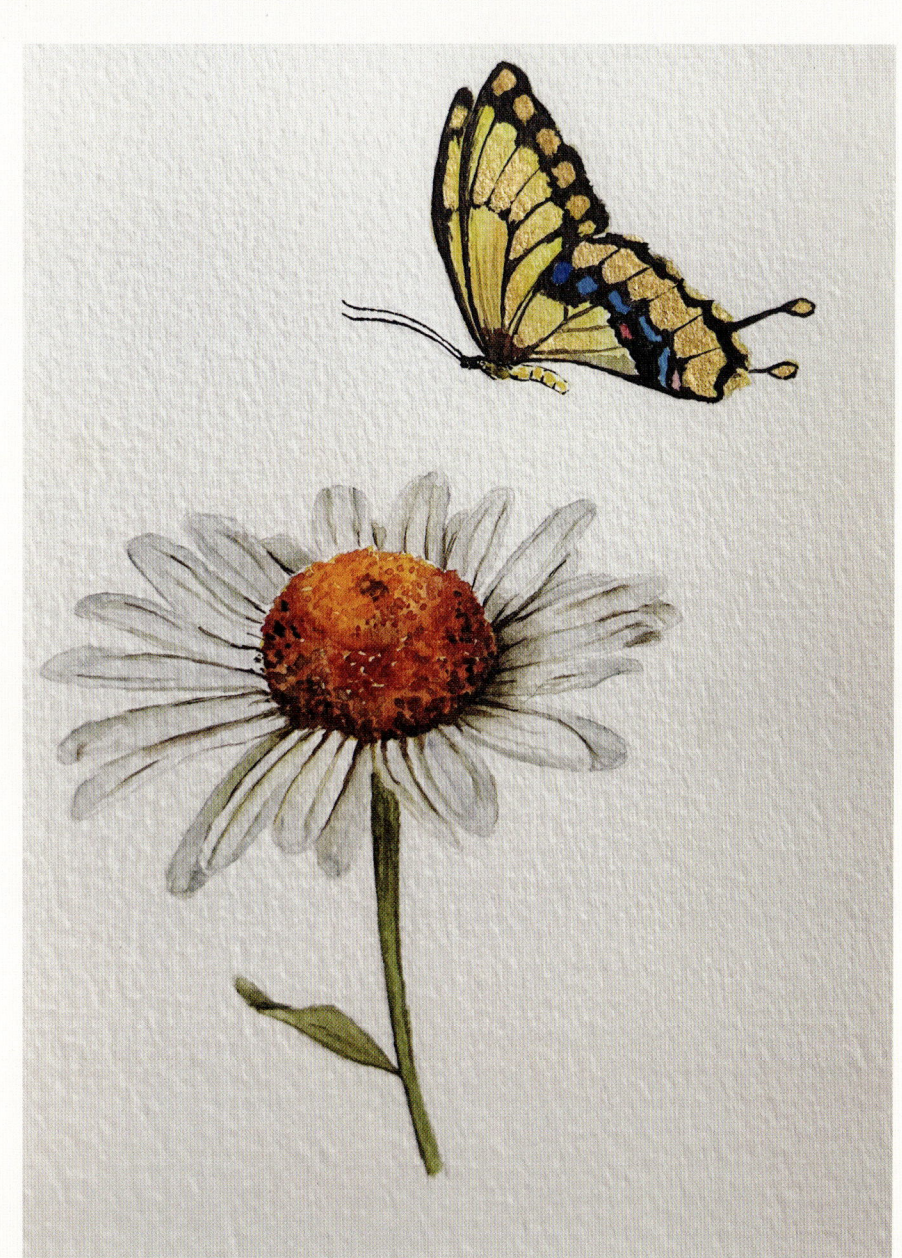

STEP 1: Shadow Areas

Dilute Dark Prussian Blue with a large amount of water. Apply this color to the shadow areas of the flower, such as between the petals and the shadow of the center on the petals. Use a number 4 round brush with the wet-on-dry technique.

STEP 2: Petal Details

Apply Dark Yellow Ochre between the petals and on the line details of the petals using a liner brush. Let dry.

STEP 3: Center of the Daisy

Apply Cadmium Yellow to the center of the flower with a wet paper using a number 8 round brush. In the bottom side of the center, apply Yellow Ochre in a bouncing technique with a liner brush. Let the colors dry.

STEP 4: Center Details

With a number 4 round brush, apply Orange on top and Burnt Sienna in the lower side of the center using bouncing brushstrokes. Add Burnt Sienna in the very center as well. Use the liner brush to apply a few dots. Allow to dry.

STEP 5: Petal and Detail Lines

With the liner brush, apply Burnt Umber to the bottom side of the center using a bouncing brush technique. Also, apply the same color between the petals and to the details. Ensure the lines are thin, fading towards the end of the petals.

STEP 6: Edges of Petals and Stem

When the colors are dry, apply highly diluted Dark Prussian Blue to the edges of the petals with a number 4 round brush. Blend the colors. Apply Sap Green to the stem and leaf with the same brush.

STEP 7: Stem and Leaf Details

Apply details to the stem and leaves with Dark Sap Green. Use a liner brush for this process. Let dry.

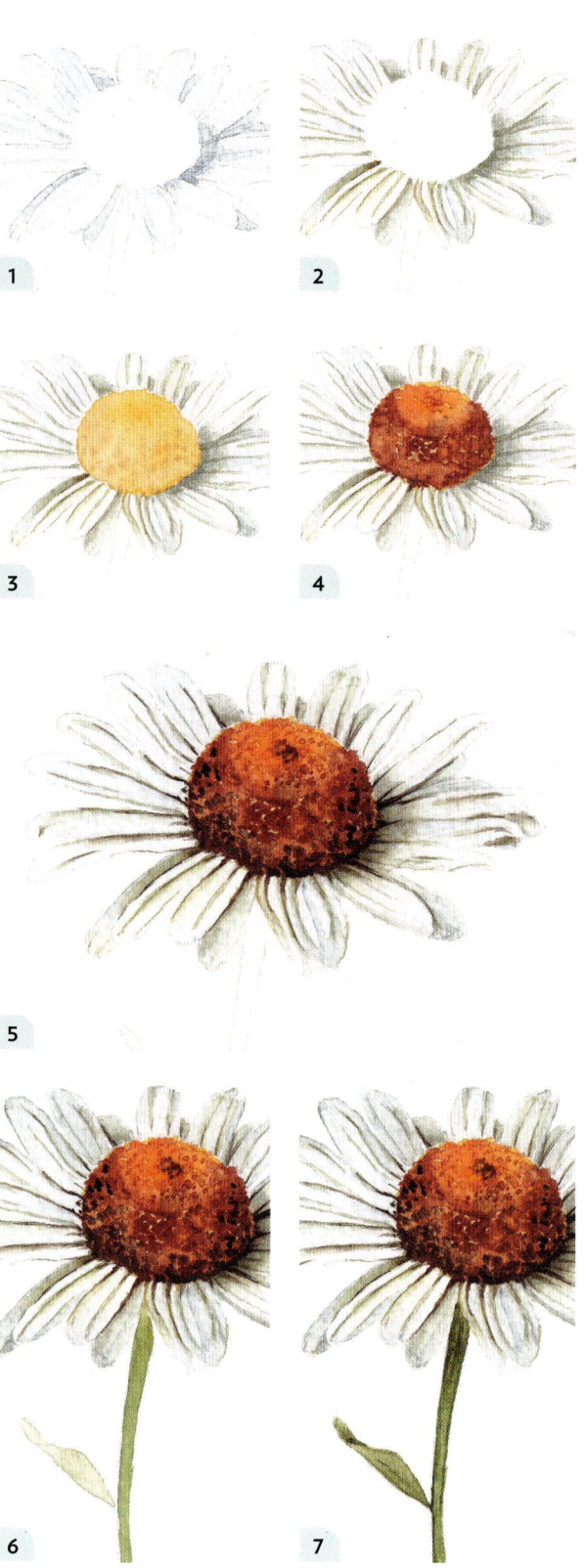

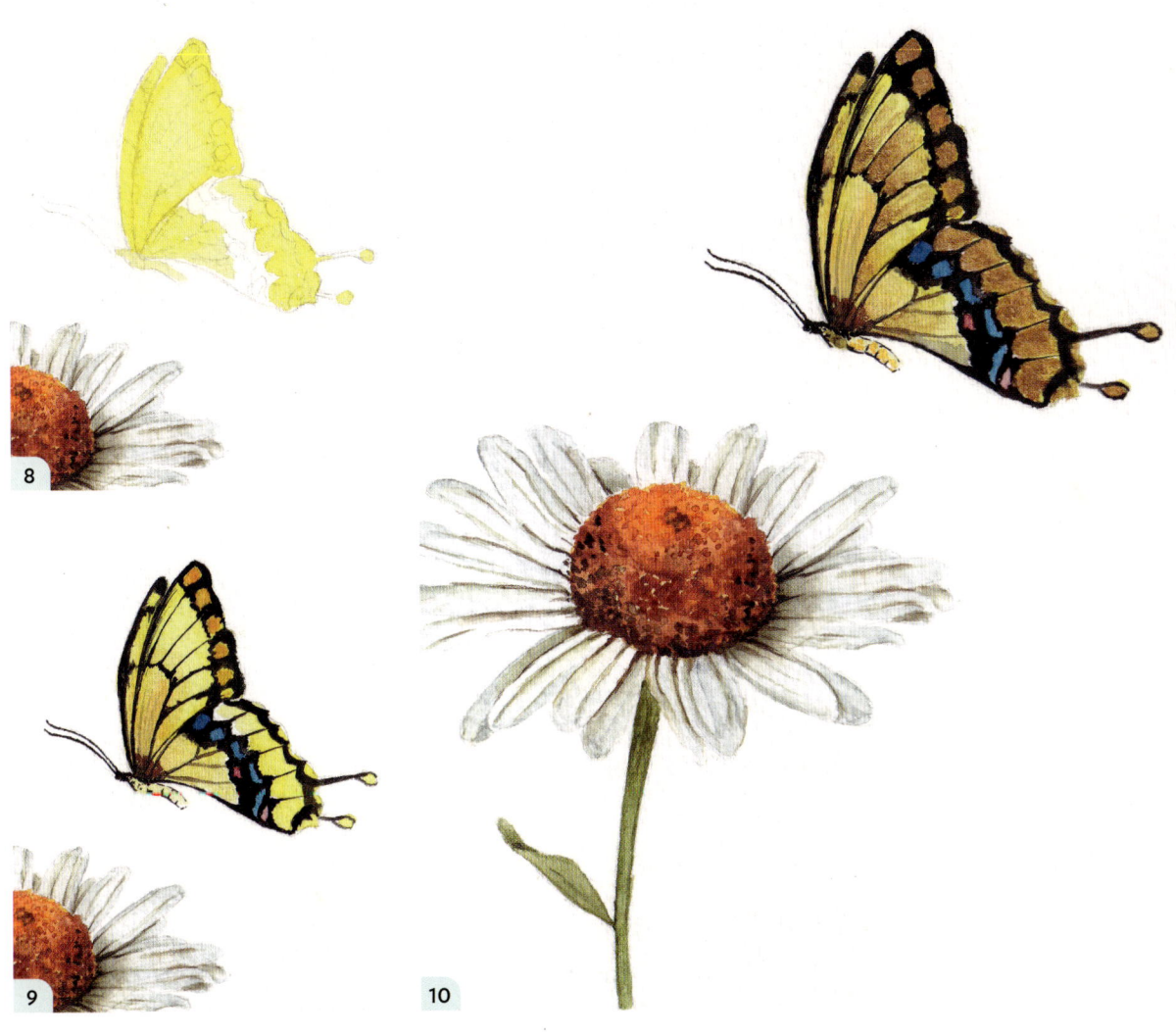

STEP 8: Butterfly Wings

Wet the wings of the butterfly and apply Cadmium Yellow with a number 8 round brush, leaving the center of the bottom set of wings white. Allow to dry.

STEP 9: Butterfly Details

Give details to the butterfly using Cobalt Blue and Red with a liner brush. Add Burnt Sienna near the body and Black details. Use the liner brush for all the processes.

STEP 10: Golden Details

Add golden details to the wings. Apply Gold Metallic color to the wing's edges and create a gradient feel in the middle. Use a liner brush for this step.

ECHINACEA AND BUTTERFLIES

Echinacea, also known as Coneflowers, are lovely flowers that attract butterflies. I attempted to capture their beauty in a painting featuring pinkish blooms and two adorable butterflies. These steps use a mix of wet-on-wet and wet-on-dry techniques. Let's enjoy creating art together.

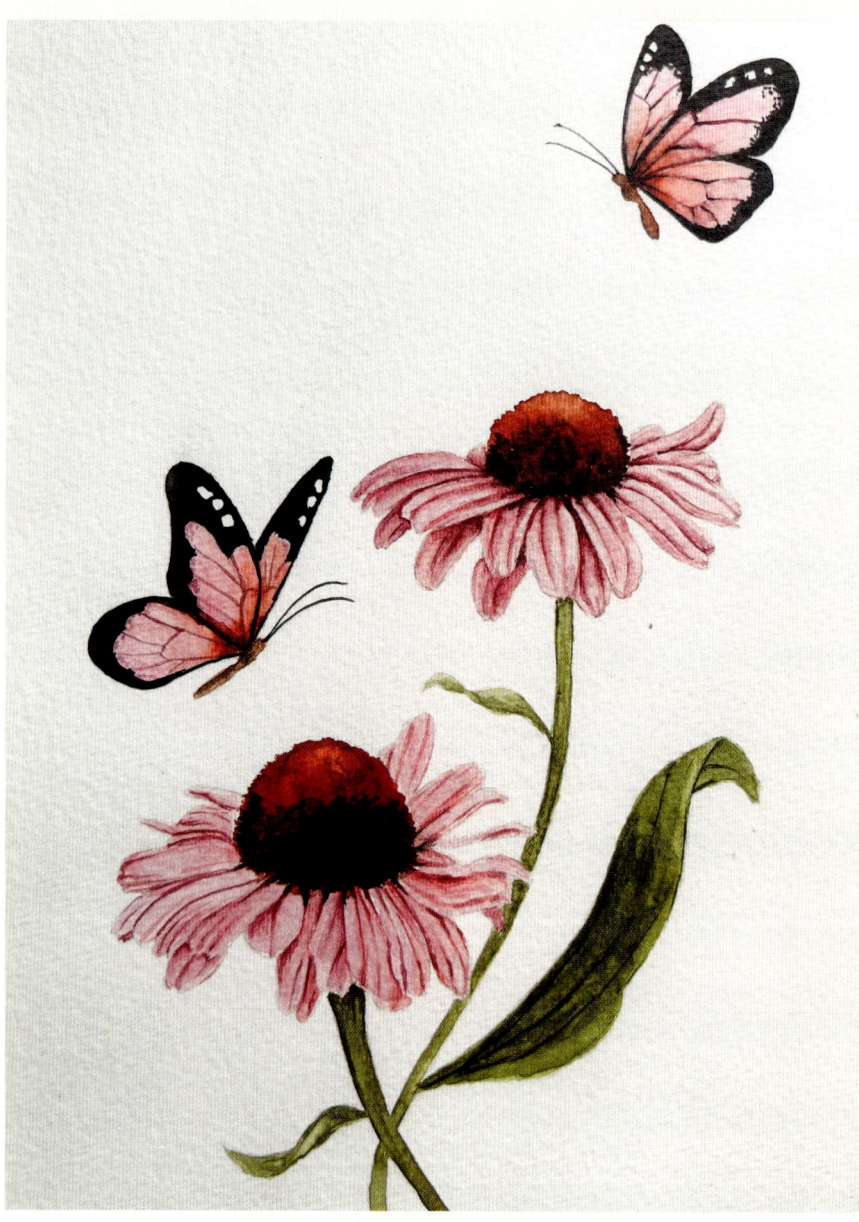

Brushes

Number 8 round brush
Number 4 round brush
Liner brush

Color Palette

Pink

Vermilion

Burnt Sienna

Red

Sap Green

Burnt Umber

Black

Color Recipes

RED-TINTED PINK:
50% Pink +
50% Vermilion

DARK RED PINK:
40% Pink + 40%
Vermilion + 20%
Burnt Umber

OLIVE GREEN: 60%
Sap Green + 40%
Burnt Sienna

DARK GREEN: 80%
Sap Green + 20%
Burnt Umber

DARK RED: 60% Red
+ 40% Burnt Sienna

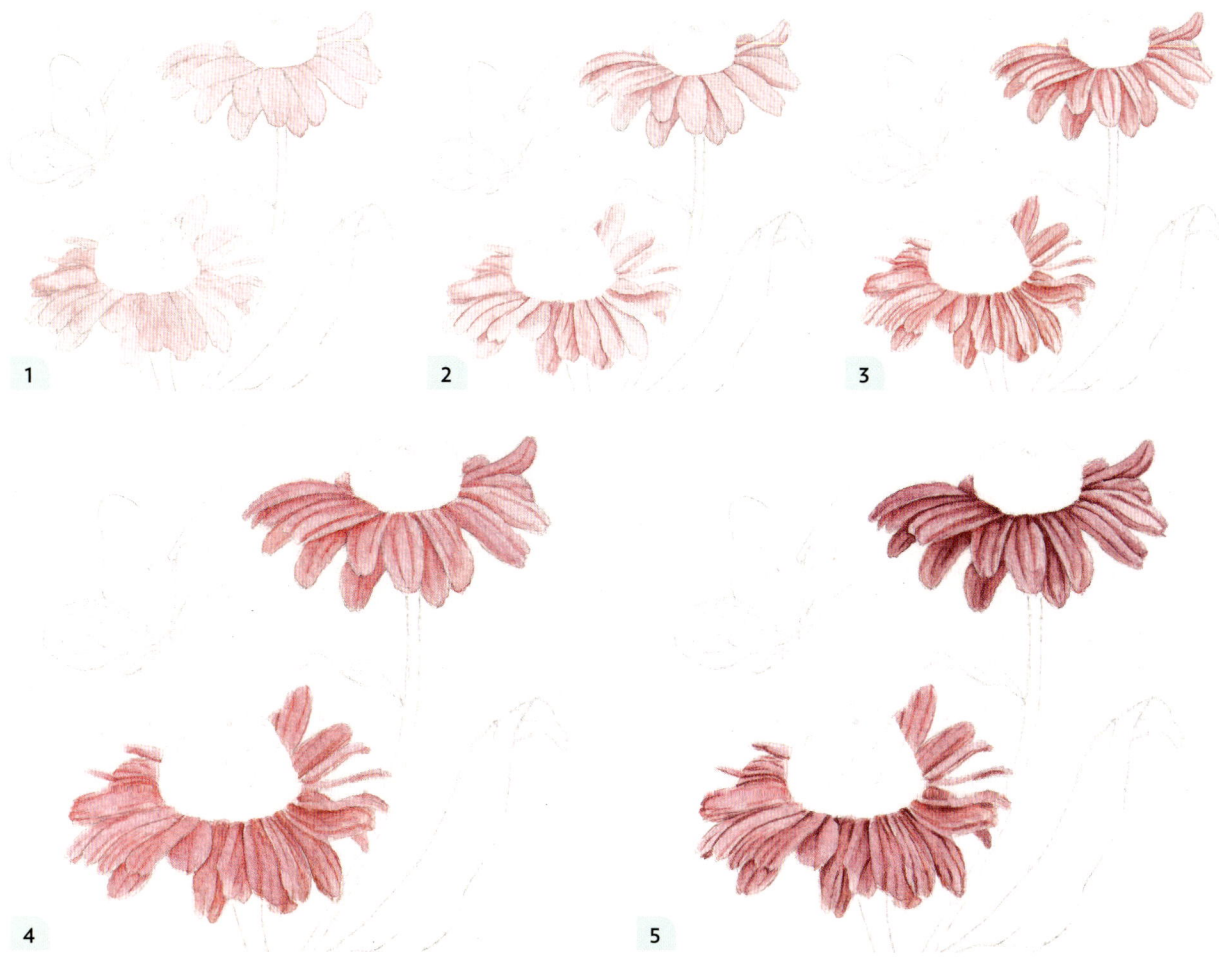

STEP 1: Base Coat for Petals

Wet the areas of the petals with water. Using a number 8 round brush, apply a mixture of Pink and Vermilion to create a Red-tinted Pink. Cover all the petals with this base coat and allow it to dry.

STEP 2: Intensify with Red

With a liner brush, add high-intensity Red-tinted Pink in between the petals to enhance contrast and definition.

STEP 3: Adding Depth to Petals

When dry, apply Dark Red Pink to the petals for detailing, using a liner brush. This step adds depth and dimension to the flower.

STEP 4: Second Layer on Petals

Once the colors are dry, use a number 4 round brush to apply medium-intensity Red tinted Pink all over the petals, creating a darker value. This adds richness to the overall appearance. Let dry.

STEP 5: Refining Petal Details

With a liner brush, apply Dark Red Pink in between and on the petals, following the reference picture for guidance. This step refines the details and emphasizes the lines on the petals.

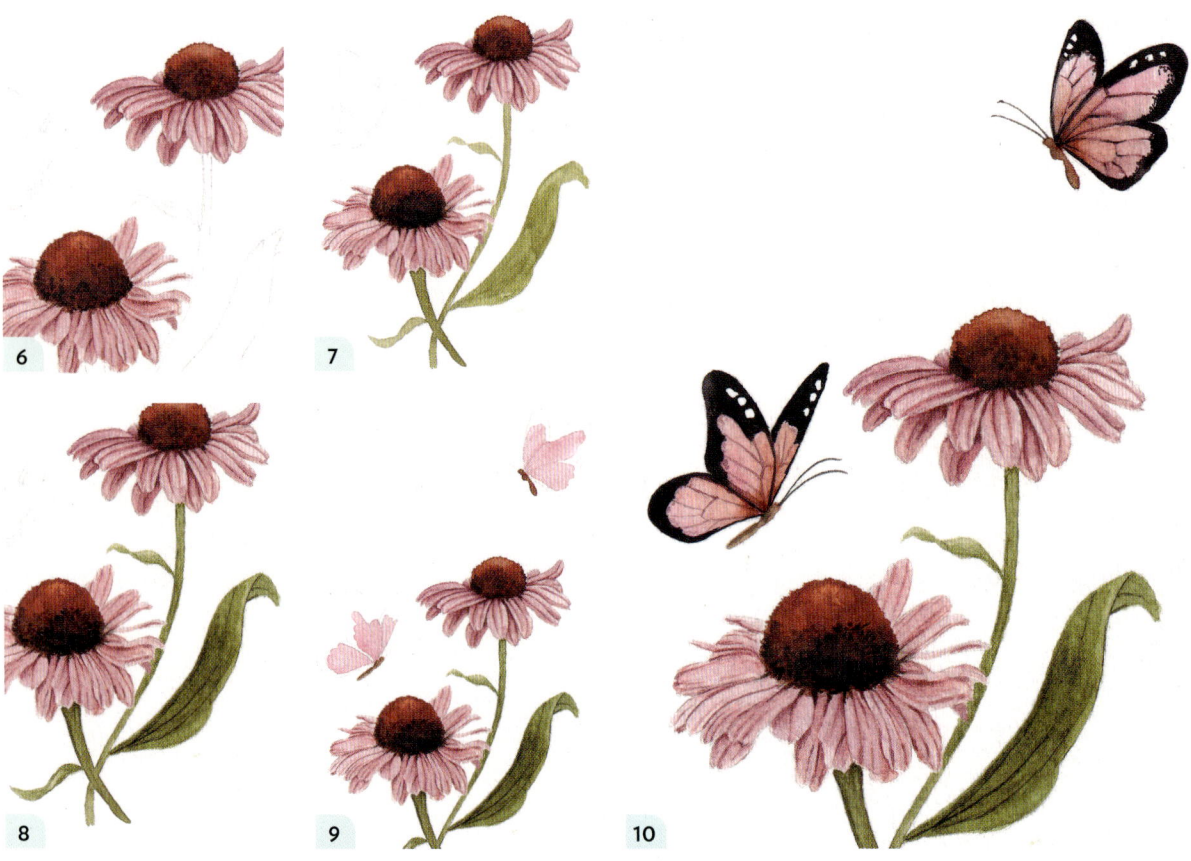

STEP 6: Center of the Flower

Wet the center of the flower with water and apply Dark Red color using a number 4 round brush. Utilize a bouncing brushstroke technique for an organic appearance. Additionally, use a liner brush to apply Burnt Umber to the bottom side of the center, employing the bouncing brush technique.

STEP 7: Further Detailing the Center

Once the previous layer is dry, apply Burnt Umber to the bottom side of the center and to the starting point of the petals. Use a liner brush to add tiny lines to the petals. Fill the stem and leaves with Olive Green using a number 4 round brush.

STEP 8: Detailing Leaves and Stem

Use Dark Green color with a liner brush to add details to the leaves and stem. This step enhances the realism of the foliage. Allow to dry.

STEP 9: Painting the Butterflies

Apply Red-tinted Pink to the butterflies using a number 4 round brush. Additionally, apply Burnt Umber to the body of the butterflies.

STEP 10: Enhancing Butterfly Wings

When dry, apply Dark Red to the wing areas near the body, blending smoothly. Add Dark Pink to create veins on the wings. Use Black color to outline the edges of the wings and the antennas of the butterflies. This step adds the finishing touches to the butterflies.

POPPIES AND BUTTERFLIES

Poppies are typically bright red flowers, but in this painting, I've introduced variations using a mix of wet-on-wet and wet-on-dry techniques to simplify the process for you. While the butterflies showcase fantasy colors, feel free to use your favorite hues. Remember, this demonstration aims to enhance your artistic vision, so follow along to explore new possibilities in your painting.

Brushes

Number 8 round brush
Number 4 round brush
Liner brush

Color Palette

- Red
- Cadmium Yellow
- Dark Red
- Alizarin
- Black
- Olive Green
- Pink
- Orange
- Yellow Ochre
- Turquoise Blue
- Prussian Blue

Color Recipes

ALIZARIN: 70% Red + 30% Cobalt Blue

DARK RED: 40% Red + 60% Burnt Sienna

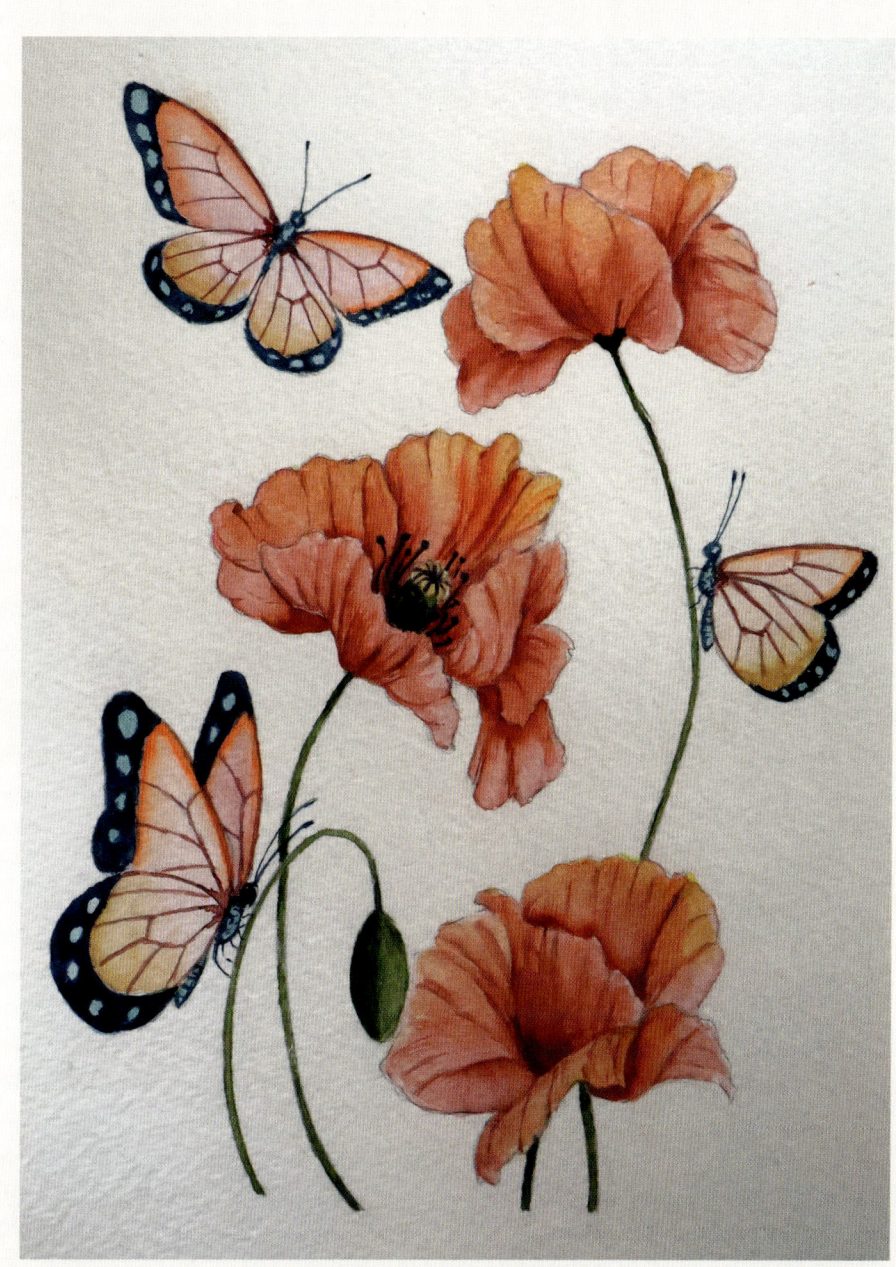

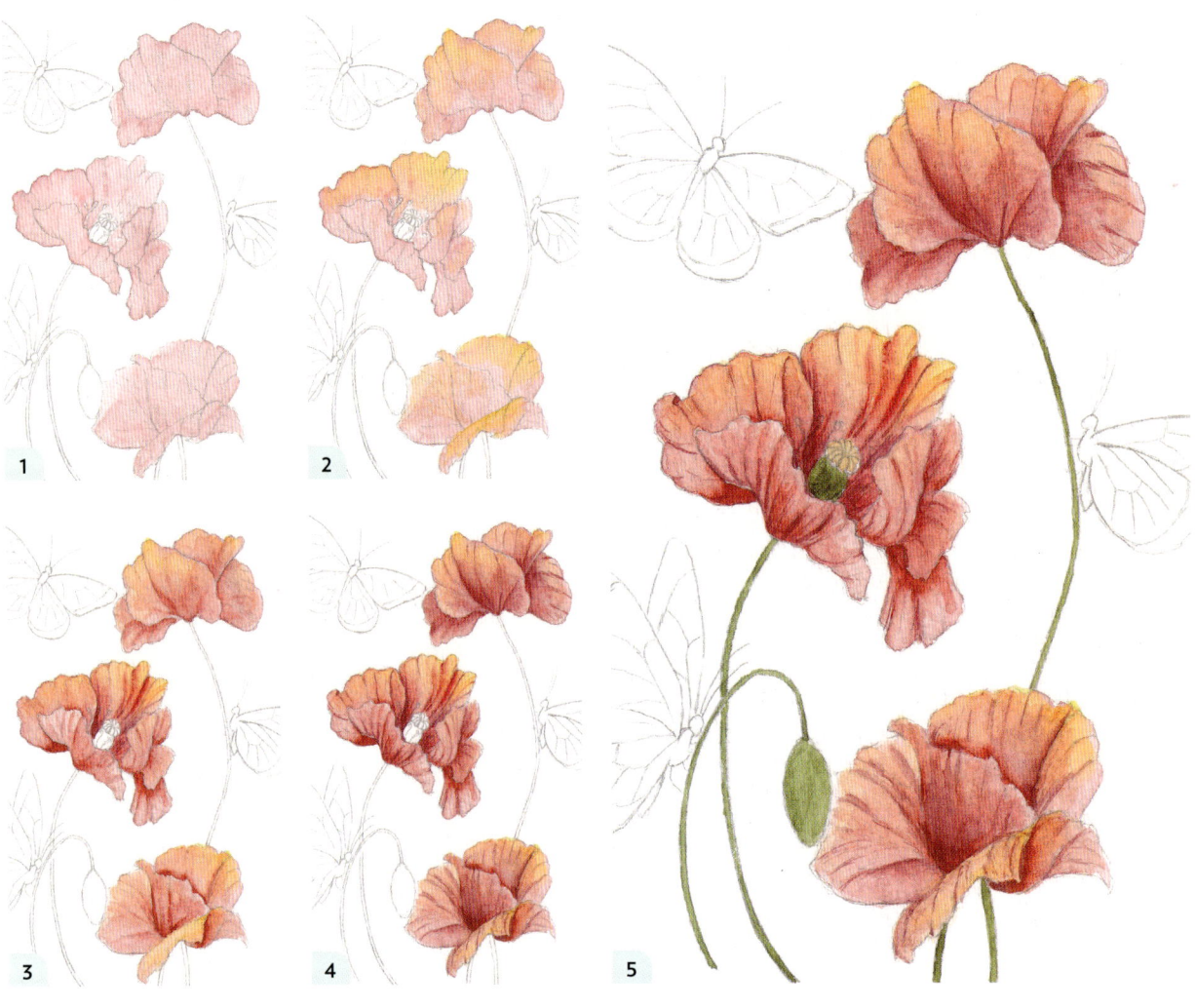

STEP 1: Base Coat for Flower Petals

Using the wet-on-wet technique, paint all the flower petals with Red in low intensity using a number 8 round brush. Let dry.

STEP 2: Highlighting the Petals

Use a number 4 round brush to apply Cadmium Yellow on the sides of the petals.

STEP 3: Application of Shadows

When dry, apply Alizarin in the shadow areas of the flowers with a small number 4 round brush. Let dry.

STEP 4: Enhancing Petal Details

Give details of the petals with Alizarin and Dark Red with a liner brush.

STEP 5: Centering the Flower and Stems

When the colors are dry, apply Olive Green to the center of the flower and stems. Use a liner brush to ease the process. Allow to dry.

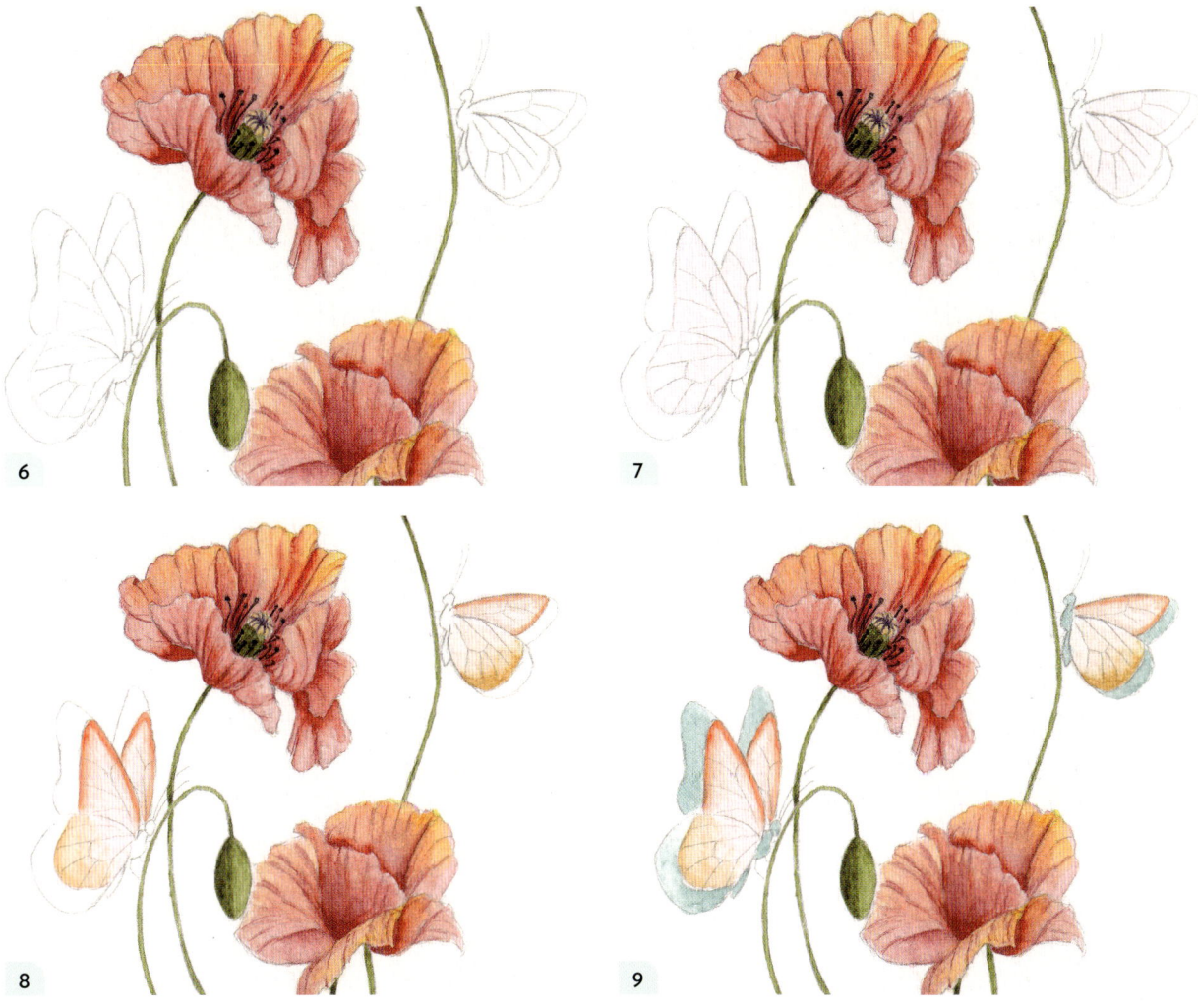

STEP 6: Intensifying the Flower

Use high-intensity Olive Green in the center and stems with a liner brush.

STEP 7: Accenting the Flower

Apply Black to the stamens and bottom area of the flowers.

STEP 8: Accenting Butterfly Wings

Using the wet-on-wet technique, apply pink color on the wings of the butterfly with a number 4 round brush. Allow to dry.

STEP 9: Coloring Butterfly Wings

Apply Orange on the top wing edges and Yellow Ochre to the bottom wing edges. Check the reference for details. Blur the edges with an empty brush.

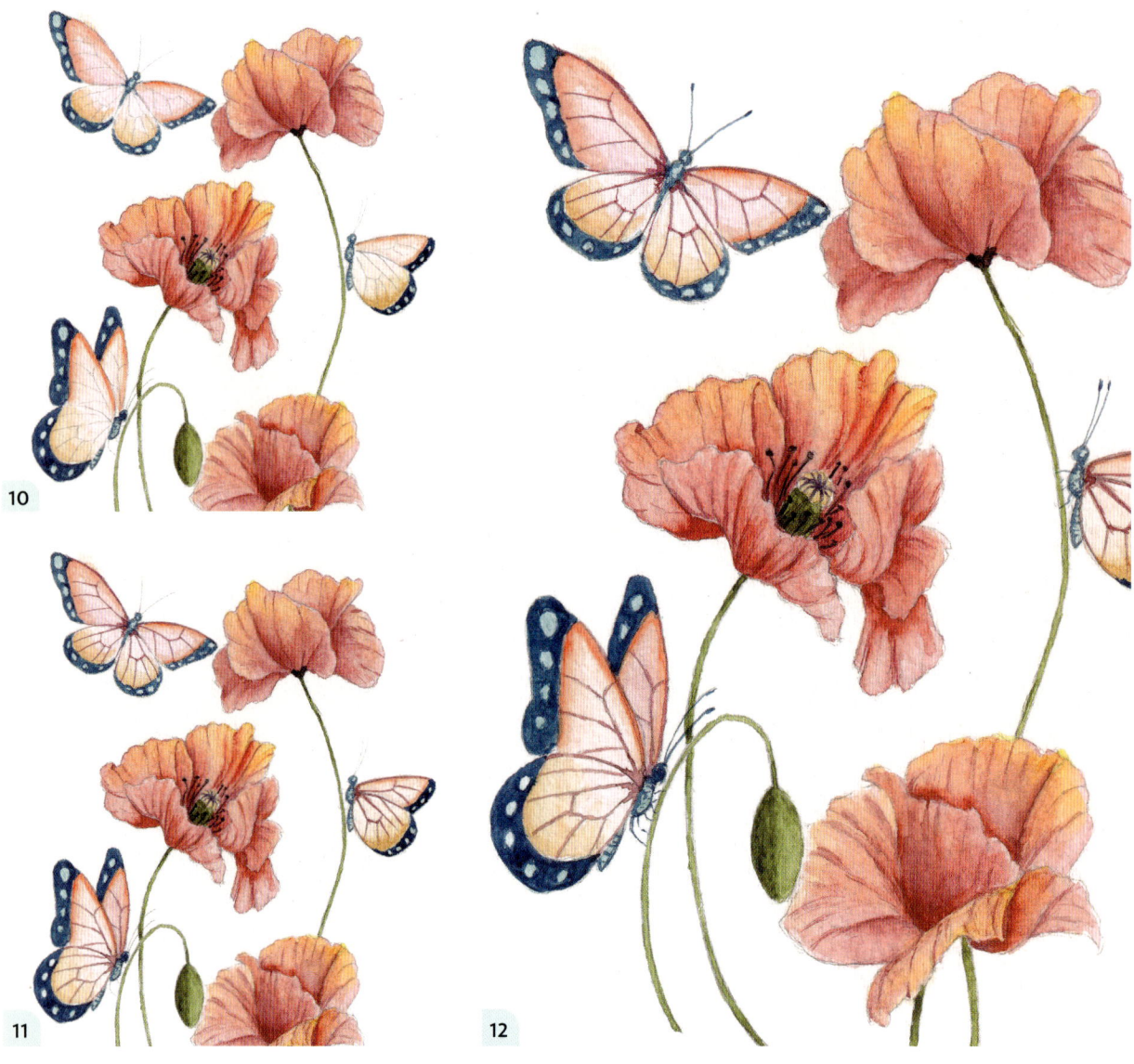

STEP 10: Coloring Wing Edges

When dry, apply Turquoise Blue on the edges of the wings and body with a number 4 round brush. Let dry.

STEP 11: Detailing the Wings

Using a liner brush, apply Prussian Blue in the edges by leaving tiny details in between. You can see the light-colored tiny circles in the edges of the wings. Also apply the same color on the body of the butterfly.

STEP 12: Detailing the Veins

When dry, apply Alizarin on the veins and the area near the body using a liner brush. Allow to dry. For the final touch, paint Prussian Blue on the antennae and legs of the butterfly.

Brushes

Number 8 round brush
Number 4 round brush
Liner brush

Color Palette

Pink

Purple

Cobalt Blue

Prussian Blue

Dark Pink

Violet

Dark Red

Dark Olive Green

Burnt Umber

Dark Purple

Gold Metallic

Color Recipes

PURPLE: 60% Pink + 40% Cobalt Blue

DARK PINK: 80% Pink + 20% Burnt Umber

DARK PURPLE: 80% Purple + 20% Burnt Umber

DARK RED: 40% Red + 60% Burnt Sienna

DARK OLIVE GREEN: 70% Olive Green + 30% Burnt Umber

HYDRANGEA AND BUTTERFLIES

Hydrangea flowers maintain their exquisite structure even as their colors fade, retaining their timeless beauty. As you may already know, the hydrangea's hues shift from blue to pink based on the soil's pH balance. In this demonstration, I've simplified the steps using a mix of wet-on-wet and wet-on-dry techniques, ensuring that even beginners can paint a stunning hydrangea with both colors effortlessly.

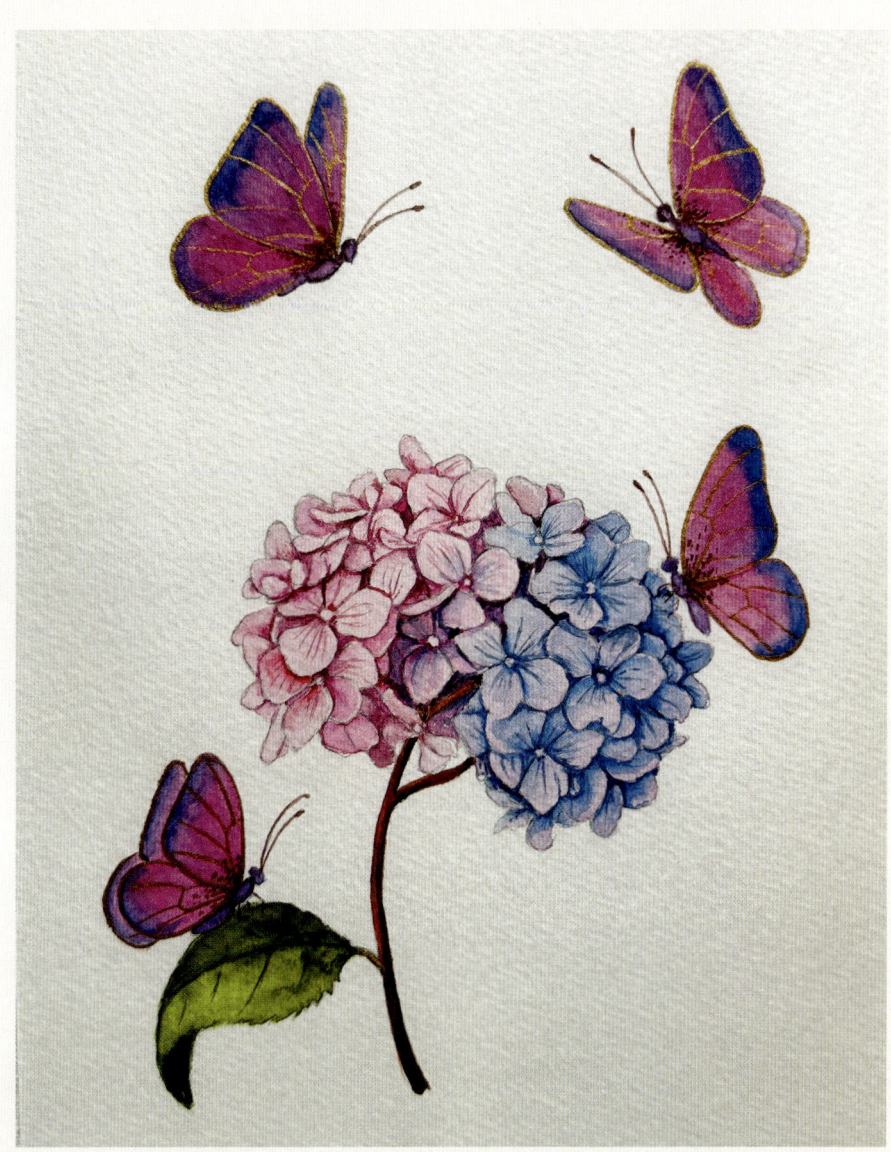

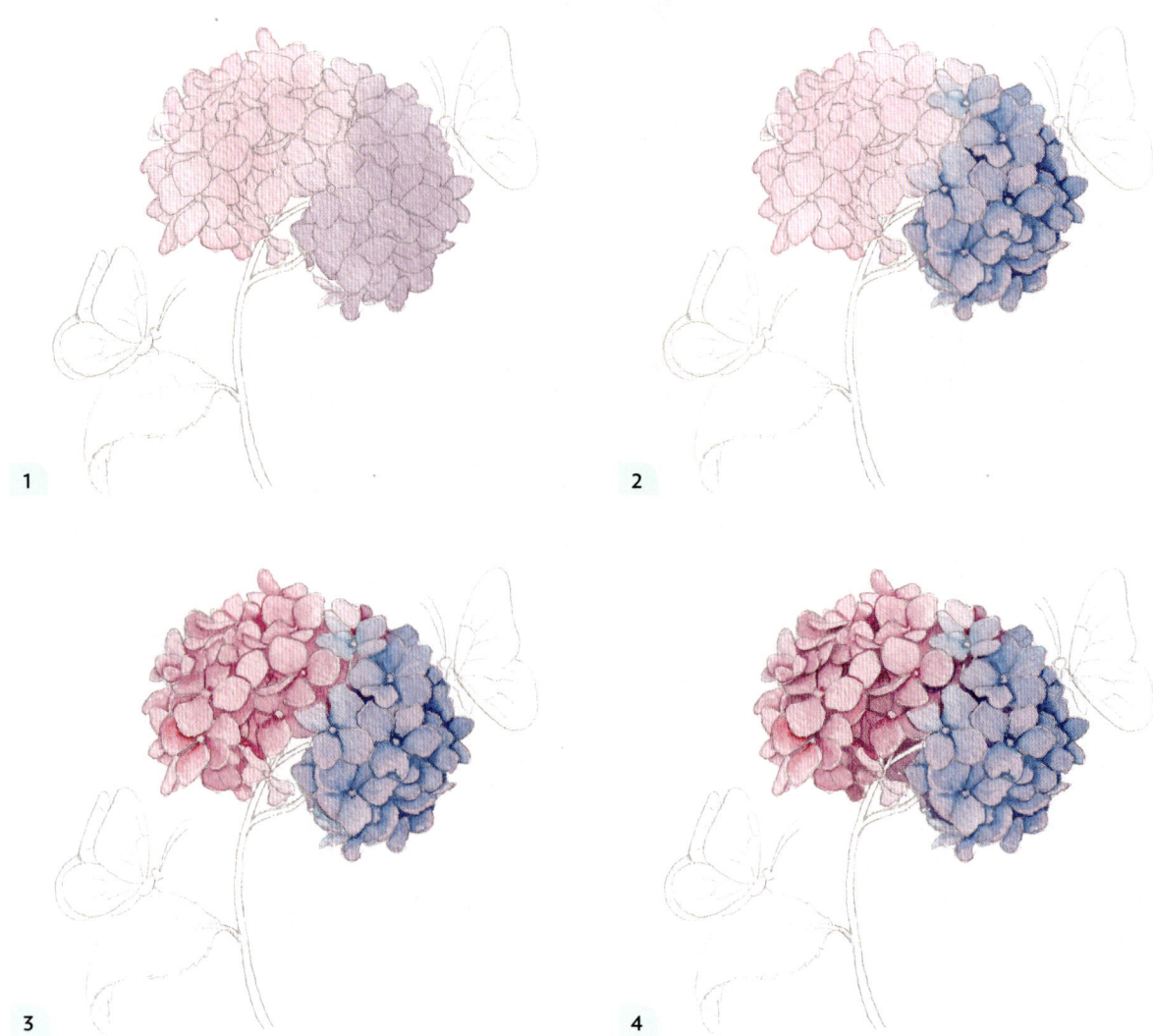

STEP 1: Base Layer for Flowers

Wet the flower area and apply light-intensity Pink on the left side and Purple on the right using a number 8 round brush.

STEP 2: Adding Center and Petal Details

When dry, use a liner brush to apply Prussian Blue to the flower center, Cobalt Blue between the petals, and Prussian Blue in tiny spaces. Let dry.

STEP 3: Enhancing Flower Depth

Apply high-intensity Pink on the left side of the flower with a liner brush, mirroring the right side. Let dry.

STEP 4: Adding Contrast and Dimension

When dry, use a liner brush to apply Dark Pink on the left and Dark Purple on the right side of the flower. Let dry.

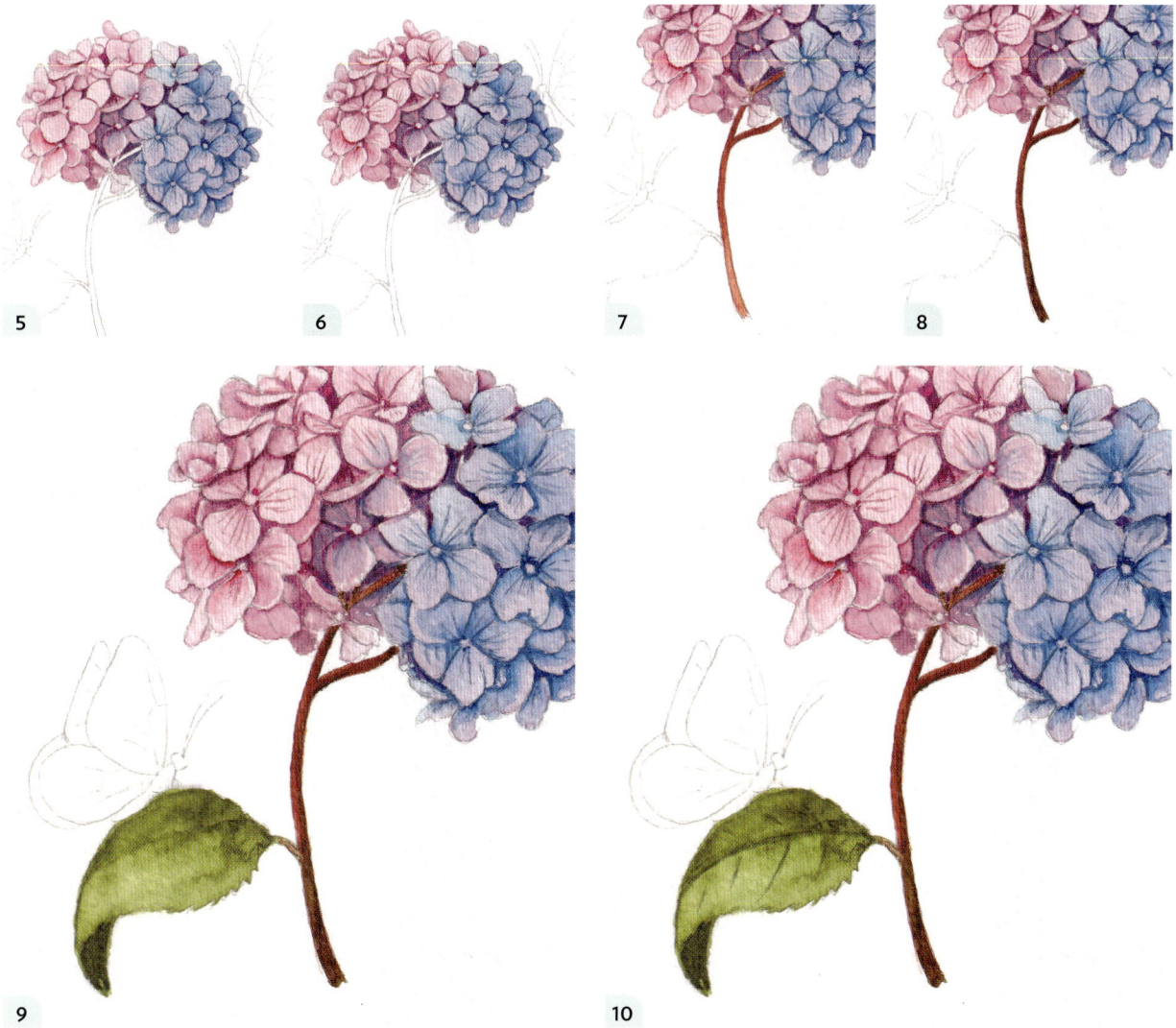

STEP 5: Petal Detailing—Right Side

Add tiny lines with Prussian Blue to detail the petals on the right side.

STEP 6: Petal Detailing—Left Side

When dry, detail the petals on the left side with Dark Pink. Allow to dry.

STEP 7: Stem Base Color

Apply Dark Red to the flower stems with a number 4 round brush.

STEP 8: Stem Shading and Texture

When dry, cover the stems with Burnt Umber from bottom to top. Let dry.

STEP 9: Base Layer for Leaves

Apply Olive Green to the leaves.

STEP 10: Leaf Detailing

When dry, add leaf details with Dark Olive Green.

STEP 11: Base Layer for Butterfly Wings
Wet the butterfly wings and apply Pink and Cobalt Blue. Let dry.

STEP 12: Butterfly Body
Use a liner brush to give the butterfly body a Purple color.

STEP 13: Wing Detailing—Inner Sections
When dry, apply Dark Purple on the wings near the body. Let dry.

STEP 14: Wing Vein Highlighting
Use a liner brush to apply Gold Metallic on the wing veins.

STEP 15: Final Touches on Butterfly Wings
When dry, apply Dark Pink on the wings near the body, detailing the body and antennae with the same color using a liner brush.

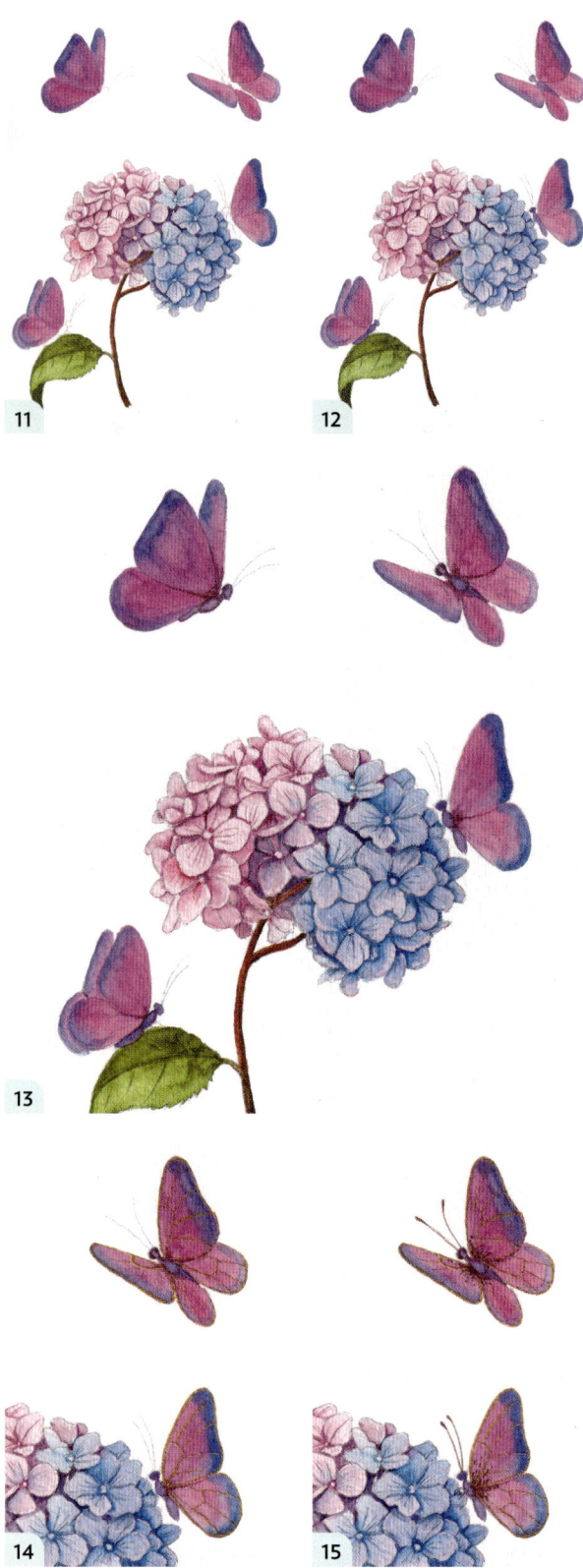

Brushes

Number 8 round brush
Number 4 round brush
Liner brush

Color Palette

- Purple
- Cadmium Yellow
- Cobalt Blue
- Reddish Purple
- Olive Green
- Dark Red
- Dark Green
- Viridian
- Pink
- Burnt Umber
- Gold Metallic

Color Recipes

PURPLE: 60% Pink + 40% Cobalt Blue

REDDISH PURPLE: 40% Pink + 40% Red + 20% Cobalt Blue

DARK PURPLE: 80% Purple + 20% Burnt Umber

DARK RED: 40% Red + 60% Burnt Sienna

DARK GREEN: 70% Green + 30% Burnt Umber

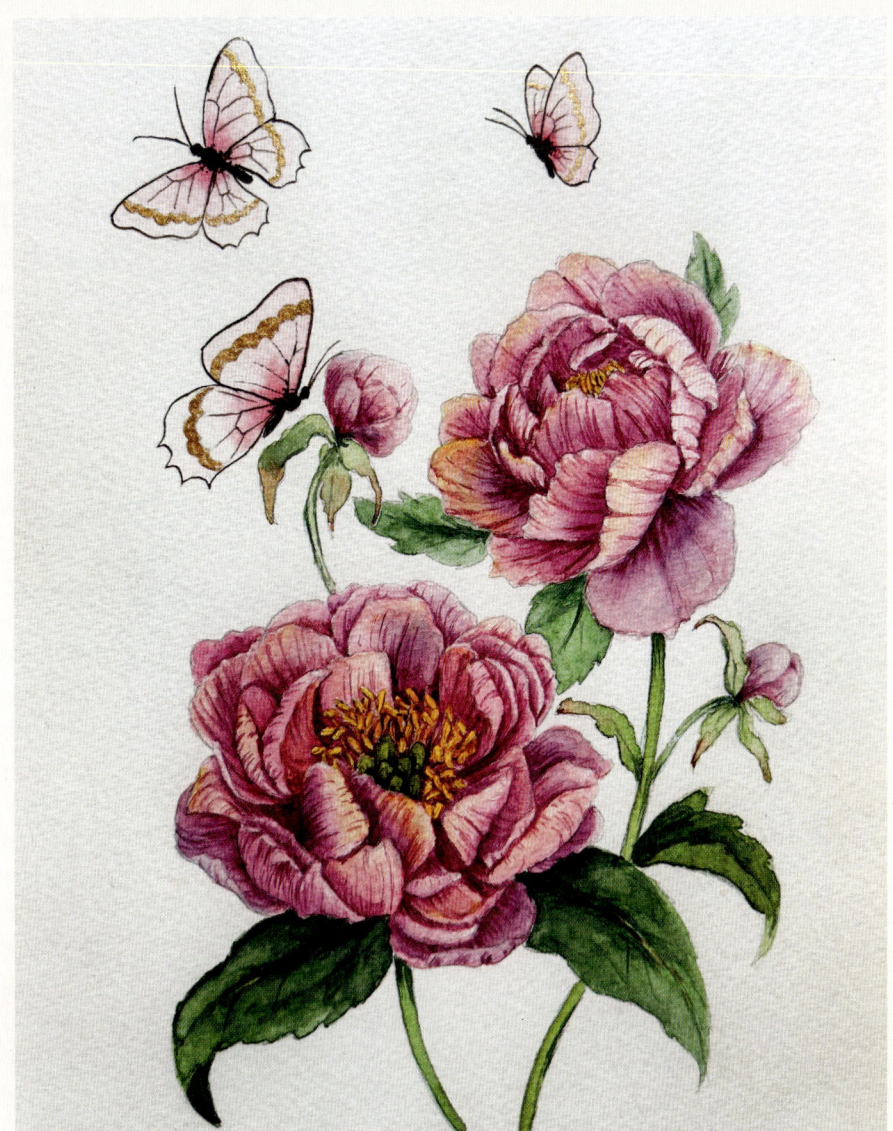

PEONIES AND BUTTERFLIES

Peonies are considered lucky flowers but can be challenging for beginners to paint. I've chosen an approach that simplifies the process, ensuring you won't feel overwhelmed while creating these beautiful blooms. I hope you enjoy the painting journey.

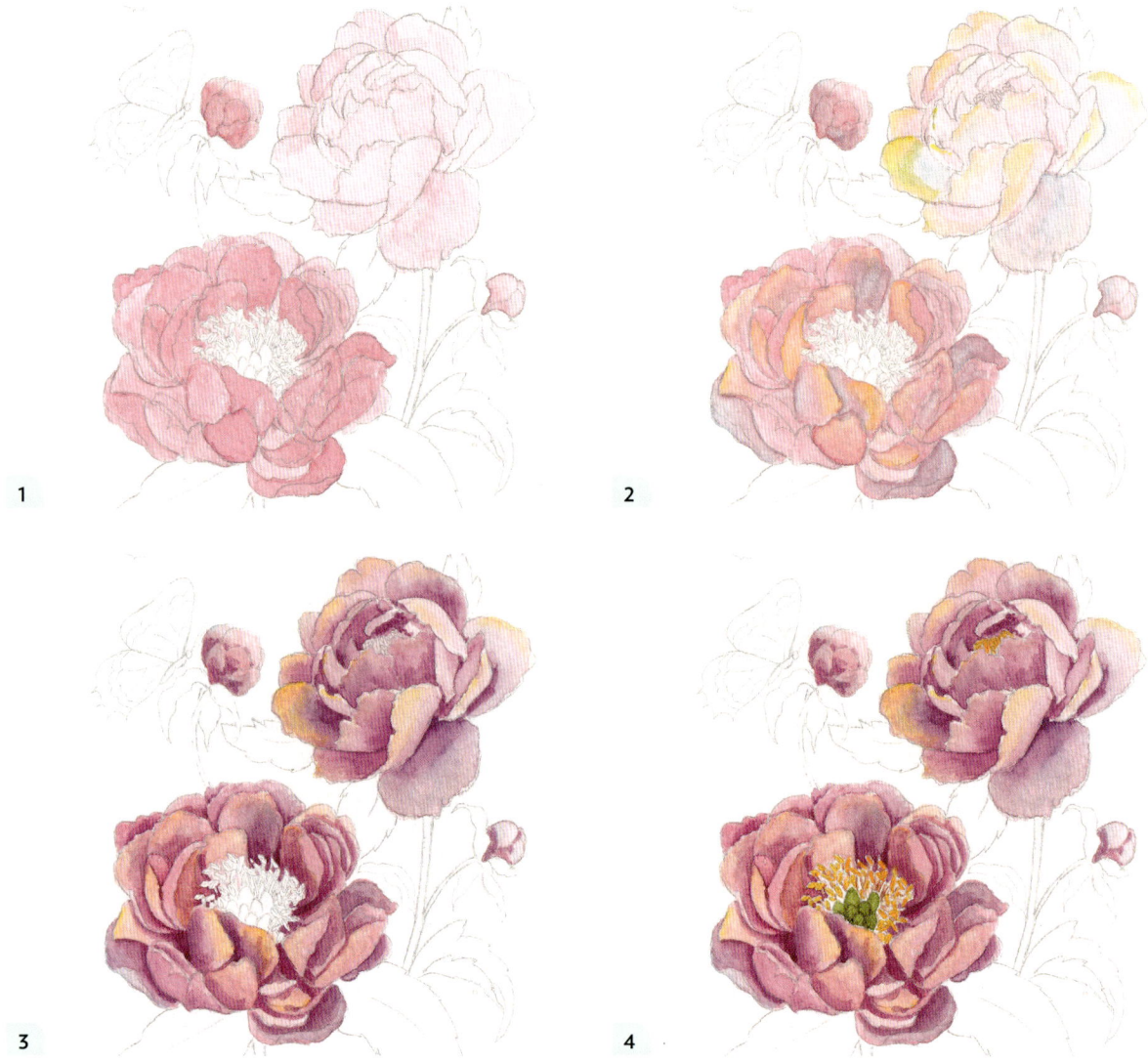

STEP 1: Base Layer for Flowers

Wet the flower area and apply a light intensity of Purple all over using a number 8 round brush. Let dry. After every step in this painting, allow the previous layer to dry.

STEP 2: Petal Highlighting and Detailing

Using a number 4 round brush, apply Cadmium Yellow to the petal tips and Cobalt Blue on the top of the petals, following the reference. Let dry.

STEP 3: Adding Depth to Petals

Enhance depth by applying high-intensity Purple to the bottom side of the petals with a number 4 round brush.

STEP 4: Center and Stamens Detailing

When dry, apply Olive Green to the flower center and Cadmium Yellow to the stamens. Allow to dry.

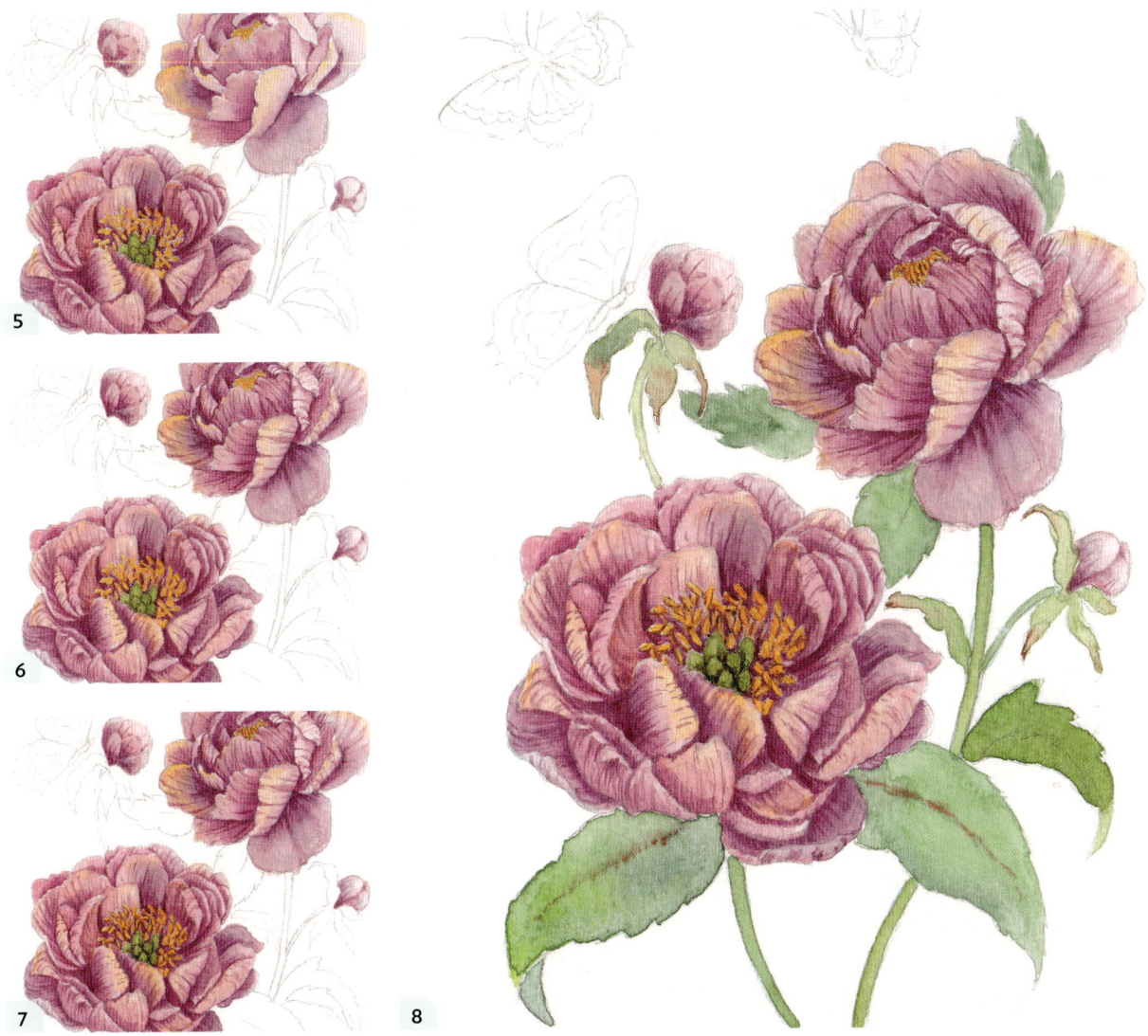

STEP 5: Front Flower Petal Detailing

Using a liner brush, add tiny lines all over the front flower petals for detailing.

STEP 6: Background Flower and Bud Detailing

When dry, repeat the same detailing process for the background flower and buds.

STEP 7: Middle-area Detailing for Flowers

Provide middle-area details by using Dark Red as a line around the stamens and Dark Green around the center with a liner brush. Let dry.

STEP 8: Base Layer for Leaves and Stem

Apply Viridian to the leaves and stem using a number 8 round brush, incorporating Burnt Sienna and Cobalt Blue for color variations. Allow to dry.

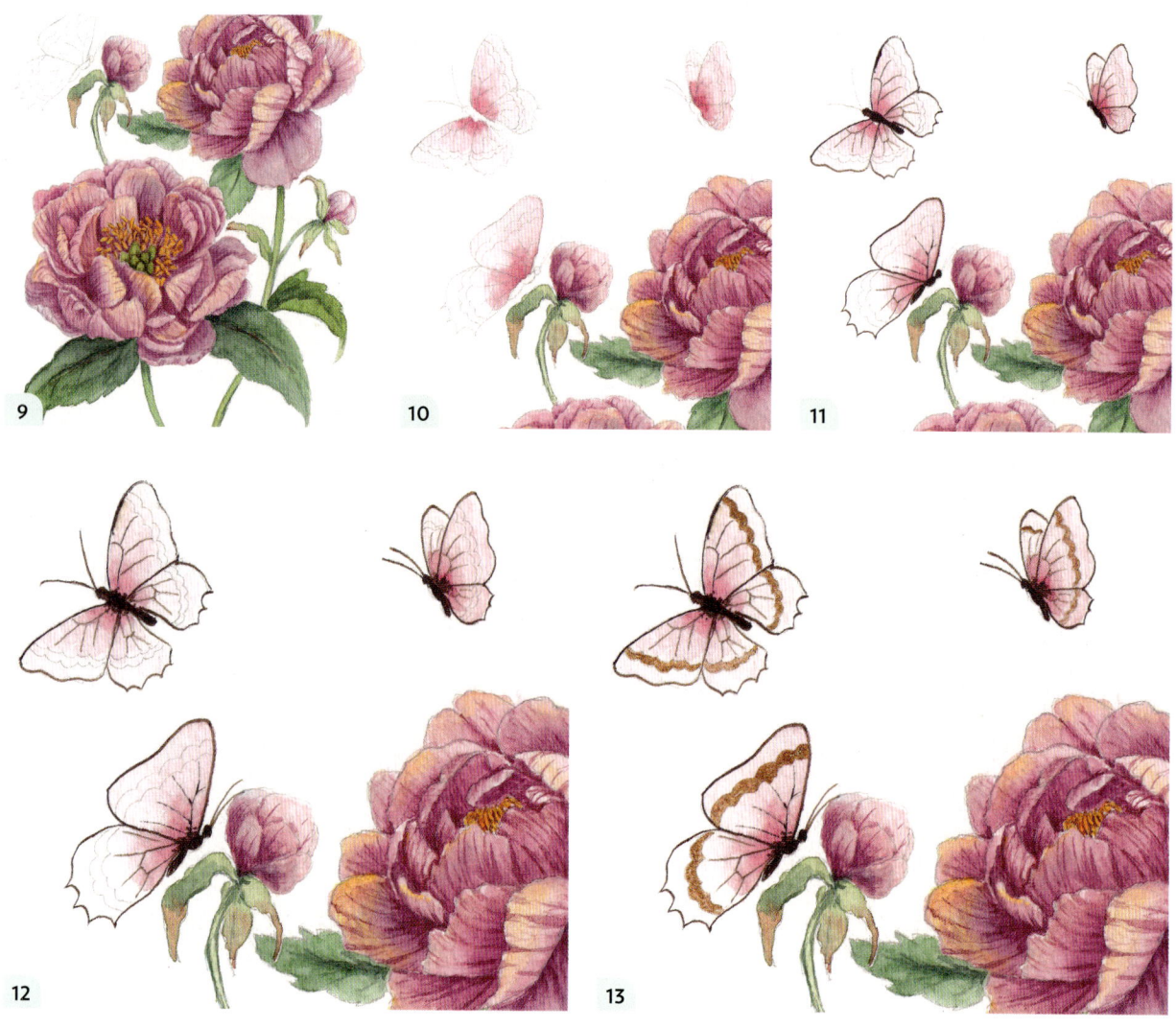

STEP 9: Leaf Depth and Detailing

Use Dark Green with a number 4 round brush to add depth to the leaves.

STEP 10: Base Layer for Butterfly Wings

Wet the butterfly wings, gradually increasing color saturation towards the inner side using a smaller-sized brush. Let dry.

STEP 11: Butterfly Body and Veins

Apply Burnt Umber to the body and veins of the butterfly with a liner brush.

STEP 12: Detailing Butterfly Wings and Antennae

When dry, detail the wings near the body area and antennae with Burnt Umber using a liner brush. Let dry.

STEP 13: Final Touches with Metallic Gold

Add Gold Metallic to the wing details of the butterfly for a finishing touch.

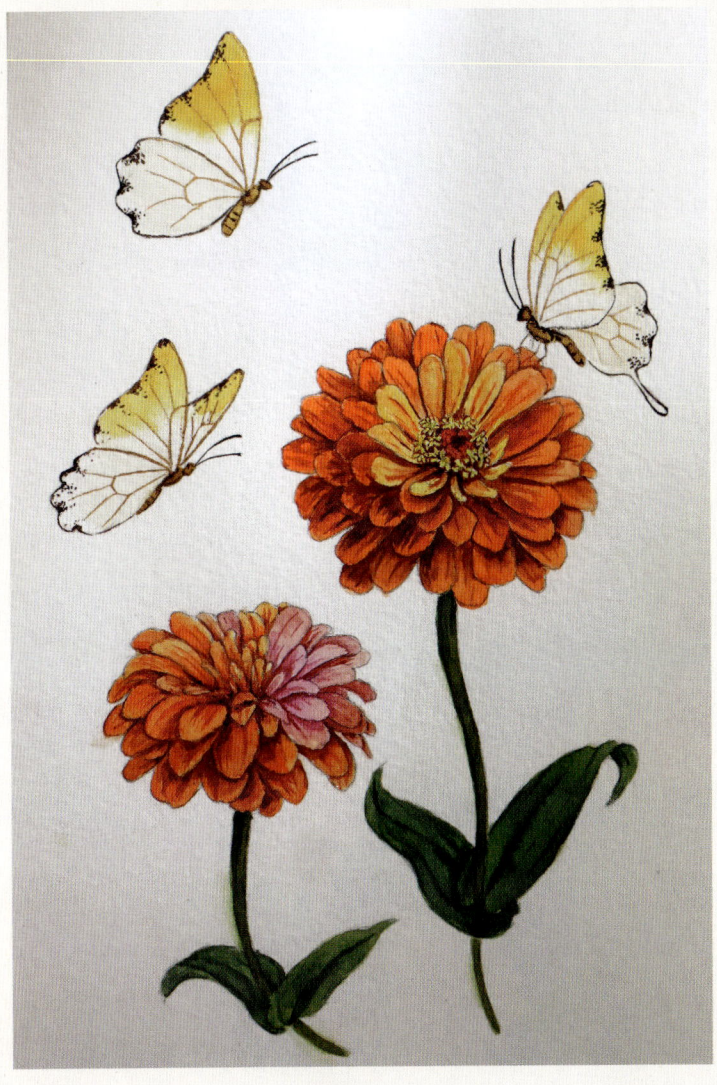

ZINNIA AND BUTTERFLIES

Another favorite of mine are the zinnias with their tight petal structure that always elicits a "Wow" from everyone. Let's paint them along with complementary butterflies gracefully fluttering around. Scan the QR code to watch me painting the Zinnia and Butterflies.

Brushes

Number 8 round brush
Number 4 round brush
Liner brush

Color Palette

- Cadmium Yellow
- Orange
- Dark Orange

- Pink
- Dark Pink
- Red
- Lemon Yellow
- Burnt Sienna
- Burnt Umber
- Olive Green

- Bluish Olive Green
- Dark Green
- Yellow Ochre
- Gold Metallic

Color Recipes

- **DARK ORANGE:** 70% Orange + 30% Burnt Umber

- **DARK PINK:** 60% Pink + 40% Burnt Umber

- **BLUISH OLIVE GREEN:** 60% Olive Green + 40% Cobalt Blue

- **DARK GREEN:** 70% Bluish Olive Green + 30% Burnt Umber

STEP 1: Base Layer for Flowers

With a number 4 round brush, use the wet-on-dry technique, applying Cadmium Yellow and Orange to the large flower and Pink and Orange to the small flower. Let dry. After every step in this painting, allow the previous layer to dry.

STEP 2: Petal Detailing—
Large and Small Flowers

For the large flower, individually apply high-intensity Orange on the outer petals and high-intensity Cadmium Yellow on the inner petals. For the small flower, use moderate-intensity Orange and Pink on individual petals. Employ a number 4 round brush for both. Allow to dry.

STEP 3: Separating Petals and Center Detailing

Use Dark Orange to separate each petal and apply Dark Pink only to the Pink petal area, using a liner brush for comfort.

STEP 4: Center and Tiny Flower Detailing

When dry, apply Red to the flower center and Lemon Yellow to the tiny flowers in the center, using a liner brush. Let dry.

STEP 5: Further Detailing Large Flower Petals

Use a liner brush to add Burnt Sienna between the tiny flowers in the center, providing details to the very center. Give details to the petals of the large flower by adding lines on top with Dark Orange. Let dry.

STEP 6: Center Detailing Continued

Apply Burnt Umber between the tiny flowers in the center of the large flower. Also, apply high-intensity Orange and Pink as details to the small flower petals, using a liner brush.

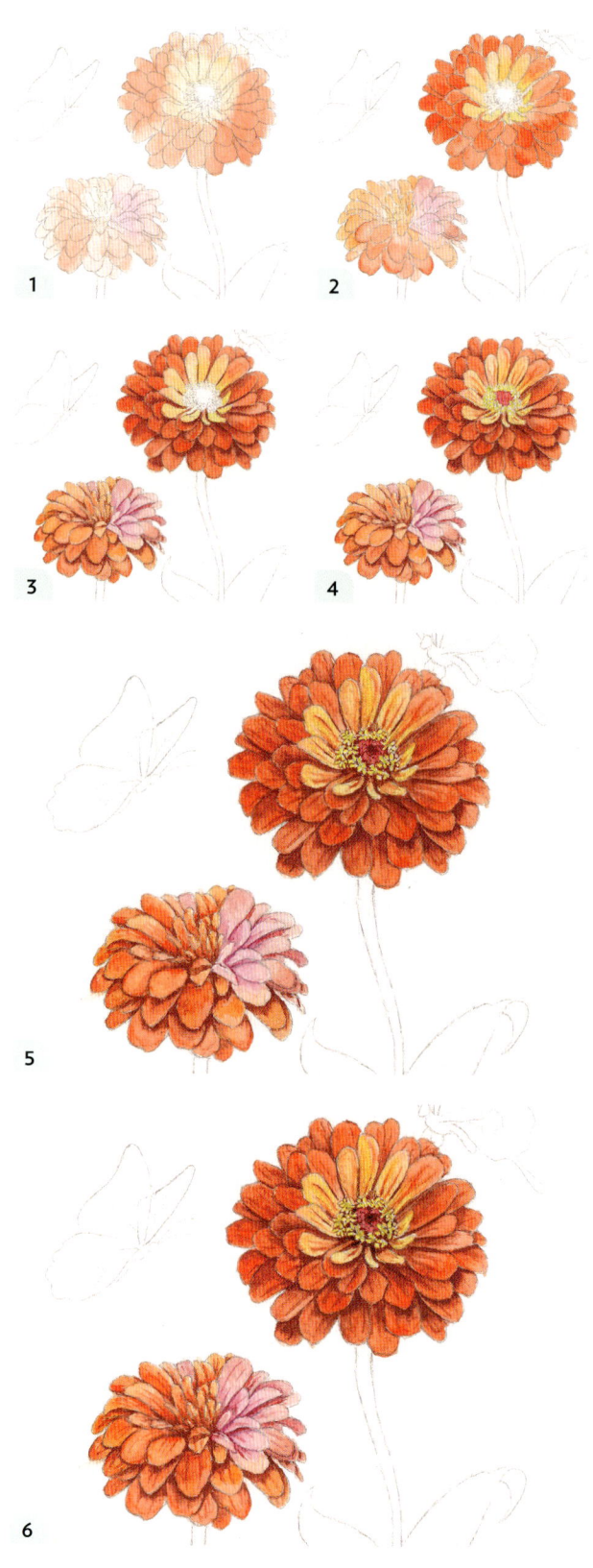

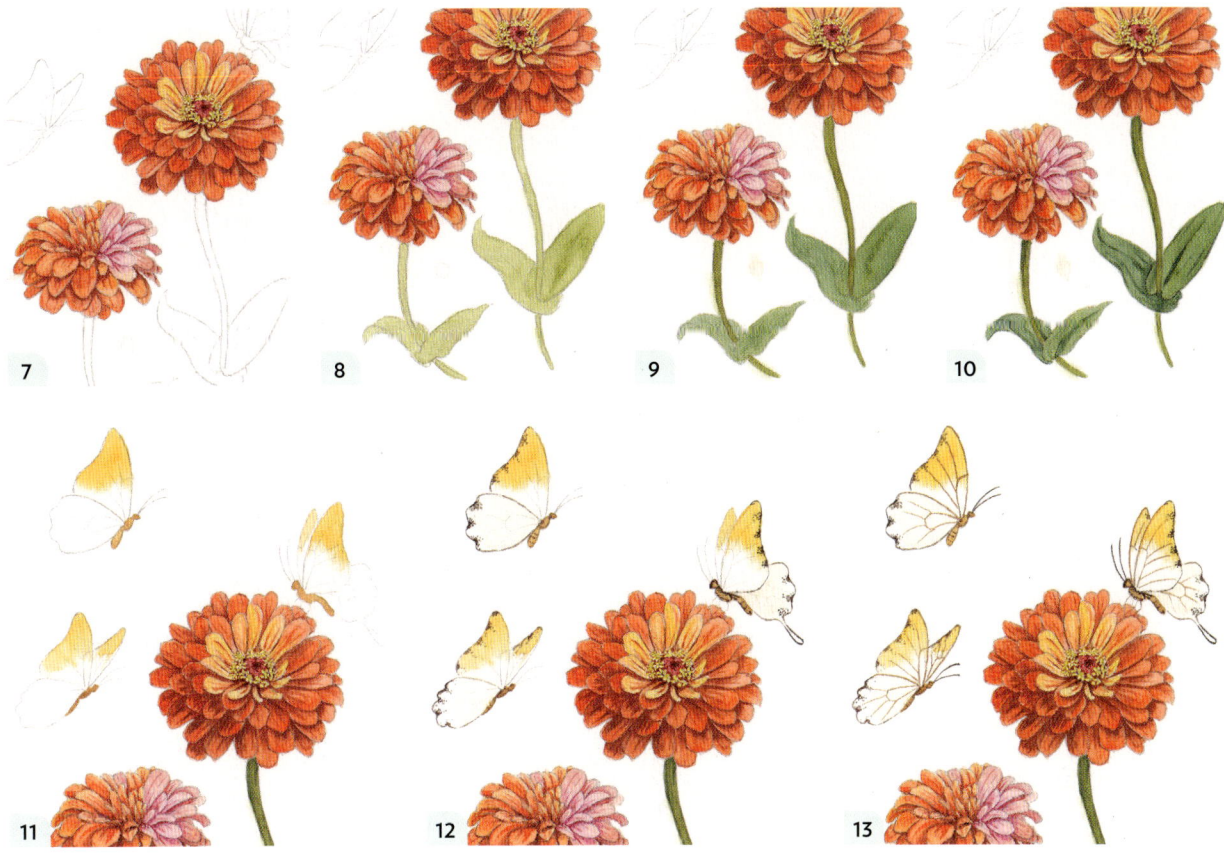

STEP 7: Adding Shadow and Depth

When dry, add a shadow to the flower on the bottom-left side by applying high-intensity Orange to that specific area. Refer to the reference for guidance and use a liner brush.

STEP 8: Base Layer for Stem and Leaves

With a number 4 round brush, apply Olive Green to the stem and leaves. Allow to dry.

STEP 9: Leaf Detailing and Stem Coloring

Use Bluish Olive Green on the leaves and apply high-intensity Olive Green to the stems. Utilize a number 4 round brush for the leaves and a liner brush for the stem. Let dry.

STEP 10: Leaf Detailing Continued

Use Dark Green to detail the leaves with a liner brush.

STEP 11: Base Layer for Butterfly Wings and Body

With a number 4 round brush, wet the butterfly wings and apply Cadmium Yellow to the top end. Also, apply Yellow Ochre to the butterfly's body using a liner brush. Let dry.

STEP 12: Detailing Butterfly Body and Wings

Apply Burnt Umber for the details on the body and side of the wings. Allow to dry.

STEP 13: Final Wing Vein Detailing with Gold

Add Gold Metallic to the veins of the wings.

BLACK-EYED SUSAN AND BUTTERFLIES

Black-eyed Susans, or Rudbeckia, are fun and easy flowers to draw. The dark center of the flower naturally creates depth, which adds to its appeal. Let's paint using a mix of wet-on-wet and wet-on-dry techniques and learn more about them. Scan the QR code to watch me paint Black-Eyed Susan and Butterflies.

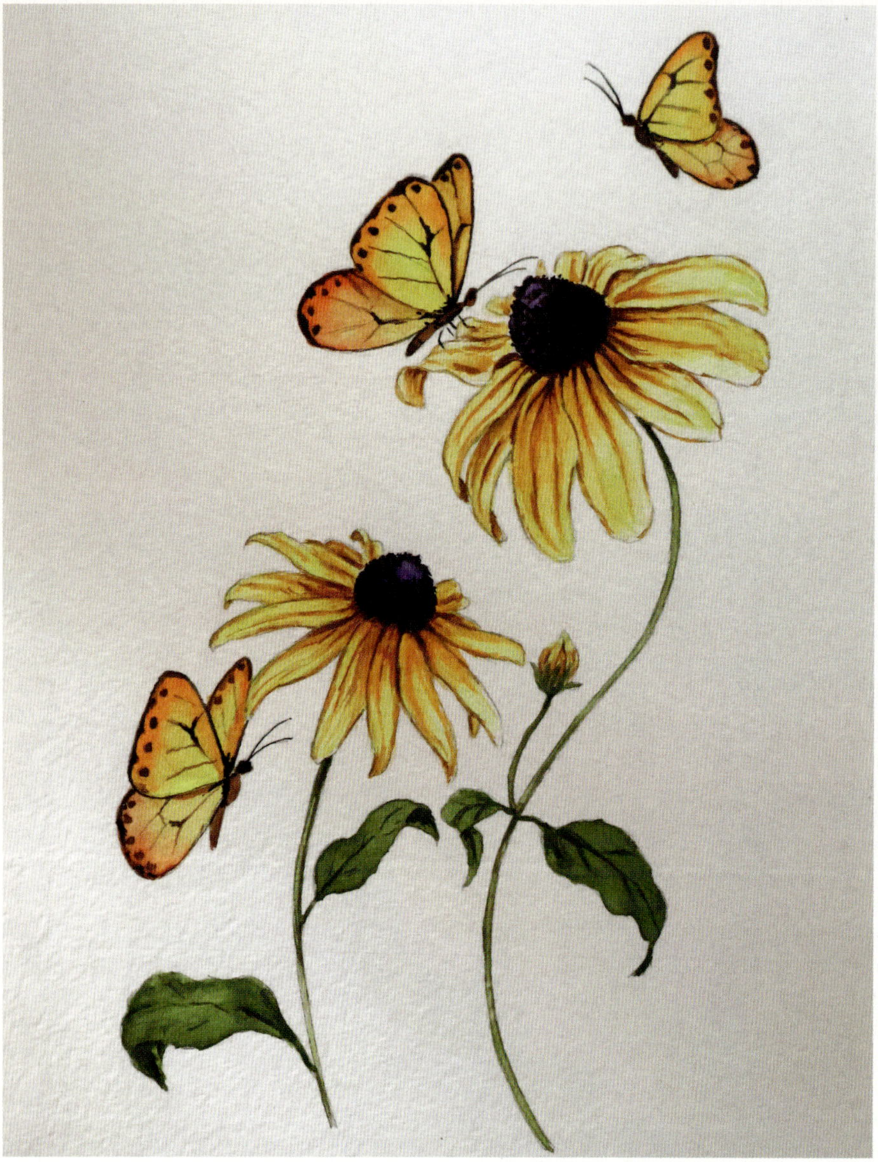

Brushes

Number 8 round brush
Number 4 round brush
Liner brush

Color Palette

- Lemon Yellow
- Cadmium Yellow
- Yellow Ochre
- Indian Yellow
- Dark Indian Yellow
- Burnt Sienna
- Violet/Indigo
- Black
- Olive Green
- Orange
- Red
- Burnt Umber

Color Recipes

INDIAN YELLOW: 50% Cadmium Yellow + 50% Orange

DARK INDIAN YELLOW: 60% Indian Yellow + 40% Burnt Umber

STEP 1: Base Layer for Flower Petals

Using the wet-on-wet technique, begin by applying Lemon Yellow to the flower petals with a low-intensity, using a number 8 round brush for the flower and number 4 for the buds. Allow to dry.

STEP 2: Adding Depth with Cadmium Yellow

Add Cadmium Yellow towards the center of the petals. Let dry.

STEP 3: Detailed Work with Indian Yellow

Using a liner brush, introduce Indian Yellow for detailed work on the petals and spaces in between.

STEP 4: Creating Shadows with Dark Indian Yellow

When dry, apply Dark Indian Yellow to the petals and spaces in between using a liner brush to create depth and shadows.

STEP 5: Center Detailing with Violet/Indigo

With a number 4 round brush, use the wet-on-wet technique to place Violet in the center of the flower.

STEP 6: Intricate Center Details

When dry, utilize the bouncing brush technique and a liner brush to apply Black to the center as intricate details. Allow to dry.

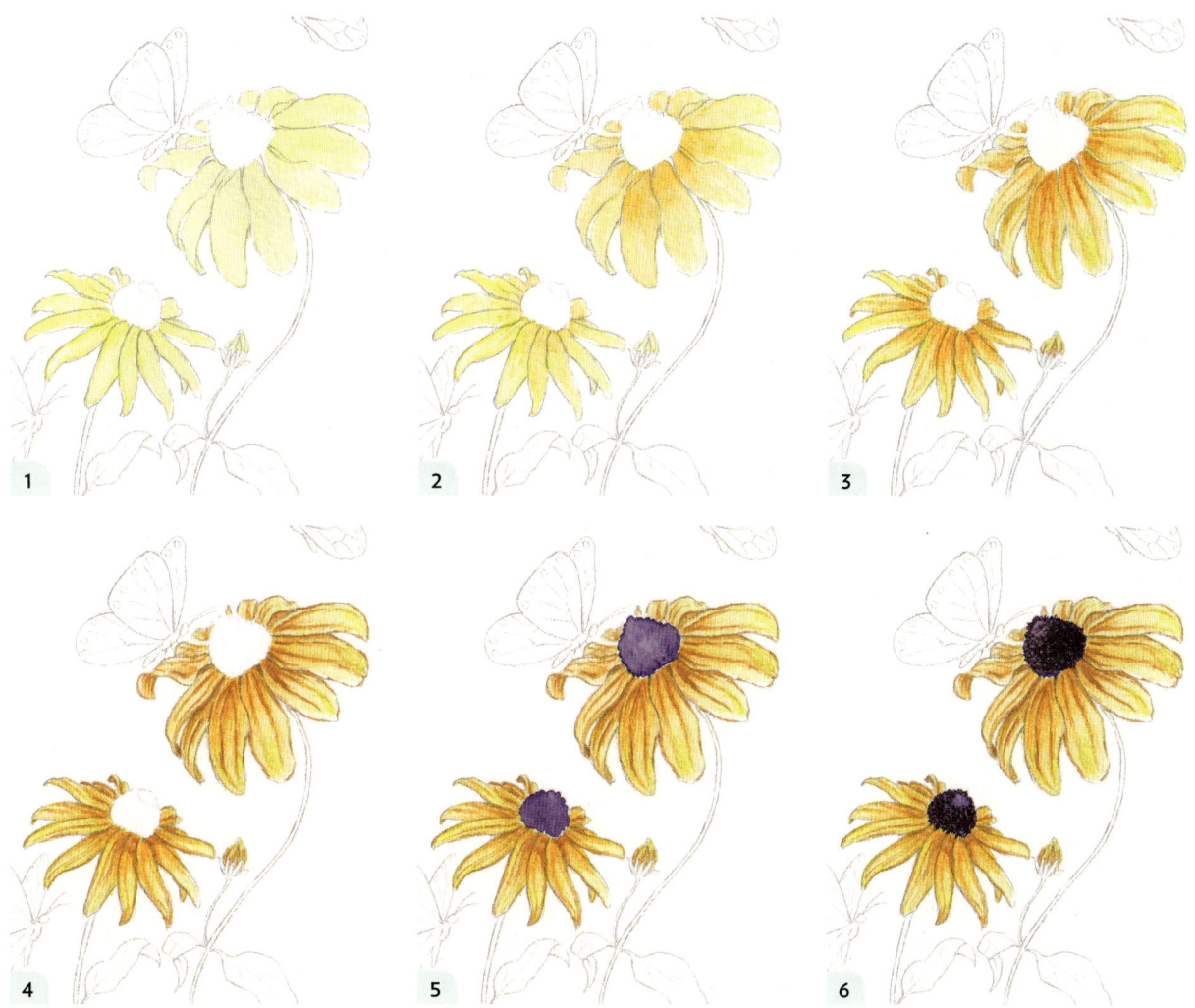

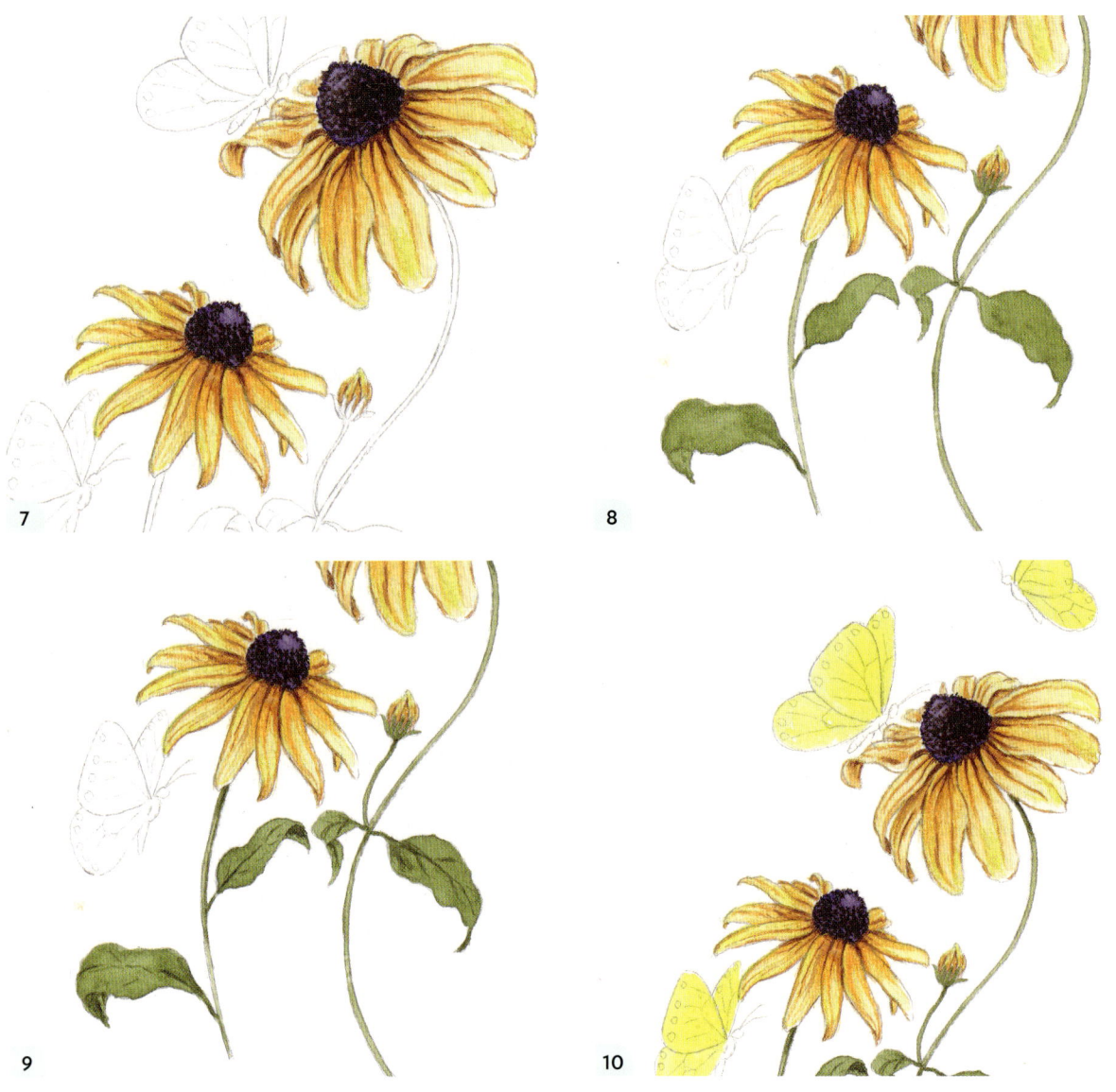

STEP 7: Realism Enhancements with Burnt Sienna

Enhance realism by applying Burnt Sienna around the center, the closest parts of the petals, and the spaces in between.

STEP 8: Base Layer for Stems and Leaves

When dry, paint the stems and leaves with Olive Green. Let dry.

STEP 9: Leaf and Stem Detailing

Add more details to the stems and leaves by incorporating high-intensity Olive Green.

STEP 10: Base Layer for Butterfly Wings— Upper Wings

For the butterfly wings, use the wet-on-wet technique and use a number 8 round brush to apply Lemon Yellow. Let dry.

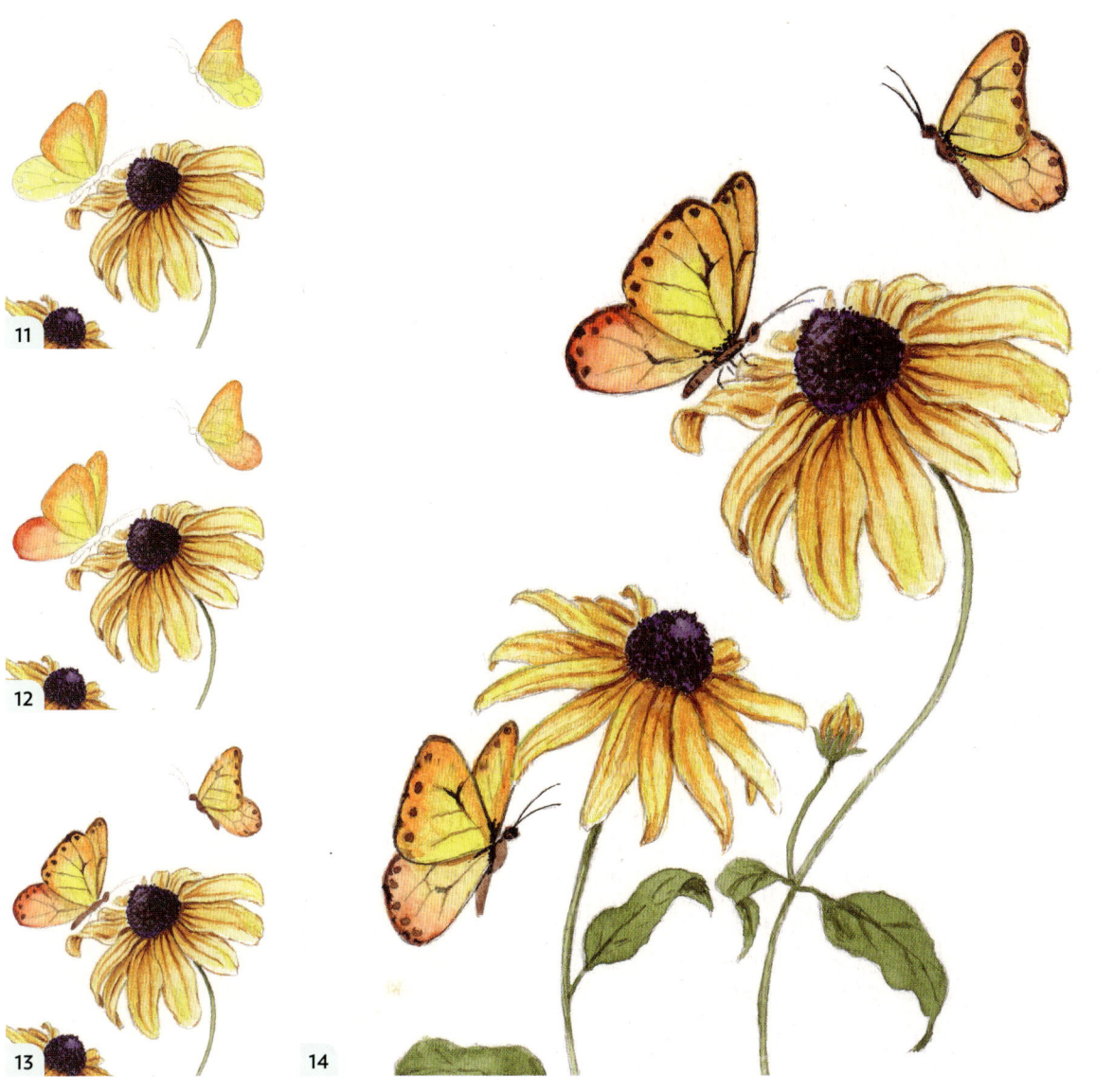

STEP 11: Adding Color to Upper Butterfly Wings

Apply Orange to the upper wings (refer to the reference) using a number 4 round brush.

STEP 12: Adding Color to Lower Butterfly Wings

When the color dries, on the lower wings, apply Red with a number 4 round brush. Allow to dry.

STEP 13: Detailing Butterfly Body and Veins

Give the body its color with Burnt Umber, and paint the veins using a liner brush.

STEP 14: Final Details on Butterfly Body and Wings

When dry, as a final step, use Black to add details to the body and wings. Also, paint the antennae using a liner brush.

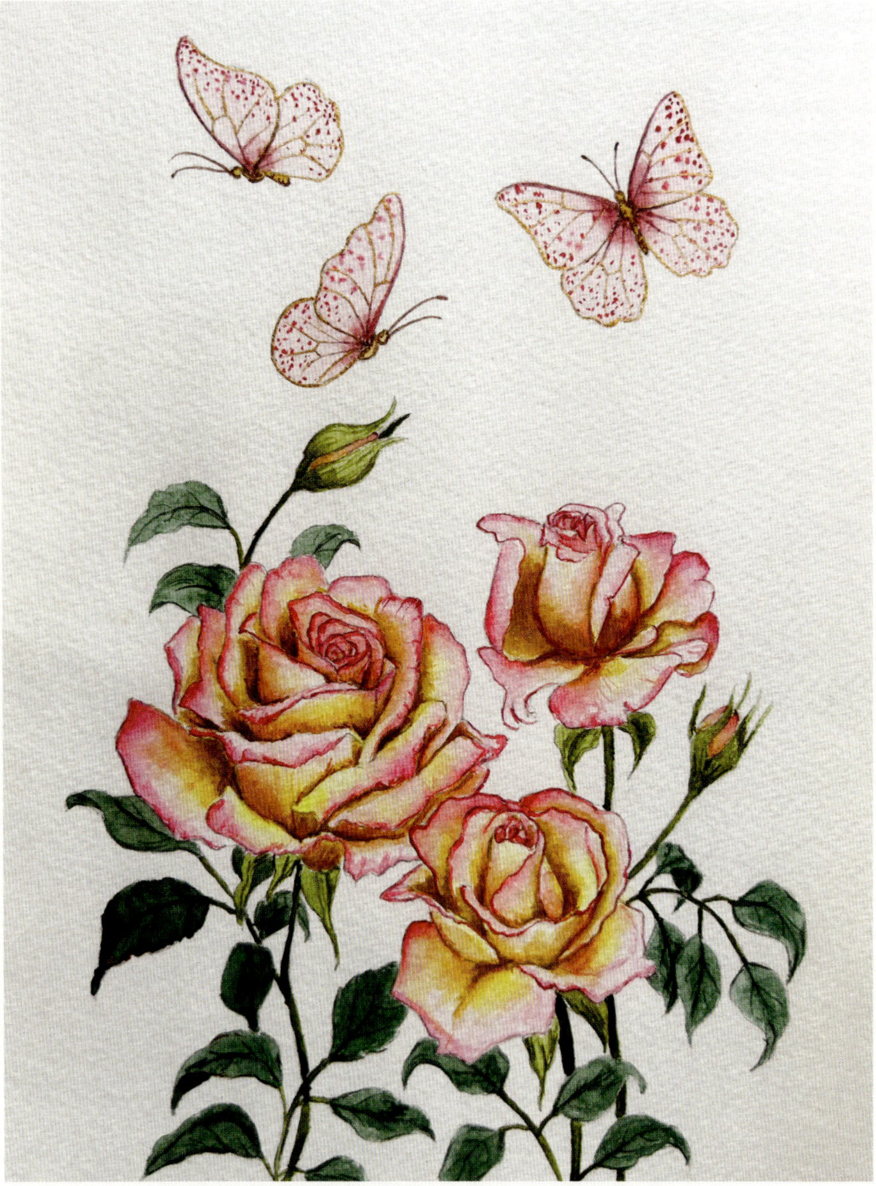

Brushes

Number 8 round brush
Number 4 round brush
Liner brush

Color Palette

- Lemon Yellow
- Pink
- Naples Yellow
- Yellow Ochre
- Dark Yellow
- Dark Green
- Viridian
- Olive Green
- Dark Pink
- Gold Metallic

Color Recipes

DARK YELLOW: 80% Cadmium Yellow + 30% Burnt Umber

DARK GREEN: 60% Viridian + 40% Burnt Sienna

DARK PINK: 80% Pink + 20% Burnt Umber

ROSES AND BUTTERFLIES

I feel that roses and butterflies are the most romantic composition. Here I have painted a double-shaded rose to bring more realism. We've previously painted a rose, and this time, we'll explore a different style with unique detailing using a mix of wet-on-wet and wet-on-dry techniques.

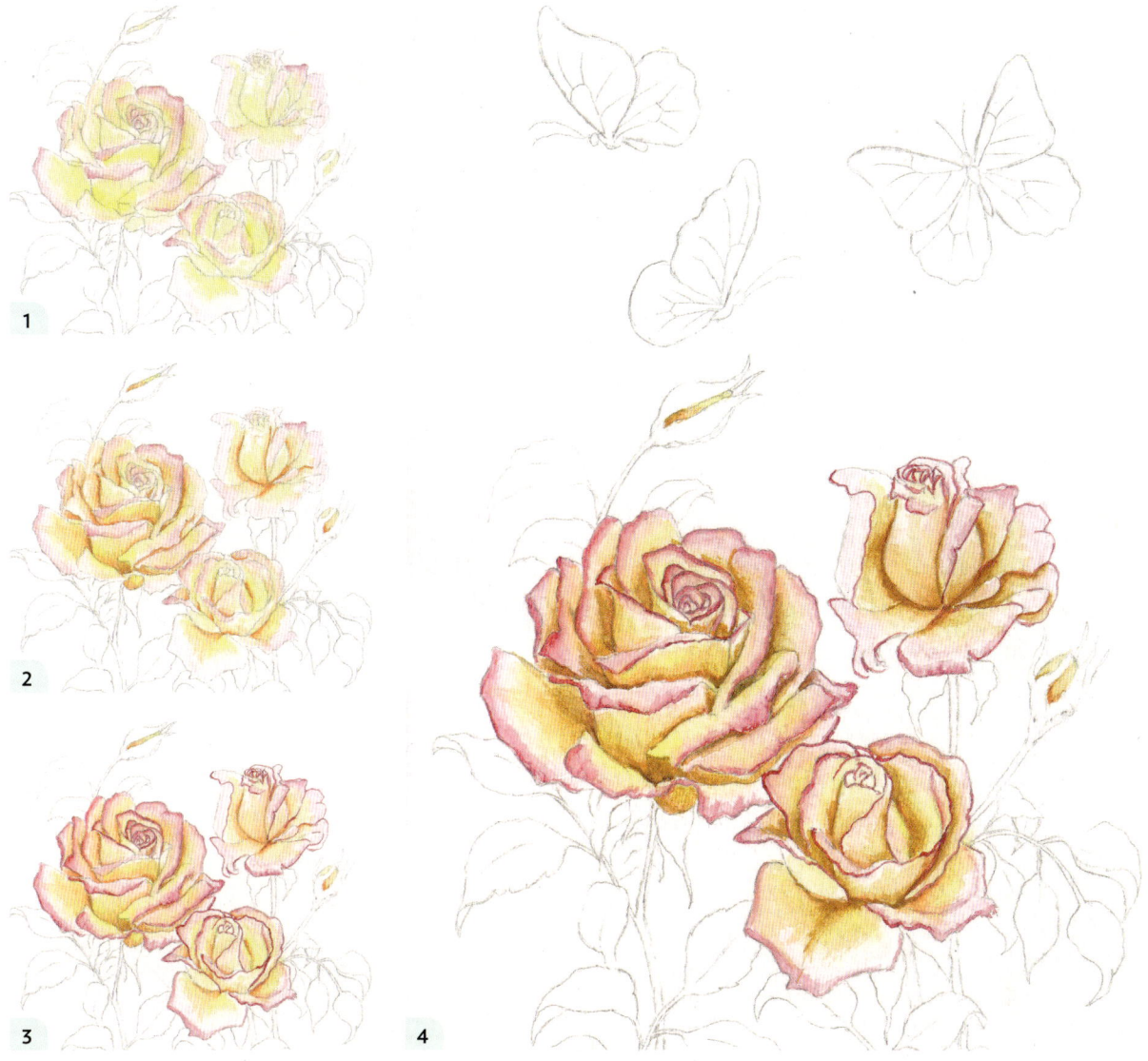

STEP 1: Base Layer for Flower Petals
Wet the designated area and paint one flower at a time using number 8 and number 4 round brushes. Use Lemon Yellow on the petals, emphasizing the edges with Pink.

STEP 2: Differentiating Petals with Yellow Ochre
Use a liner brush to apply Yellow Ochre between the petals for differentiation. Let dry.

STEP 3: Adding High-intensity Pink to Petal Edges
Apply high-intensity Pink along the edges of the petals using a liner brush. Allow to dry.

STEP 4: Detailing Stalk and Buds with Yellow Ochre
Use Yellow Ochre on the stalk for shadows and details, ensuring application to the buds as well.

STEP 5: Intensifying Pink on Flower Petals

When the color dries, apply Pink on the flower petals, intensifying towards the tips and tapering the color towards the inner sides for variation. Let dry.

STEP 6: Creating Shadows with Dark Pink

Apply Dark Pink between the petals to create shadows. Allow to dry.

STEP 7: Base Layer for Buds, Stems, and Petal Retainers

Paint the buds, stems, and petal retainers with Olive Green, adding Viridian with a number 4 round brush and a liner brush.

STEP 8: Detailing Leaves with Dark Green

When dry, detail the leaves with Dark Green. Let dry.

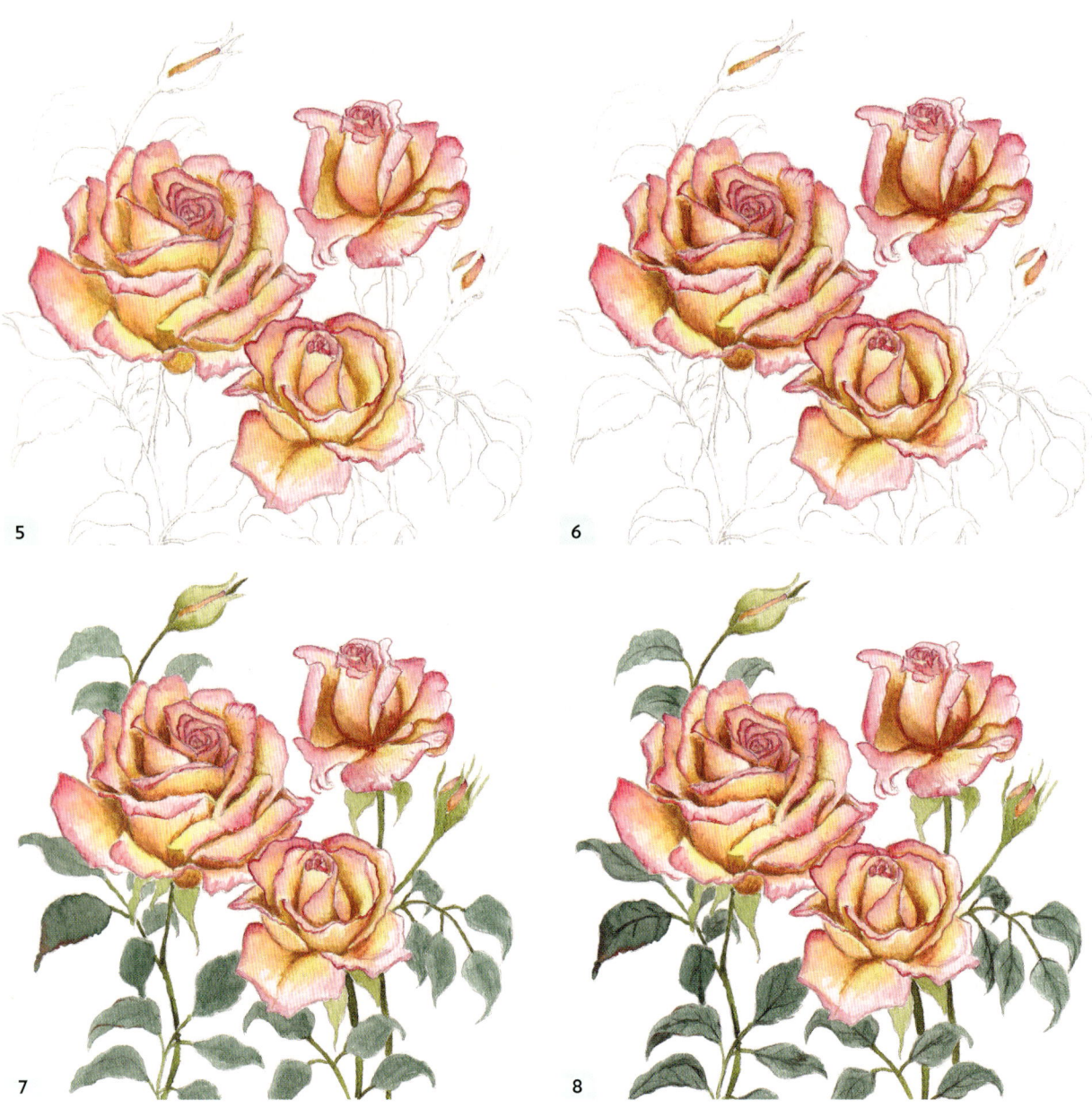

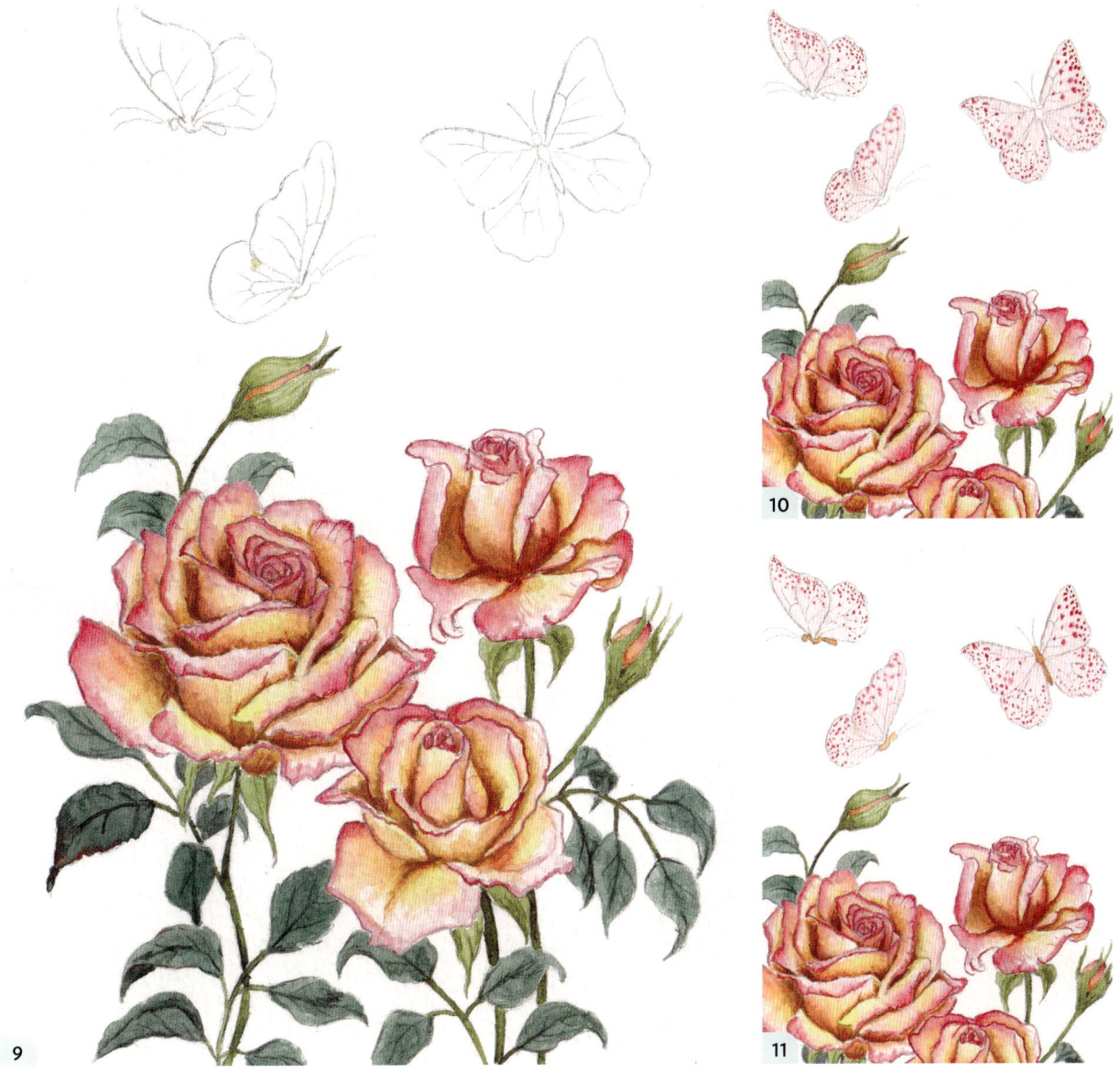

STEP 9: Enhancing Olive Green Areas

Apply high-intensity Olive Green to the areas painted with Olive Green.

STEP 10: Base Layer for Butterfly Wings

Paint the butterfly wings with wet-on-wet Pink. Before drying, add high-intensity Pink as dots.

STEP 11: Coloring Butterfly Body with Yellow Ochre

Add Yellow Ochre to the butterfly body. Let dry.

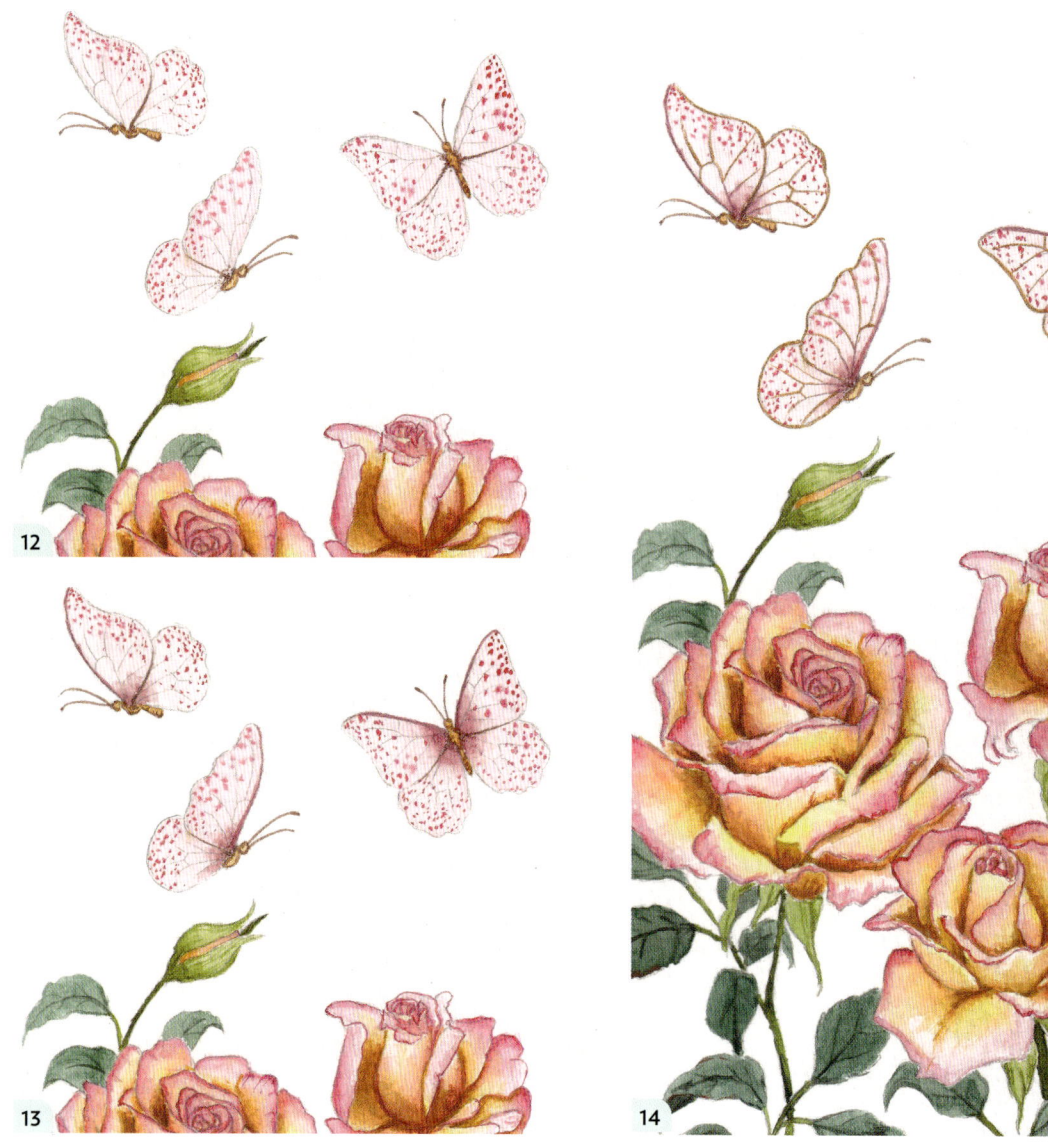

STEP 12: Detailing Butterfly Body and Wings with Dark Pink

Use Dark Pink for the antennae, wing shadows, and body details. Allow to dry.

STEP 13: Adding Detail to Butterfly Wings

Apply Dark Pink on the wings near the body and on the main veins (costal margin).

STEP 14: Final Touch with Gold Metallic Detailing

When dry, add Gold Metallic on the butterfly veins for a finishing touch.

COSMOS GARDEN AND BUTTERFLIES

Cosmos flowers are the easiest, yet most beautiful, to paint. I always enjoy painting them, as their unique and special petal structures evoke a sense of admiration for nature every time I encounter them. Scan the QR code to watch me paint Cosmos Garden and Butterflies.

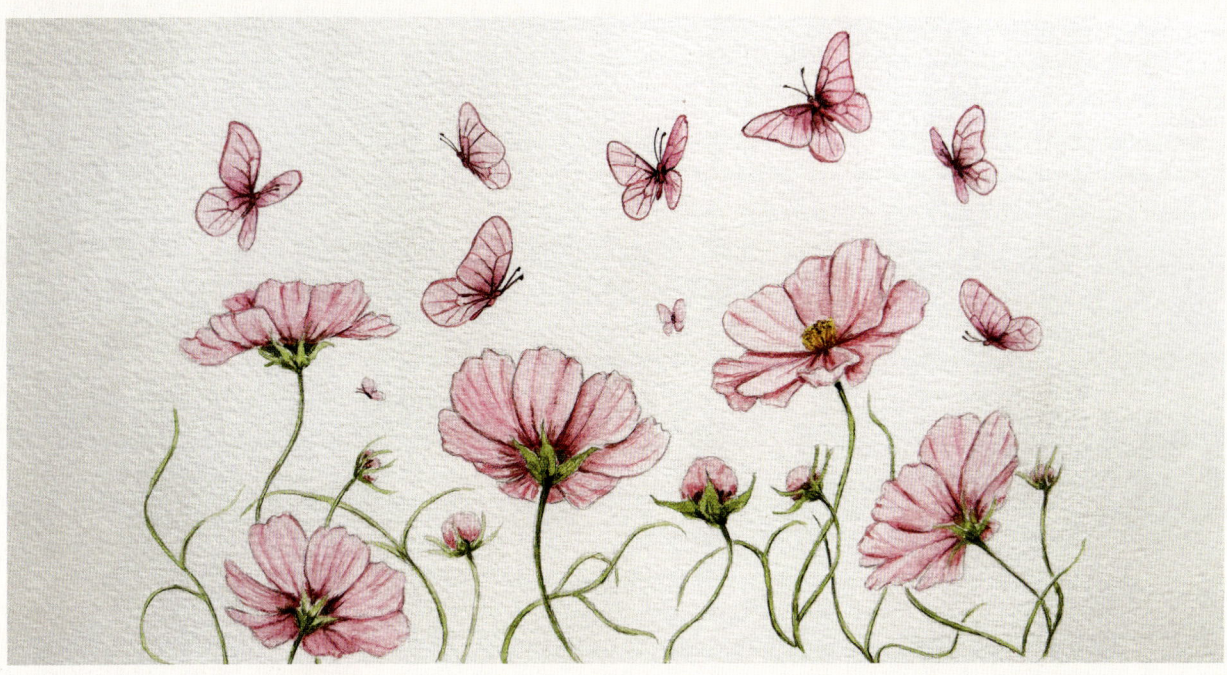

Brushes

Number 8 round brush
Number 4 round brush
Liner brush

Color Palette

- Rose
- Dark Rose
- Cadmium Yellow
- Yellow Ochre

- Burnt Sienna
- Hunter Green
- Olive Green
- Dark Green
- Burnt Umber
- Pink
- Purple
- Dark Pink

Color Recipes

DARK ROSE: 50% Rose + 50% Burnt Sienna

DARK PINK: 80% Pink + 20% Burnt Umber

PURPLE: 50% Pink + 50% Violet

HUNTER GREEN: 40% Parrot Green + 60% Burnt Sienna

OLIVE GREEN: 50% Green + 50% Burnt Sienna

DARK GREEN: 60% Green + 40% Burnt Umber

PURPLE: 60% Pink + 40% Cobalt Blue

DARK PURPLE: 80% Purple + 20% Burnt Umber

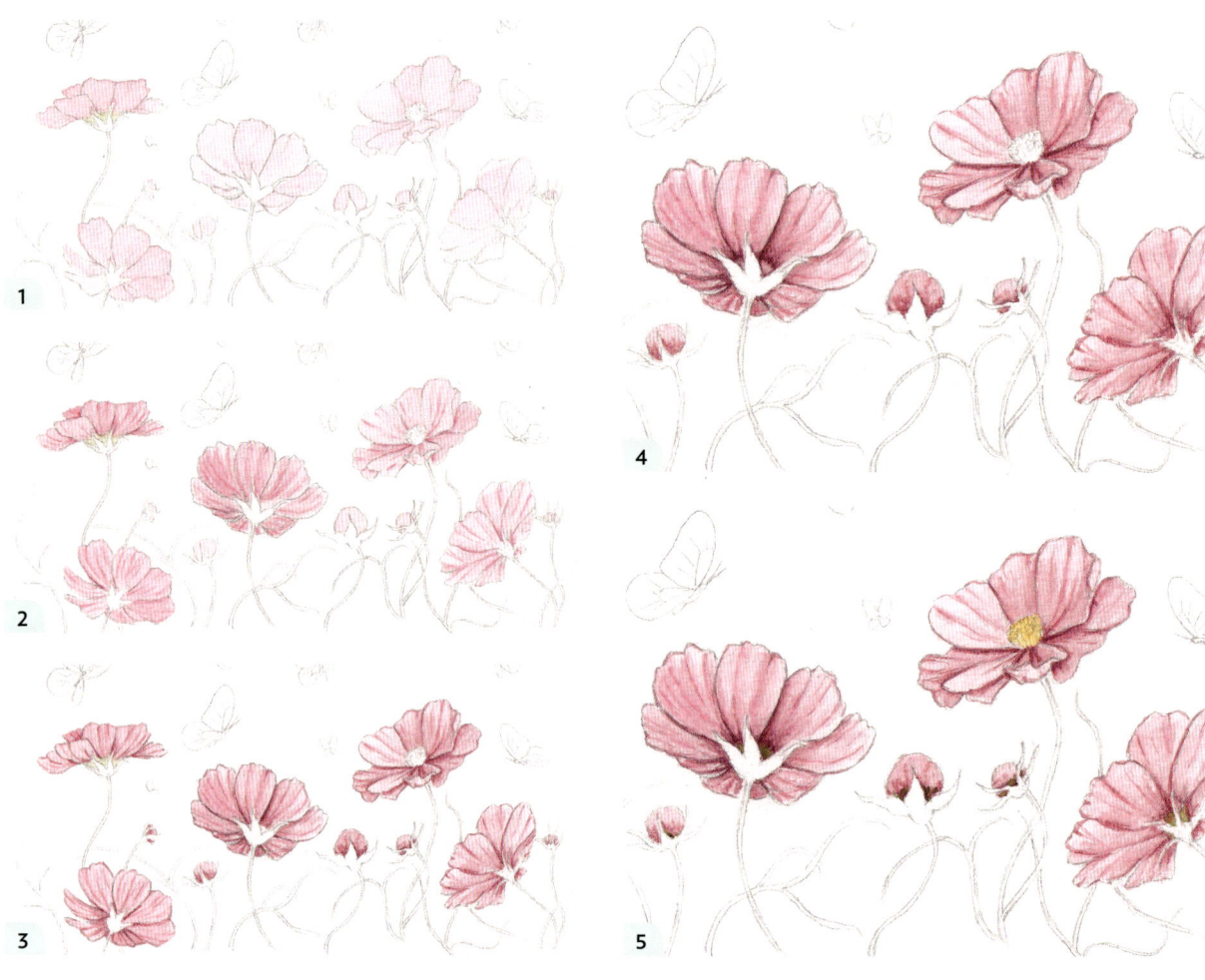

STEP 1: Base Layer for Flower Petals

Using the wet-on-wet technique, apply a low-intensity Rose to all flower petals using a number 8 round brush. Allow to dry. After every step in this painting, allow the previous layer to dry.

STEP 2: Intricate Petal Detailing

With a liner brush, add high-intensity Rose between and on the petals for intricate details. Let dry.

STEP 3: Adding Depth with Dark Rose

Enhance depth by applying Dark Rose between the petals, using a liner brush.

STEP 4: Center Detailing with Dark Rose

When dry, use a number 4 round brush to apply Dark Rose near the flower's center. Allow to dry.

STEP 5: Center and Petal Detailing Continued

Add Cadmium Yellow to the flower's center and Hunter Green to the bottom of the petals, using a liner brush.

STEP 6: Complete Petal and Sepal Coloring

When dry, apply Hunter Green to all petals and sepals with a liner brush. Allow to dry.

STEP 7: Detailing Stems with Olive Green

Intensify details on the stems with high-intensity Olive Green, using a liner brush. Let dry.

STEP 8: Creating Stem Shadows with Dark Green

Achieve a shadow effect on the stem by applying Dark Green.

STEP 9: Detailing Flower Center

When dry, use Yellow Ochre on the flower center, adding details with Burnt Sienna and Burnt Umber.

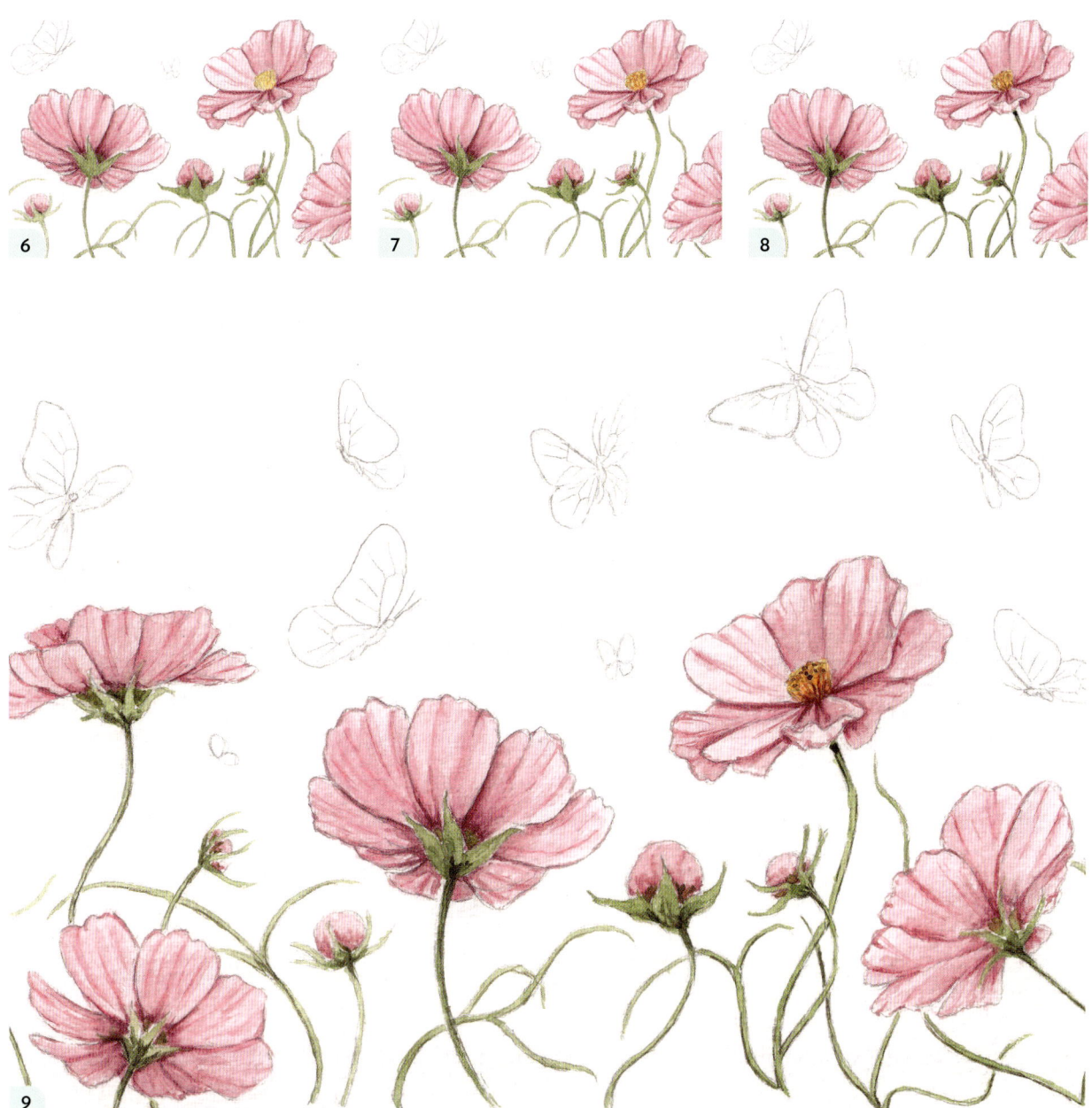

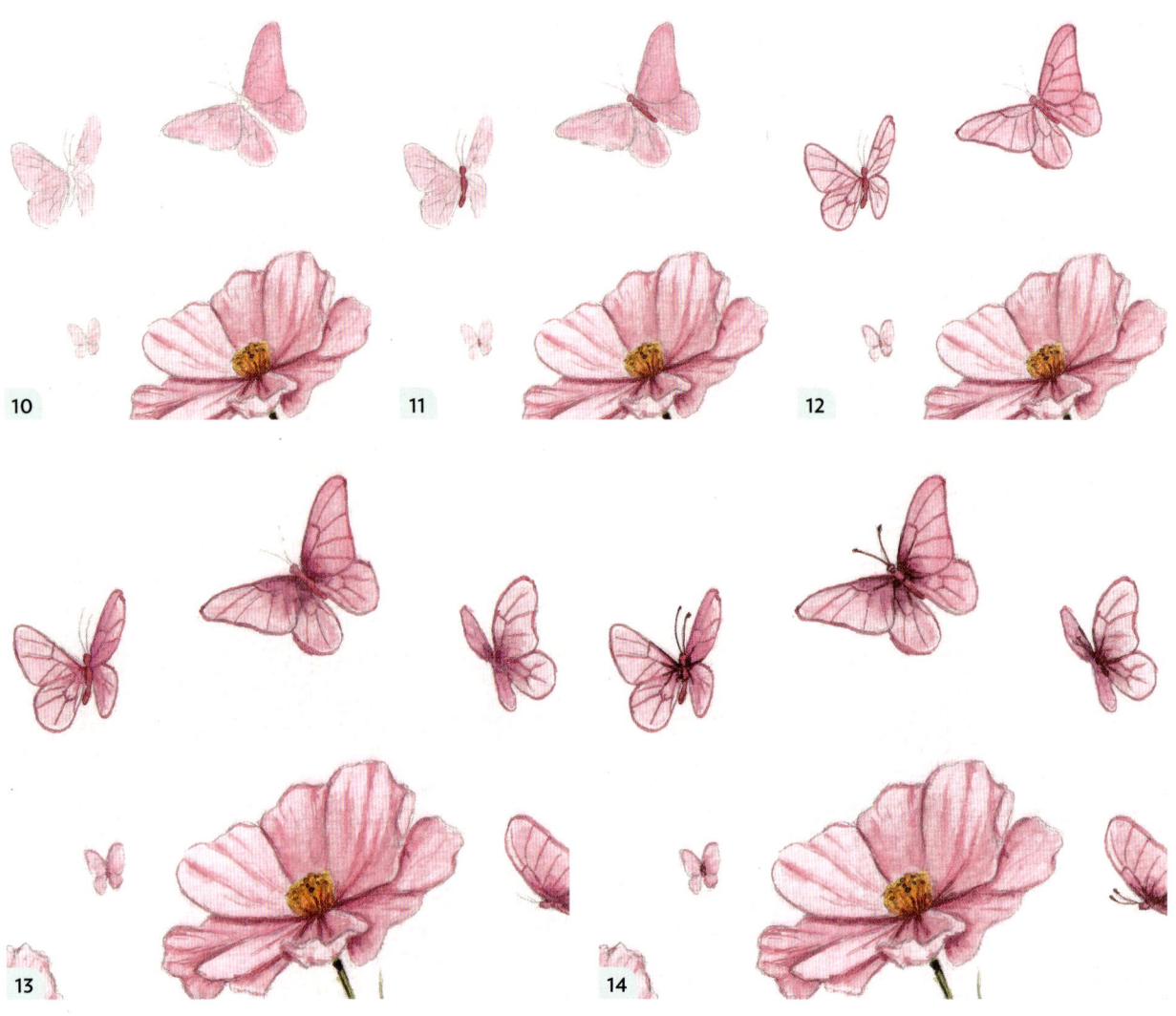

STEP 10: Base Layer for Butterfly Wings

Use the wet-on-wet technique to cover the butterfly wings with Pink, using a number 4 round brush.

STEP 11: Coloring Butterfly Body

When dry, apply high-intensity Pink to the butterfly's body. Allow to dry.

STEP 12: Vein Detailing on Butterfly Wings

Use a liner brush to add high-intensity Pink veins to the butterfly. Let dry.

STEP 13: Adding Purple Accents

Apply Purple near the body area using a small round brush.

STEP 14: Detailing Butterfly Antennae

When dry, enhance the butterfly's antennae with Dark Purple and add details using the same color.

A BOUQUET OF FLOWERS AND BUTTERFLIES

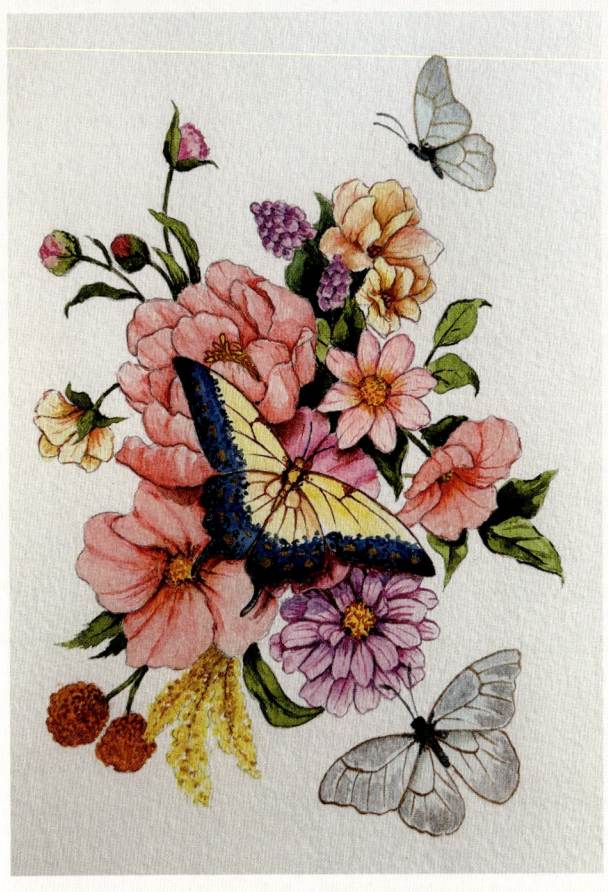

I trust you've learned the art of painting flowers effortlessly. I have included a bunch of flowers here; you will use a mix of wet-on-wet and wet-on-dry techniques and you can choose any color palette you desire. Unlike the other paintings, here I painted the butterflies first. Each flower is represented by a letter of the alphabet for easy interpretation.

Brushes

Number 8 round brush
Number 4 round brush
Liner brush

Color Palette

- Pink
- Red
- Peachy Orange
- Coral
- Purple
- Cadmium Yellow
- Yellow Ochre
- Burnt Sienna
- Burnt Umber
- Olive Green
- Cobalt Blue
- Dark Pink
- Turquoise Blue
- Turquoise Green
- Prussian Blue
- Dark Green
- Blue Metallic
- Green Metallic
- Black
- Gold Metallic

Color Recipes

- **PEACHY ORANGE:** 60% Pink + 40% Cadmium Yellow
- **CORAL:** 60% Pink + 40% Orange
- **PURPLE:** 60% Pink + 40% Cobalt Blue
- **DARK PINK:** 70% Pink + 30% Burnt Umber
- **TURQUOISE GREEN:** 50% Turquoise Blue + 50% Green
- **OLIVE GREEN:** 60% Sap Green + 40% Burnt Umber
- **DARK GREEN:** 40% Cobalt Blue + 60% Burnt Umber

Butterfly Painting Steps

STEP 1: Base Colors for Butterflies

Using the wet-on-wet technique, use a number 4 round brush to apply Cadmium Yellow to the middle portion of the middle butterfly. Apply Prussian Blue to the lower portion of the middle butterfly, Turquoise Blue to the lower butterfly, and Turquoise Green to the top butterfly. Keep the color intensity low and use a number 4 round brush for precision.

STEP 2: Adding Body Colors

When dry, add Yellow Ochre to the body of the middle butterfly. Apply Dark Green to the bodies of the top and bottom butterflies. Use a liner brush for accuracy and to prevent color bleeding. Let dry.

STEP 3: Detailing and Shadows

Apply Burnt Sienna to the body and veins of the center butterfly, extending color to the outer edges. Use high-intensity Dark Green for the body and wing shadows of the top and bottom butterflies. Allow to dry.

STEP 4: Wing Details

Use a liner brush to apply Black and Prussian Blue dots on the wings of the middle butterfly. Apply Blue Metallic to the wings of the bottom butterfly and Green Metallic color to the top butterfly.

STEP 5: Metallic and Gold Details

When dry, apply Gold Metallic to the details of the middle butterfly's wings. Use Gold Metallic to paint the veins of the top and bottom butterflies, utilizing a liner brush.

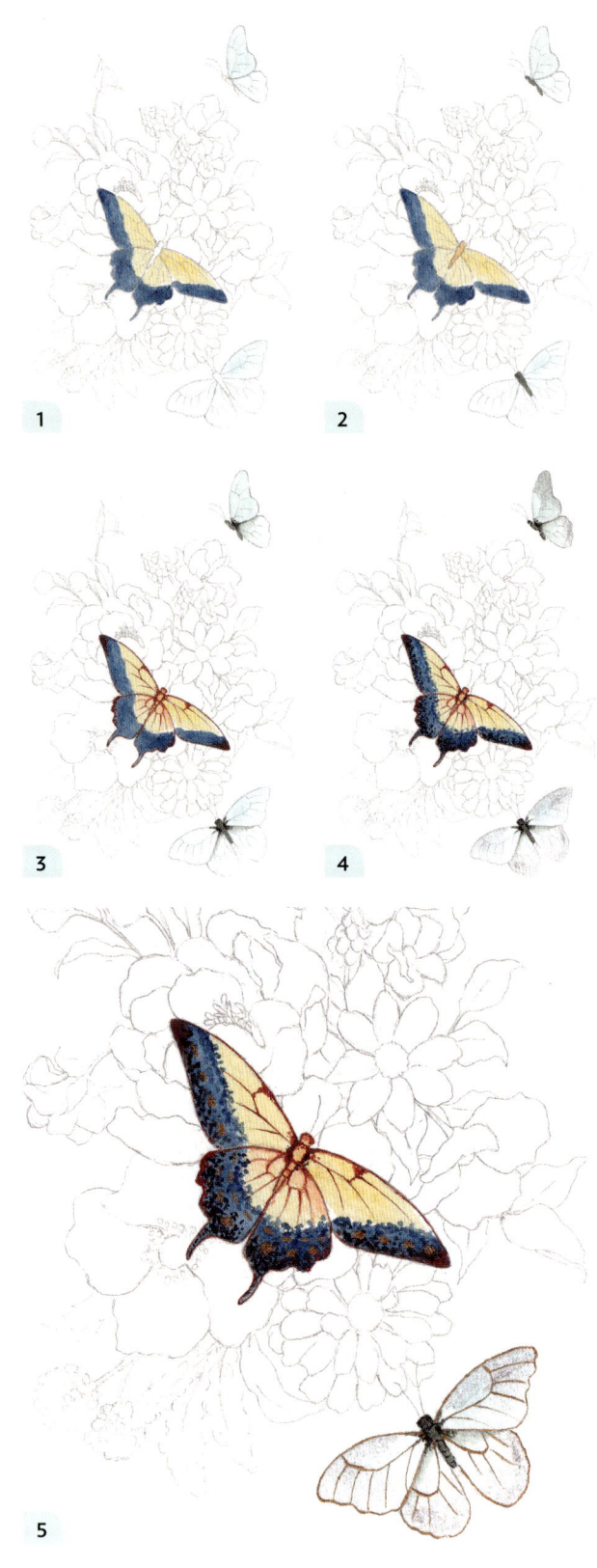

Flower Painting Steps

STEP 6: Applying Base Colors

Use number 8 and number 4 round brushes for a wet-on-wet technique to apply base colors to the flowers. Colors for each flower: A - Peachy Orange, B - Pink, C - Cadmium Yellow, D - Red, E - Coral, F - Purple, G - Orange, H - Cadmium Yellow (applied with bounce brush technique), I - Pink with a hint of Olive Green at the bottom.

STEP 7: Adding Depth to Flowers

When dry, apply high-intensity colors with a liner brush for depth. Colors for each flower: A - High-intensity Peachy Orange, C - Burnt Sienna, D- Cadmium Yellow, E - High-intensity Coral and Pink, F - High-intensity Purple. Let dry.

STEP 8: Details between Petals

Use a liner brush for high-intensity colors and smooth out with an empty brush. Colors for each flower: A - High-intensity Peachy Orange, B - High-intensity Pink, C - Burnt Sienna and Yellow Ochre,

FLOWER COLOR MAP

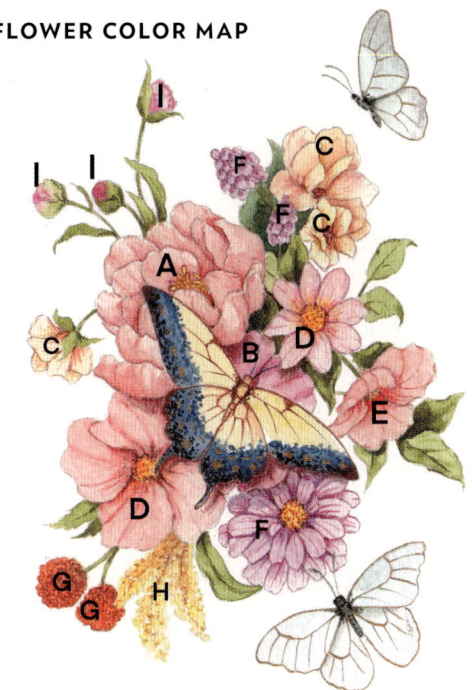

D - High-intensity Red, E - High-intensity Pink, F - High-intensity Purple and Pink, G - High-intensity Orange, H - Yellow Ochre (applied with bounce brush technique), I - High-intensity Pink (details to the top portion).

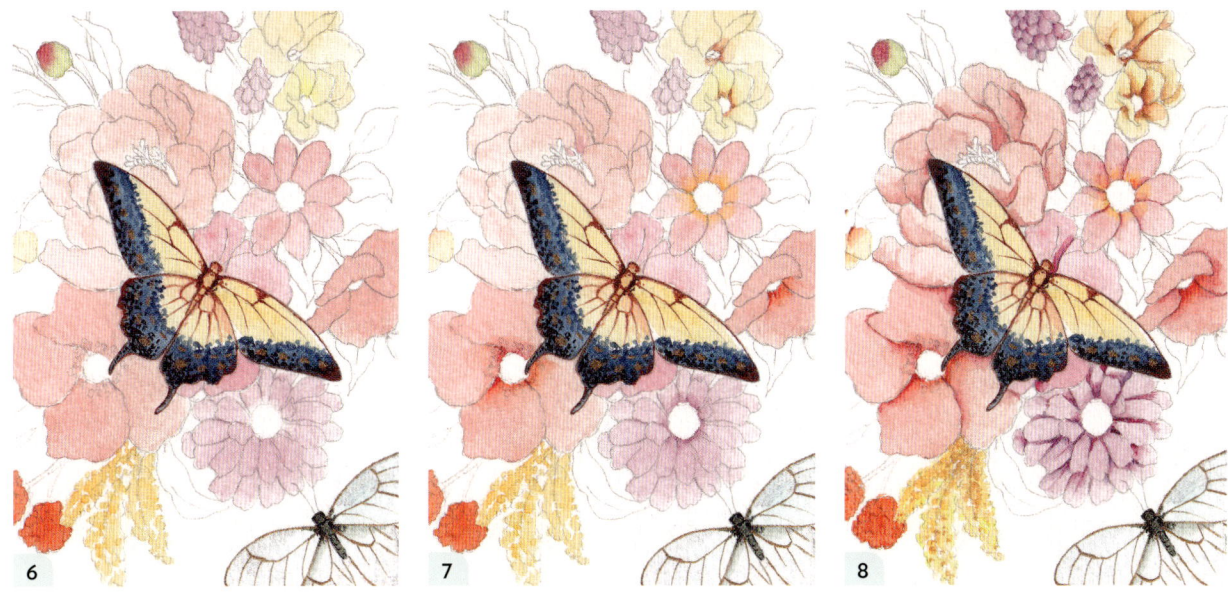

6   7   8

93

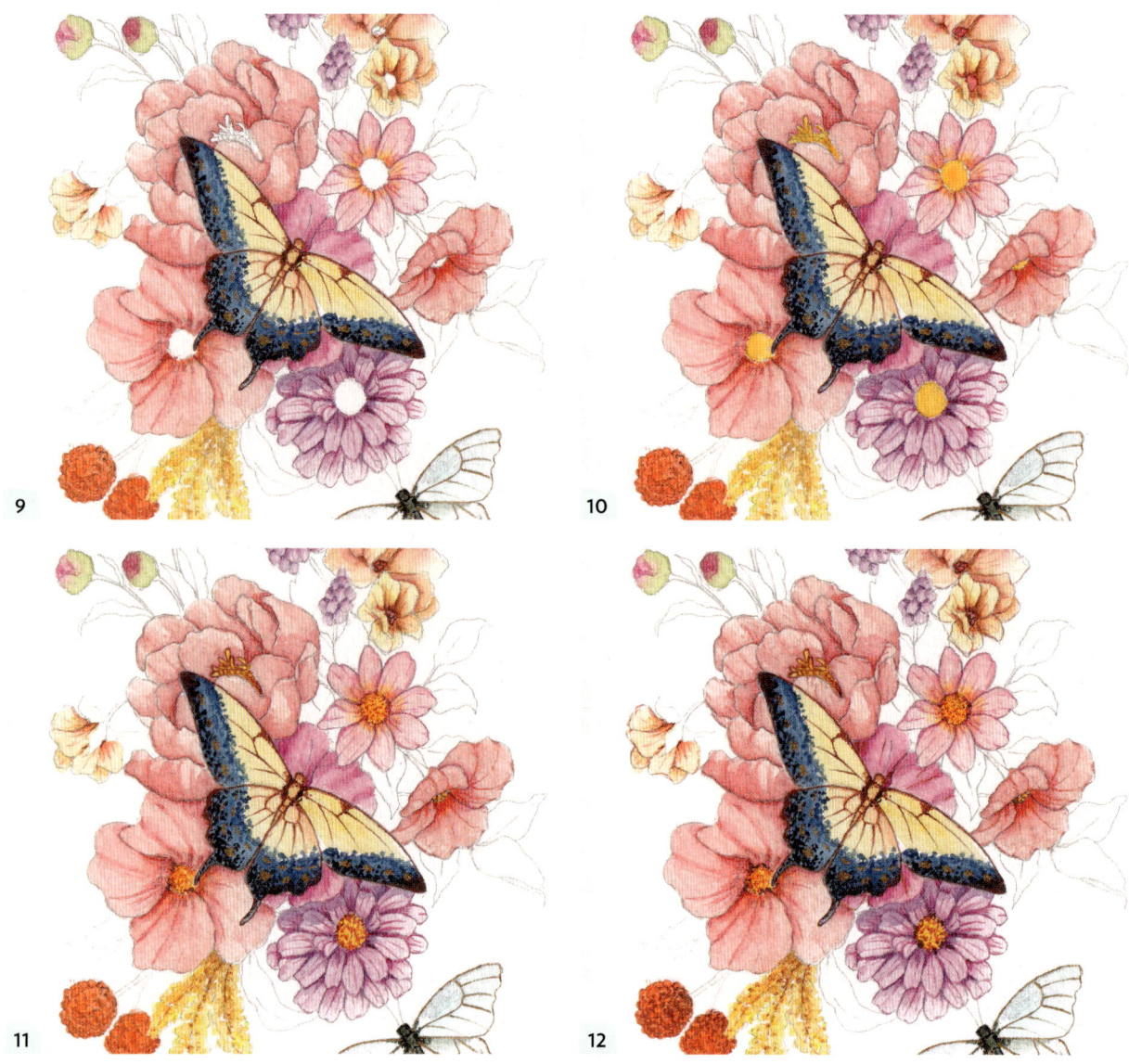

STEP 9: Texture and Details to Petals

When dry, use a number 4 round brush and liner brush for detailing. Colors for each flower: A - Peachy Orange, B - Pink, C - Coral, D - Pink, E - Coral, F - Purple and Pink, G - Burnt Sienna, I - Pink (applied to the top portion). Allow to dry.

STEP 10: Middle Portion of Flowers

Use a liner brush for detailing. Colors: Cadmium Yellow and Red. Please check reference.

STEP 11: Center Details of Flowers

When dry, apply Burnt Sienna with a liner brush. For Flower A, outline the stamens, and for others, use bounced strokes. Allow to dry.

STEP 12: Adding Depth to Petals

Use Burnt Umber between petals and starting areas for more depth. Apply Burnt Sienna to the edges of petals.

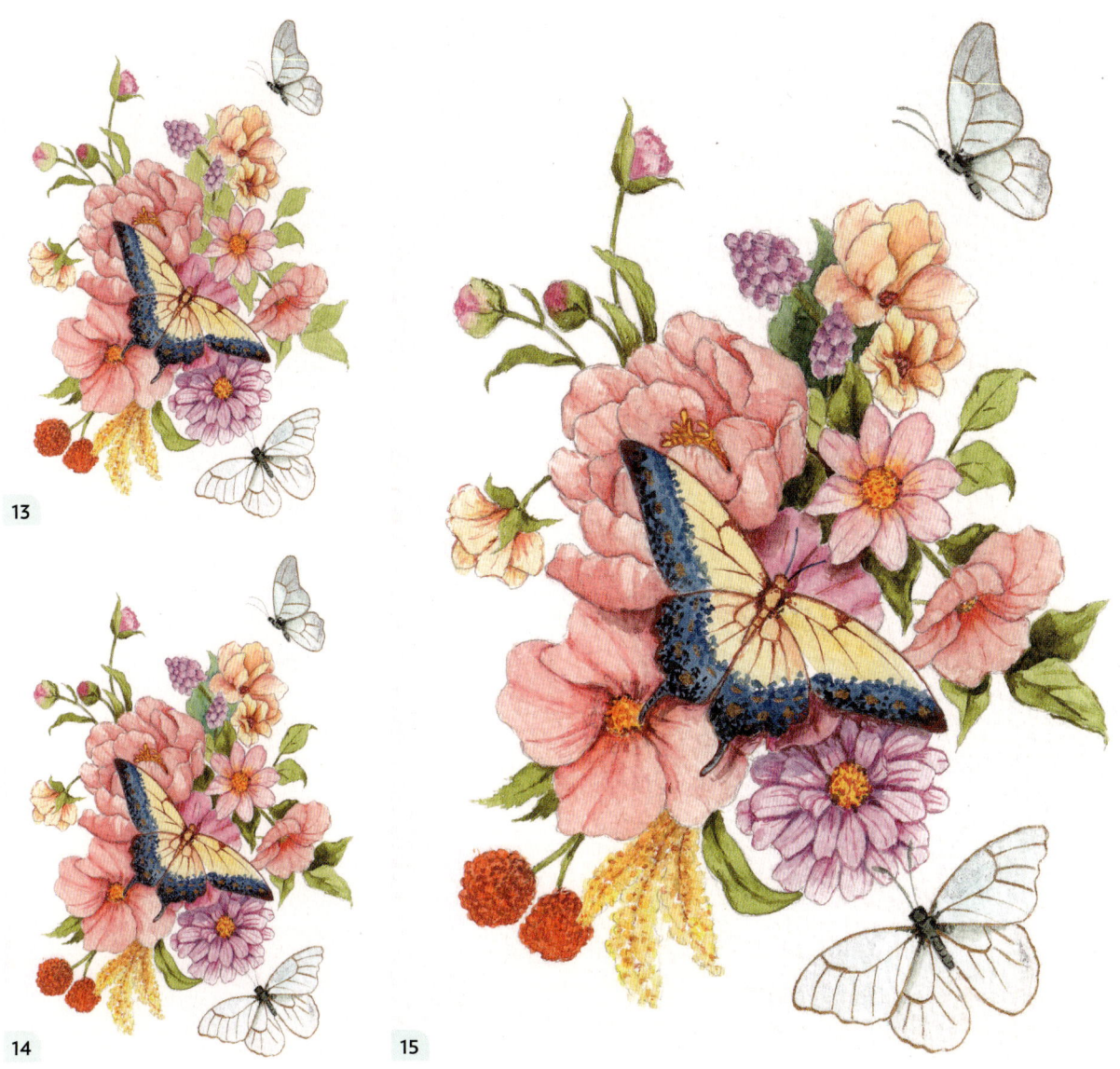

STEP 13: Painting Leaves and Stems

When dry, use Olive Green for leaves and stems with a number 4 round brush and liner brush. Let dry.

STEP 14: Background Leaf Painting

Paint the big leaf behind Flower A with Cobalt Blue and the rest with high-intensity Olive Green. Let dry.

STEP 15: Adding Shadows

Use a liner brush to apply Dark Pink to areas where the butterfly casts shadows. Apply high-intensity Olive Green to shadow areas of the leaves.

CHITHRA SHAAN is the artist behind **Littleheartcreates (www.littleheartcreates.com)** and her social media channels on Instagram, Pinterest, Facebook, and YouTube **@littleheartcreates.** She is a self-taught artist who started Littleheartcreates during the COVID-19 pandemic as a stress reliever for herself and others. She started by drawing flowers and that evolved into her current watercolor art practice.

Quarto.com | WalterFoster.com

© 2025 Quarto Publishing Group USA Inc.
Artwork and Text © 2025 Littleheartcreates

First Published in 2025 by Walter Foster Publishing,
an imprint of The Quarto Group, 100 Cummings Center,
Suite 265-D, Beverly, MA 01915, USA.
T (978) 282-9590 F (978) 283-2742

Walter Foster Publishing titles are also available at discount for retail, wholesale, promotional, and bulk purchase. For details, contact the Special Sales Manager by email at specialsales@quarto.com or by mail at The Quarto Group, Attn: Special Sales Manager, 100 Cummings Center, Suite 265-D, Beverly, MA 01915, USA.

29 28 27 26 25   1 2 3 4 5

ISBN: 978-0-7603-9143-3

Digital edition published in 2025
eISBN: 978-0-7603-9144-0

Library of Congress Control Number available

Design: Kelley Galbreath
Photography: Chithra Shaan except pages 20 and 21 are Shutterstock

Printed in China

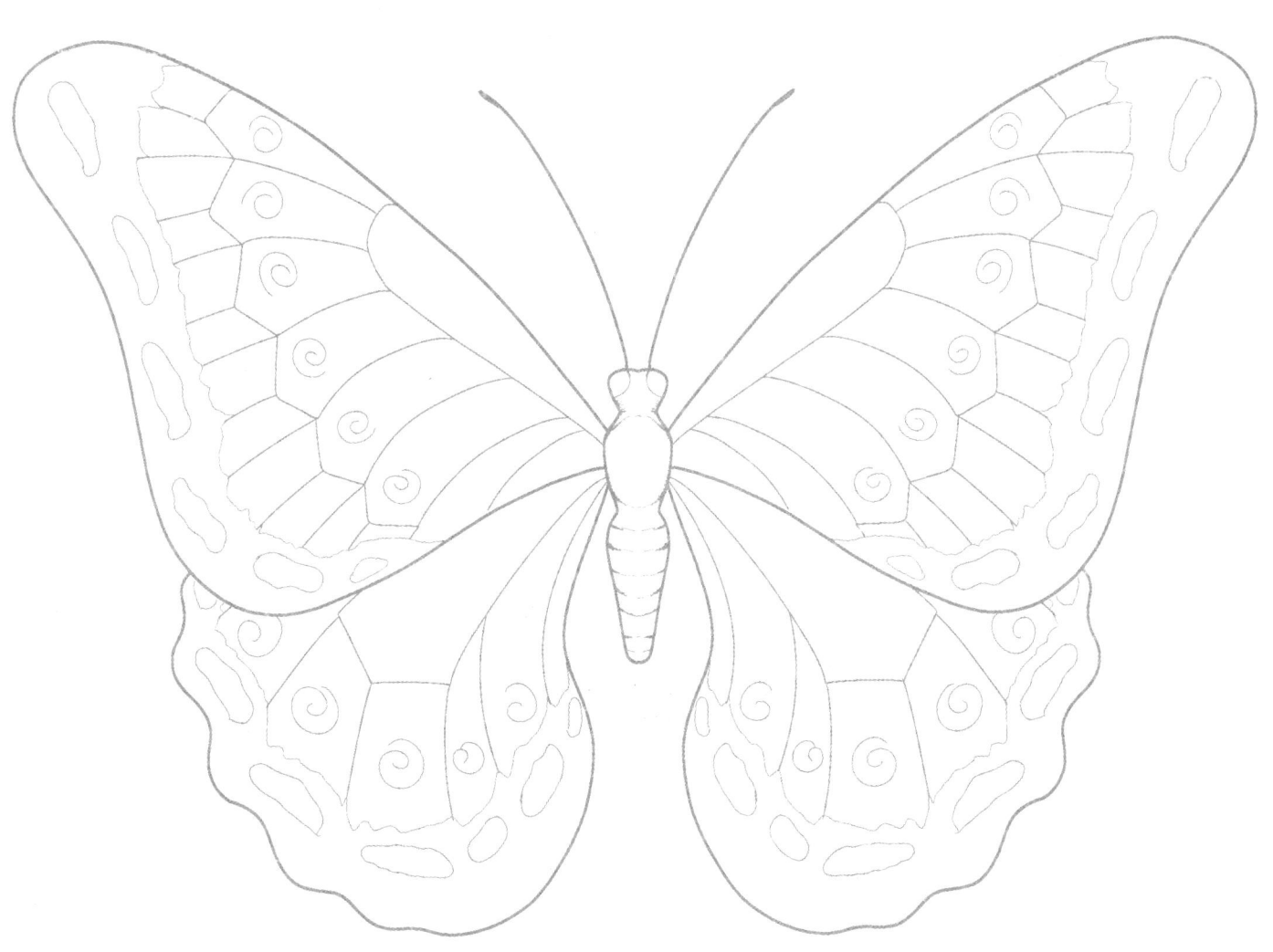

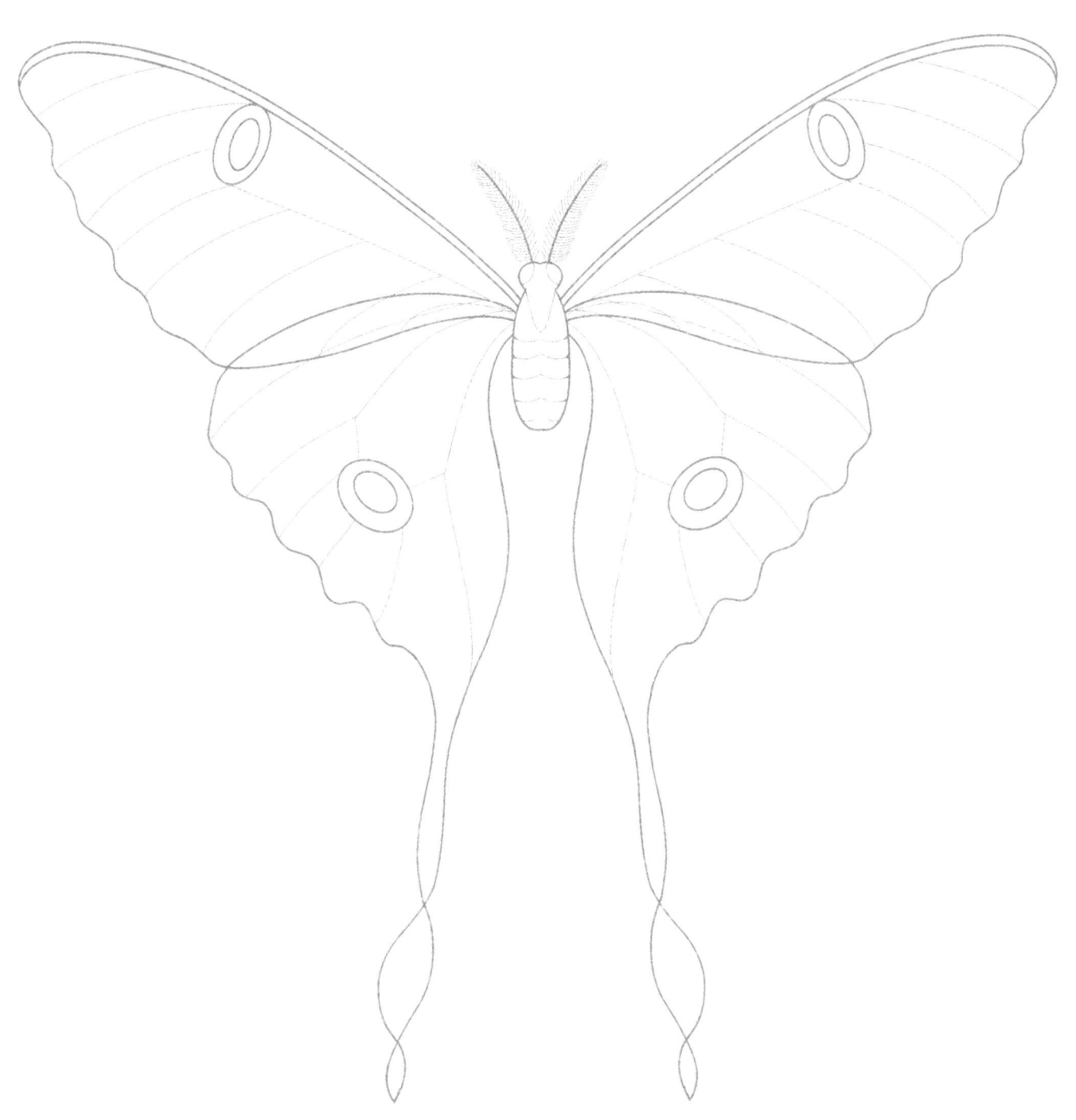

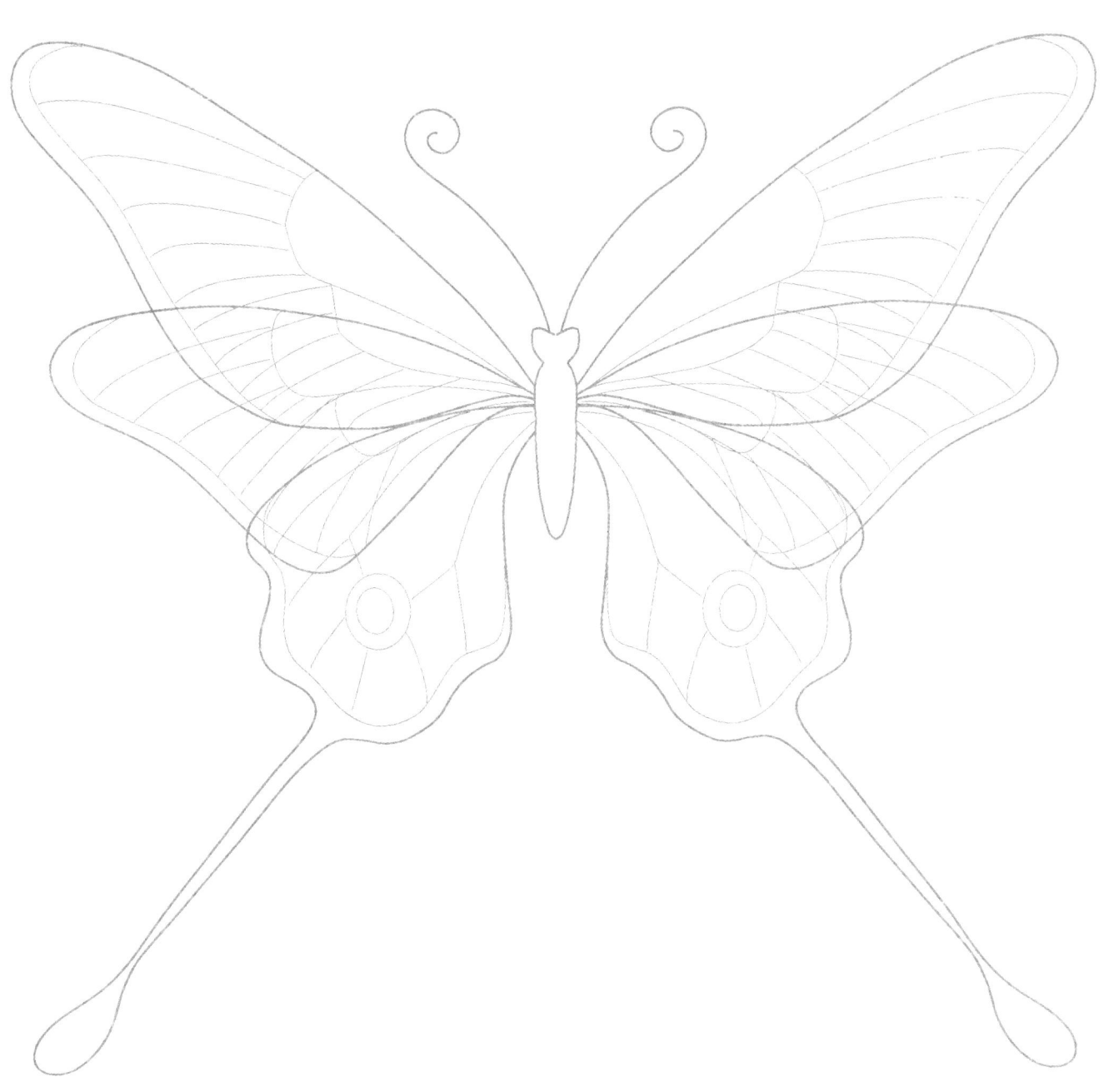

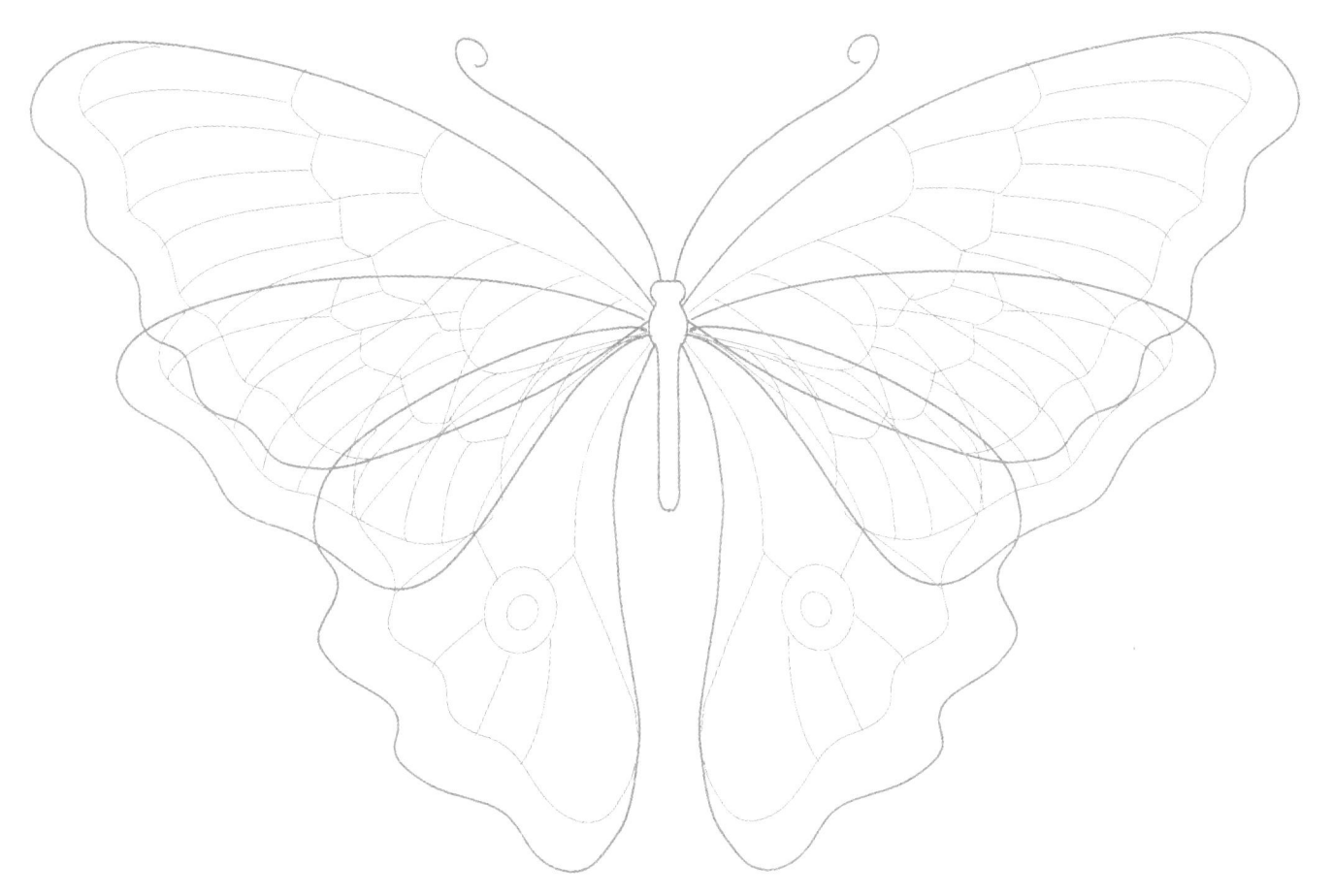

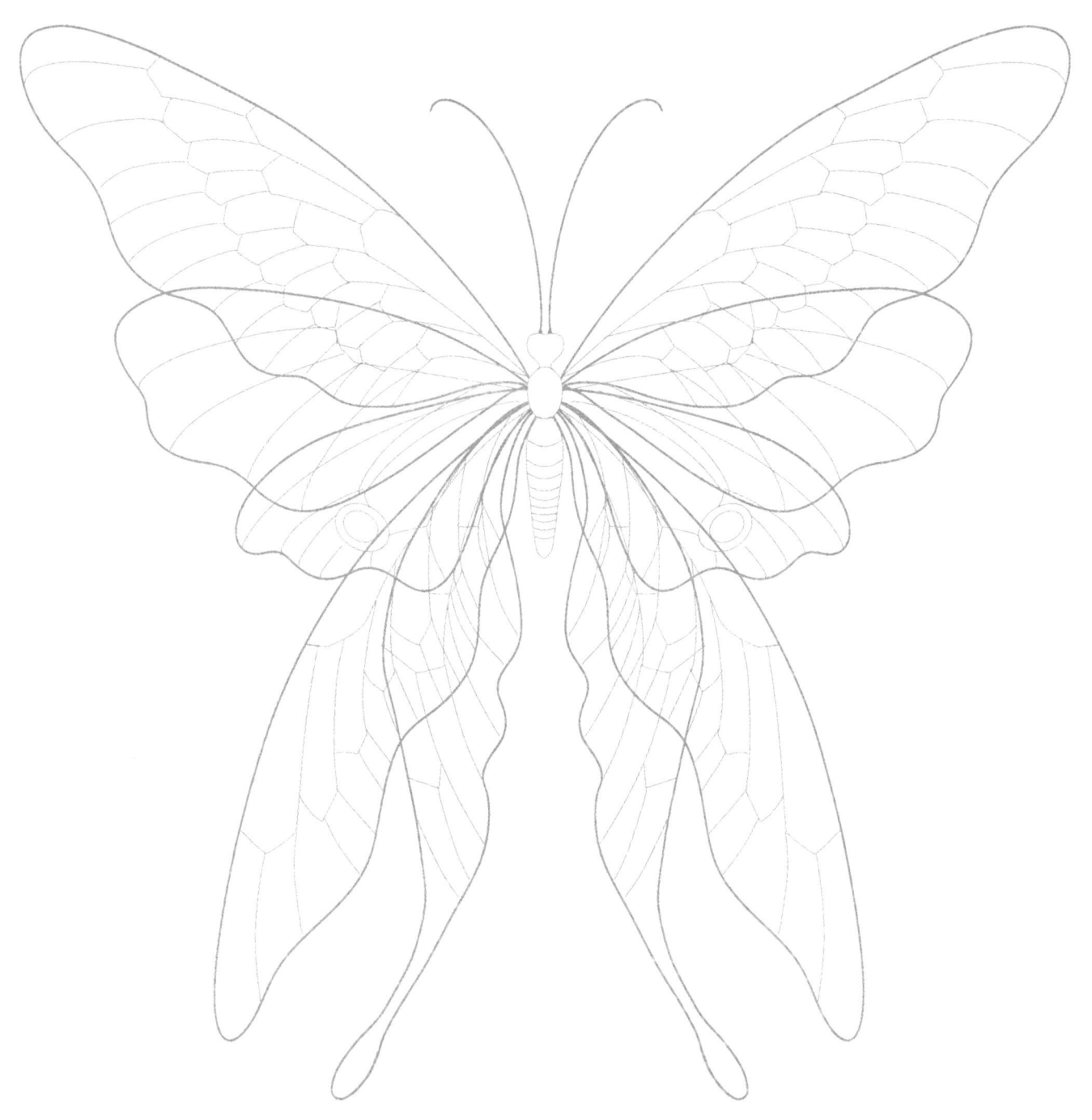

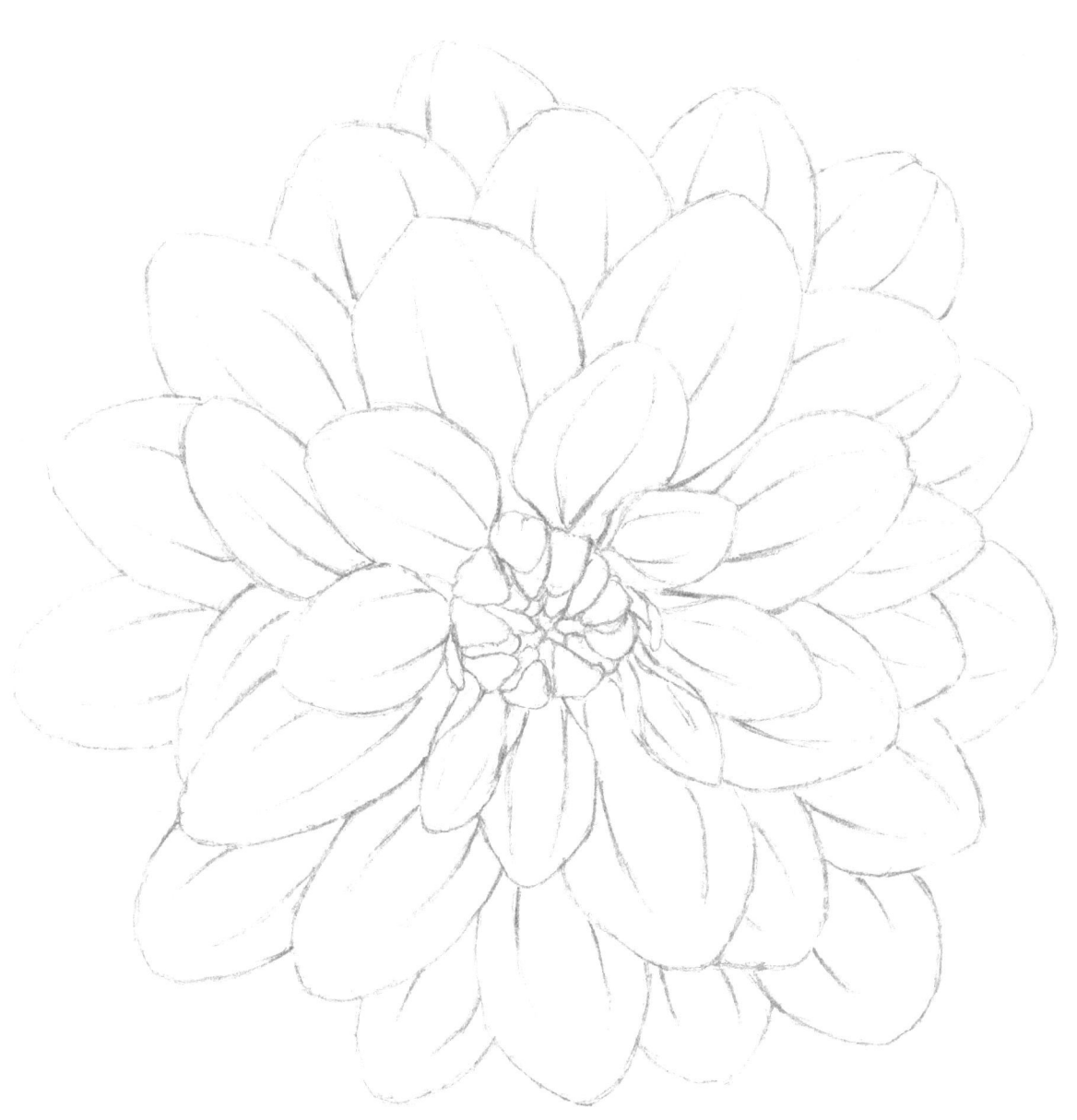

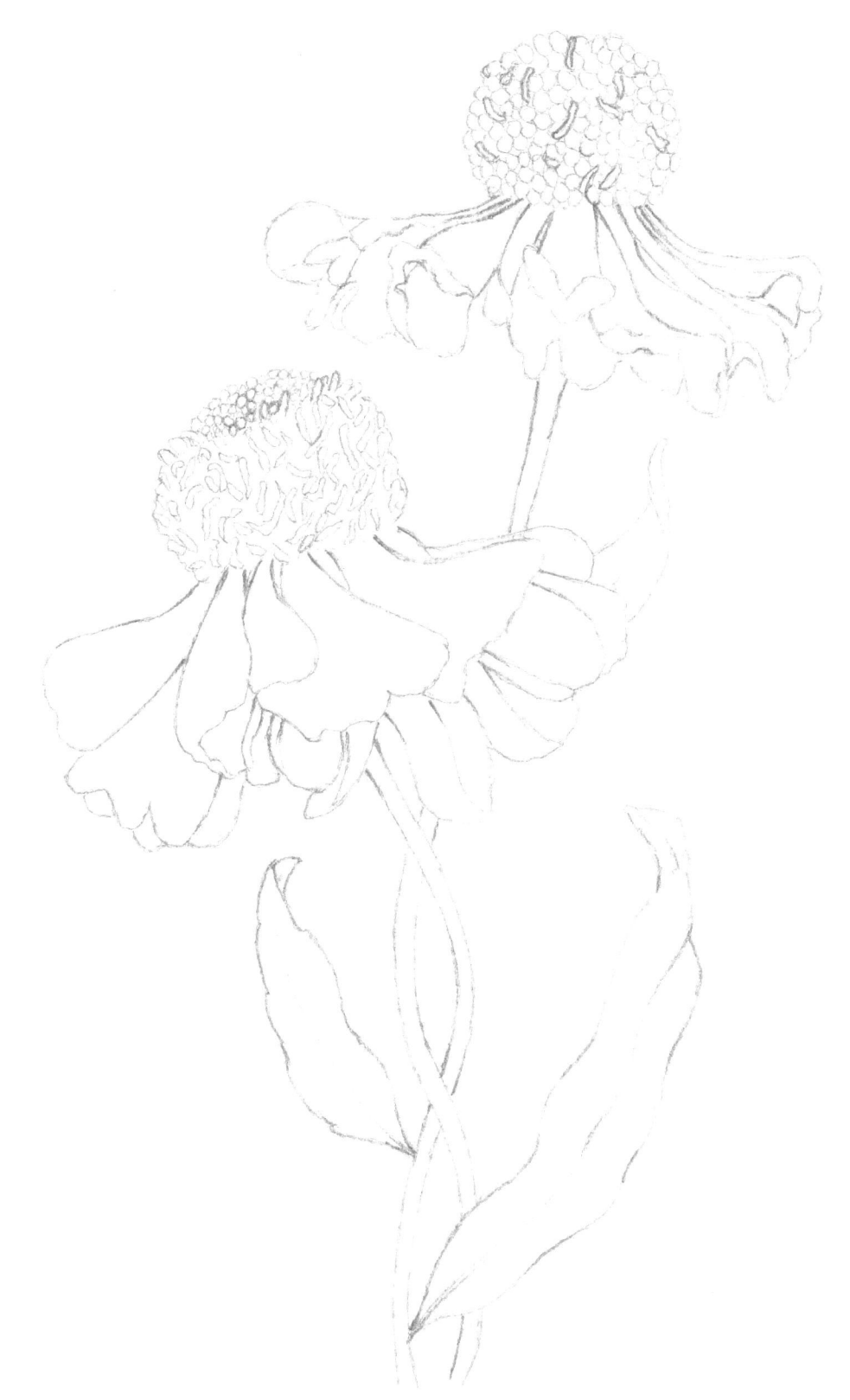

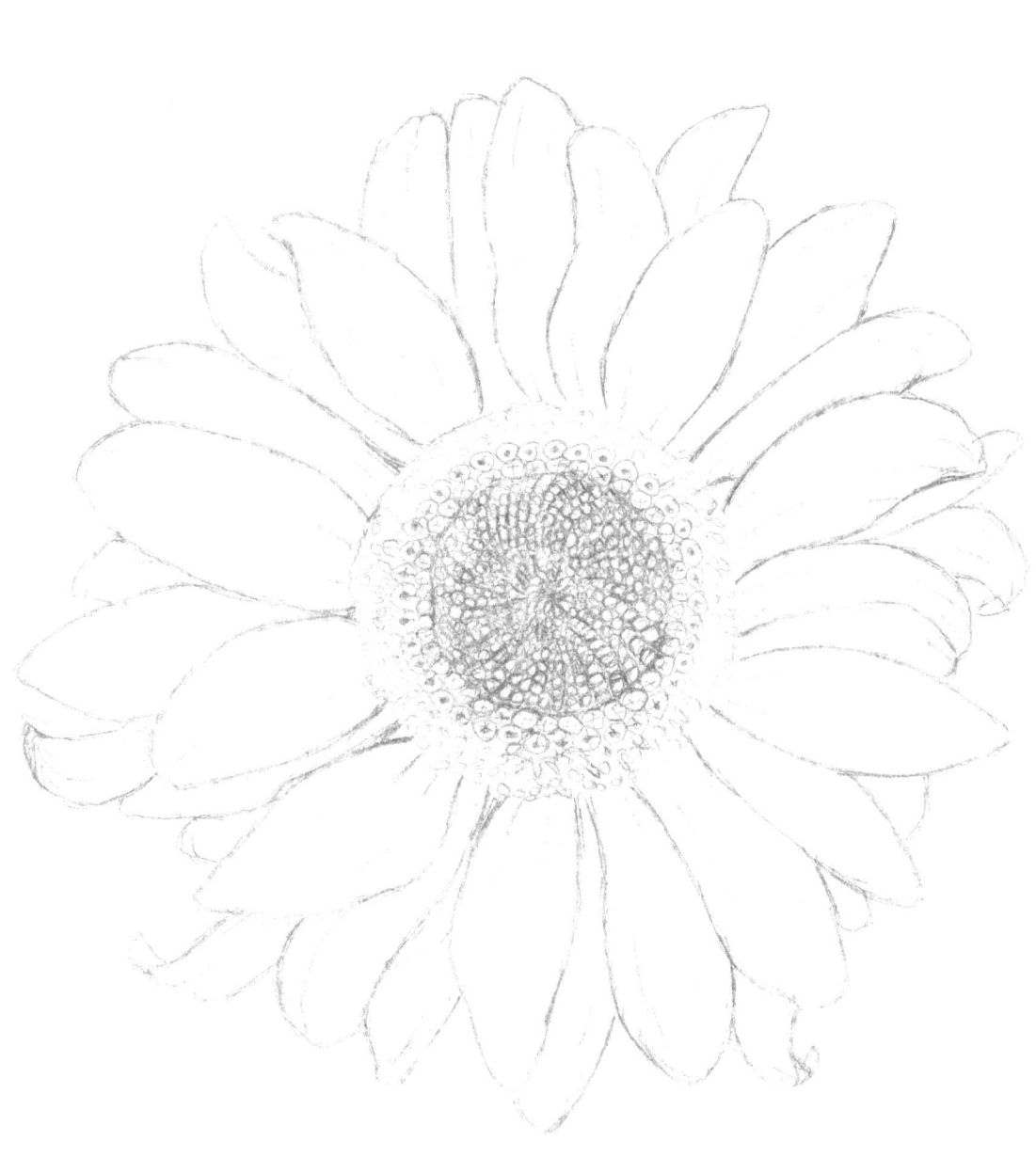

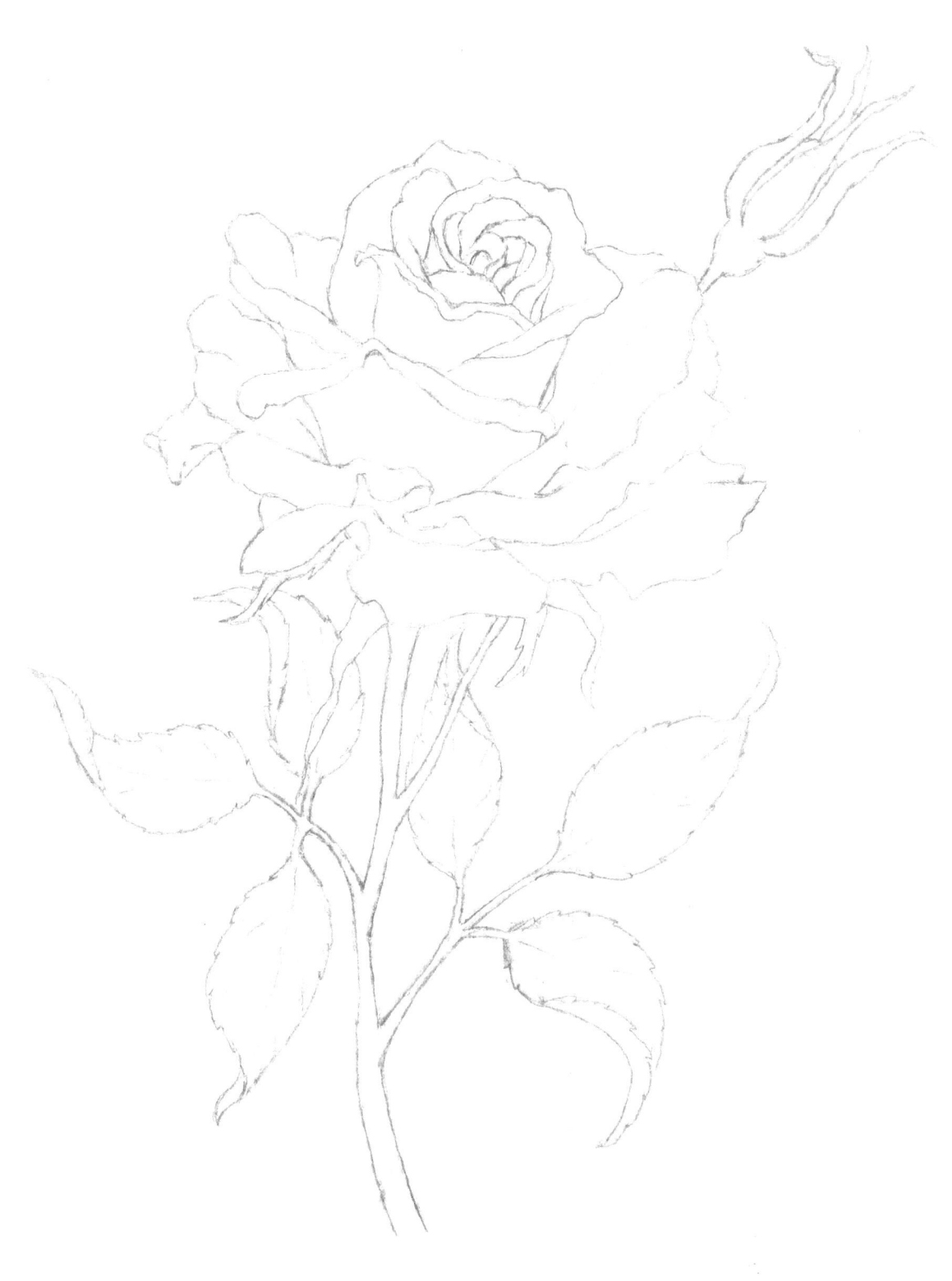

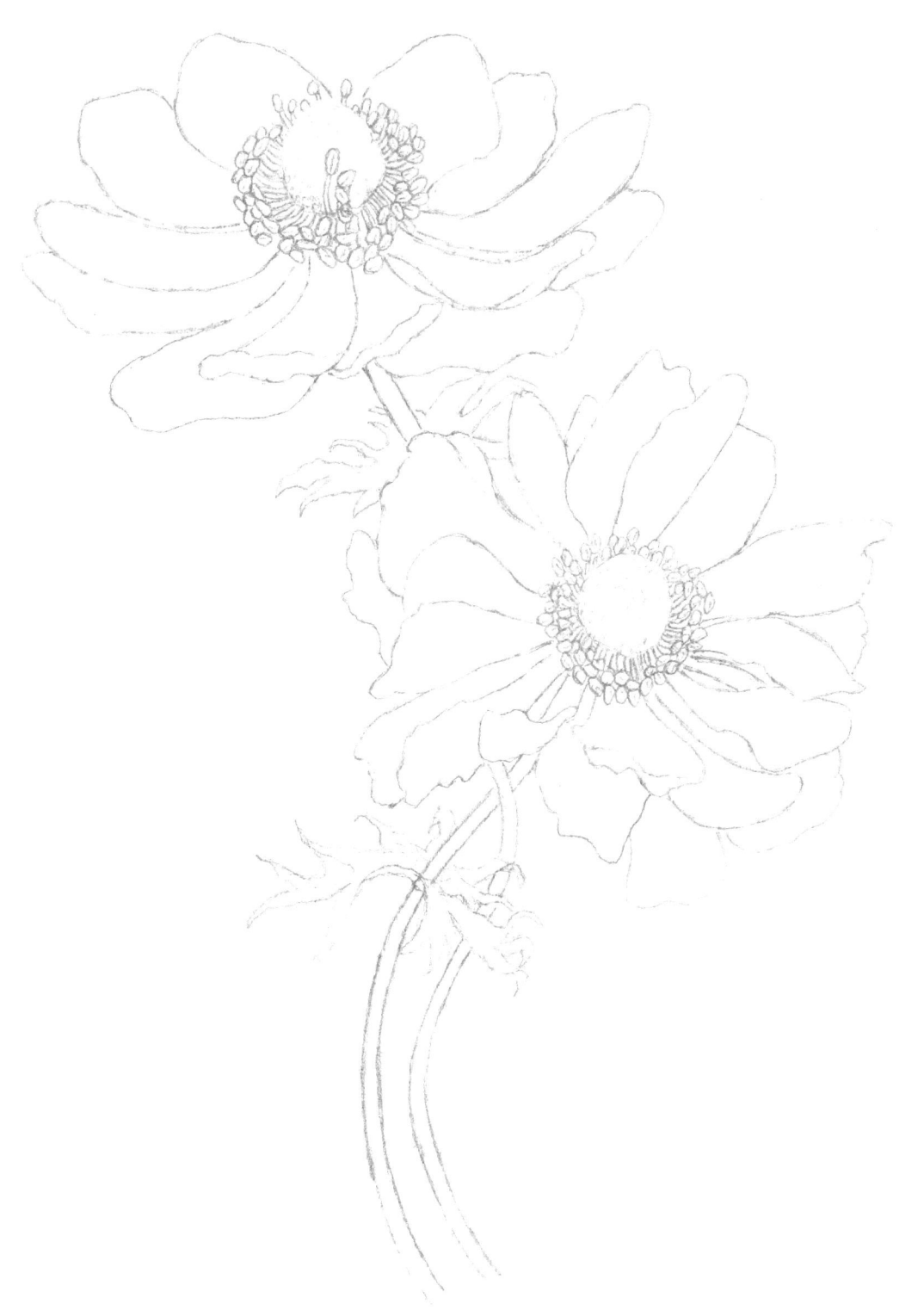

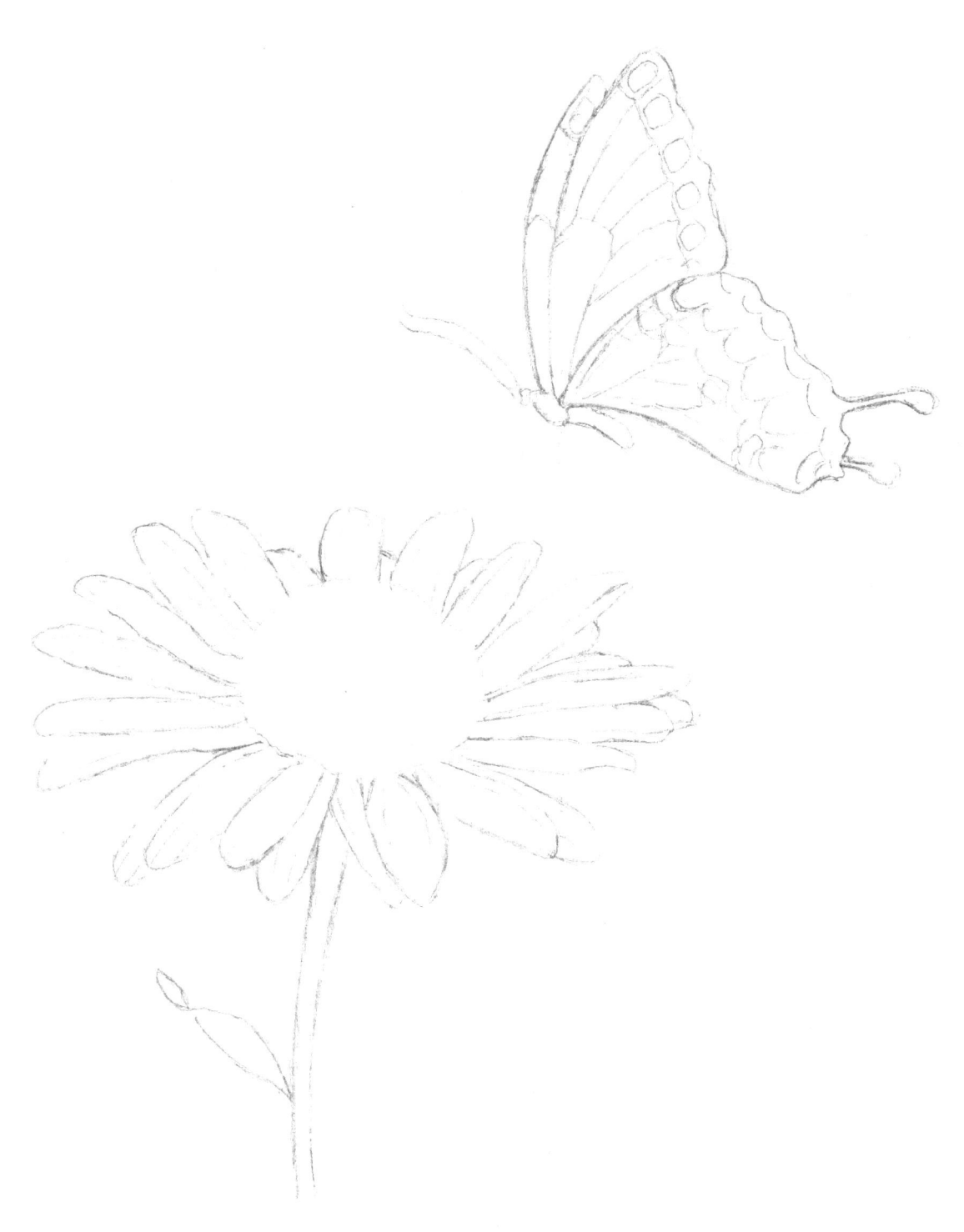

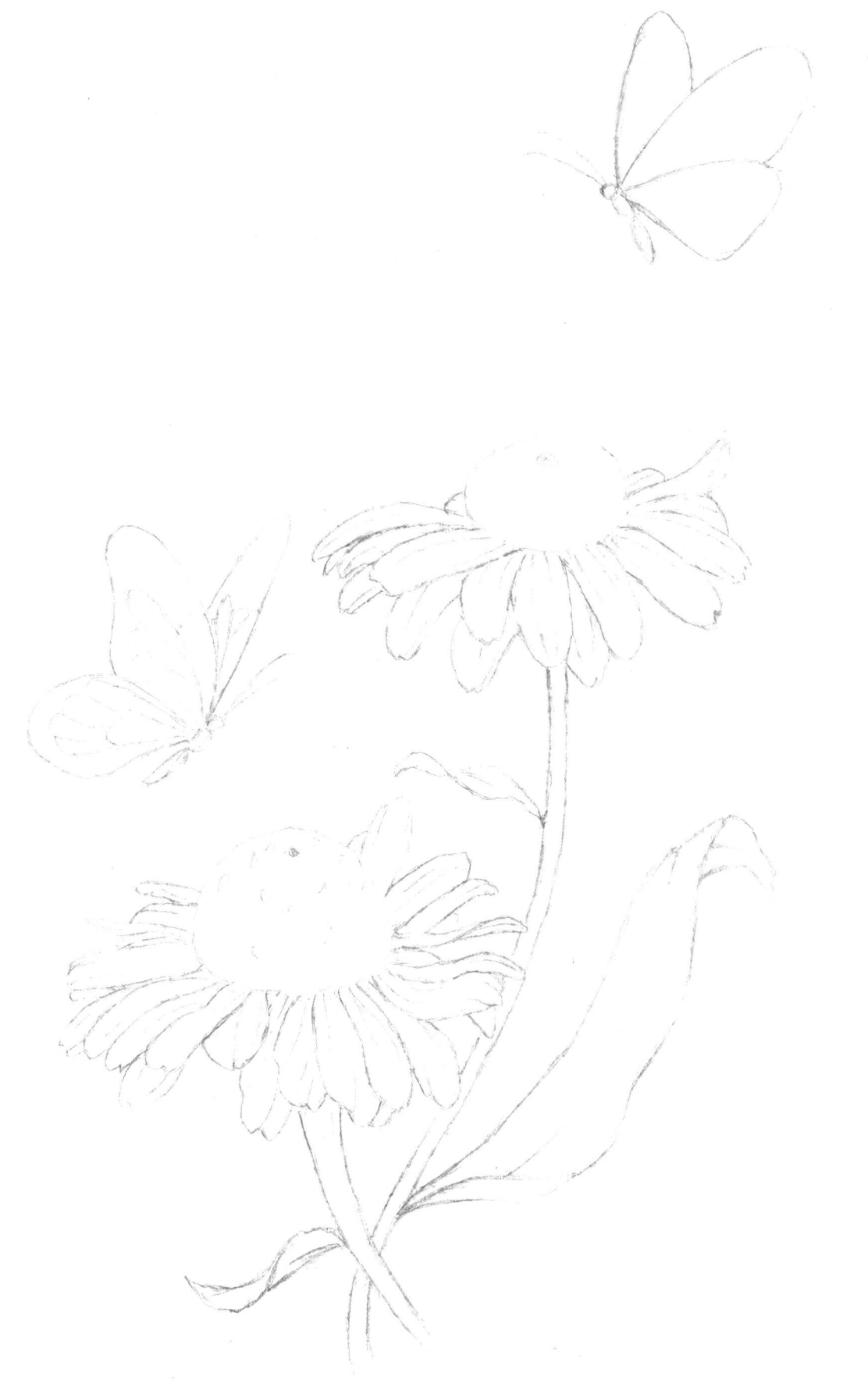

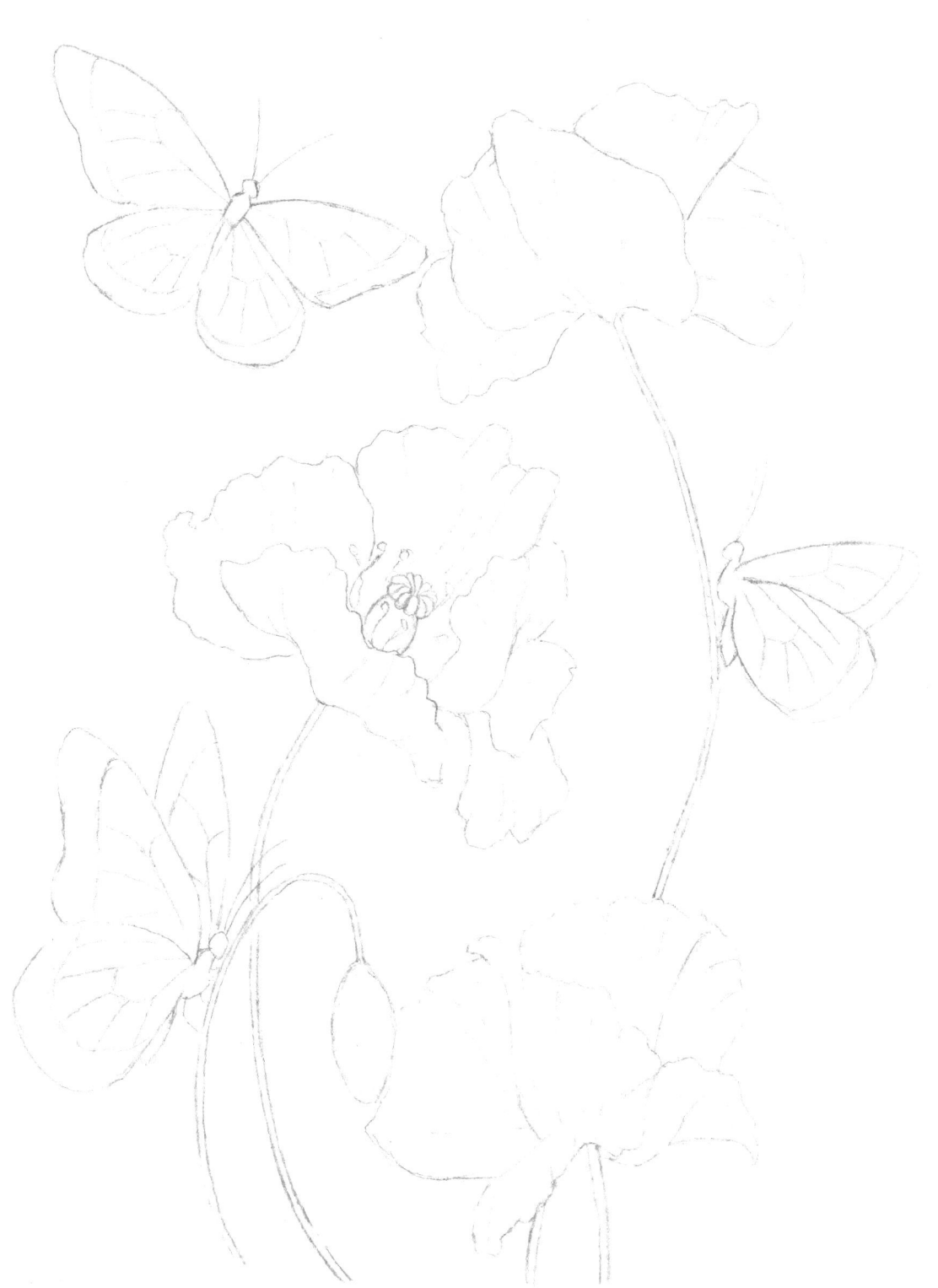

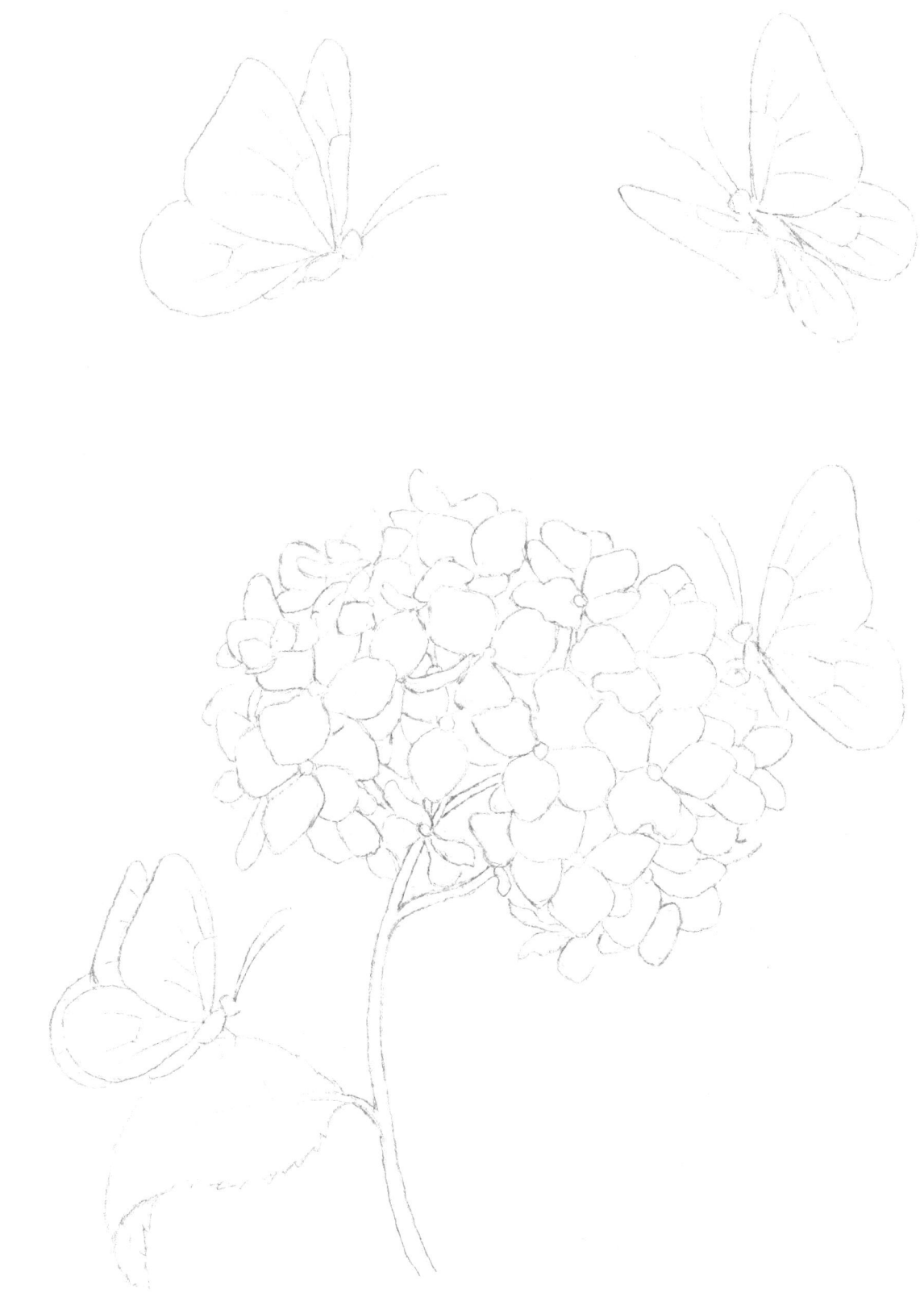

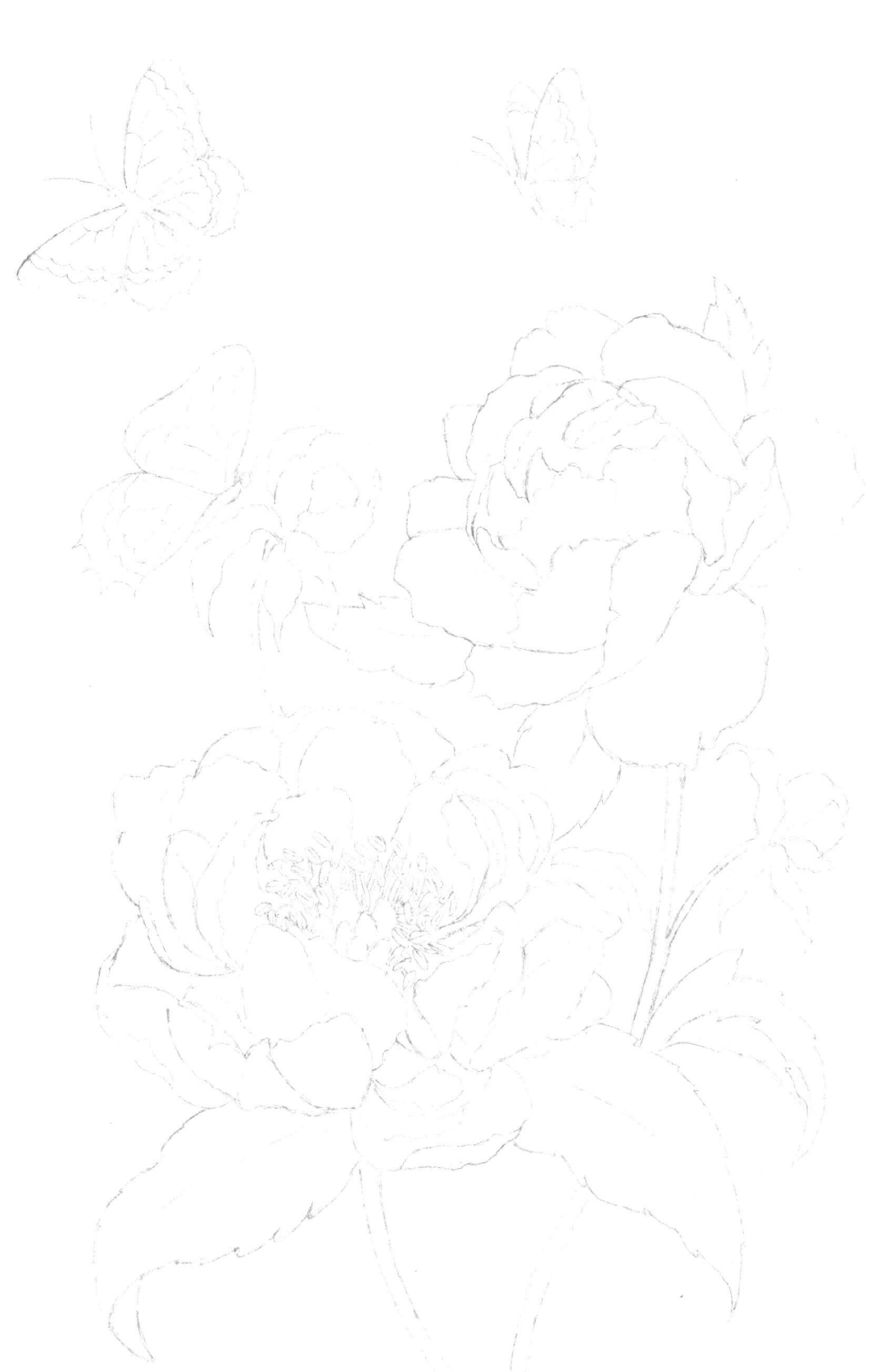

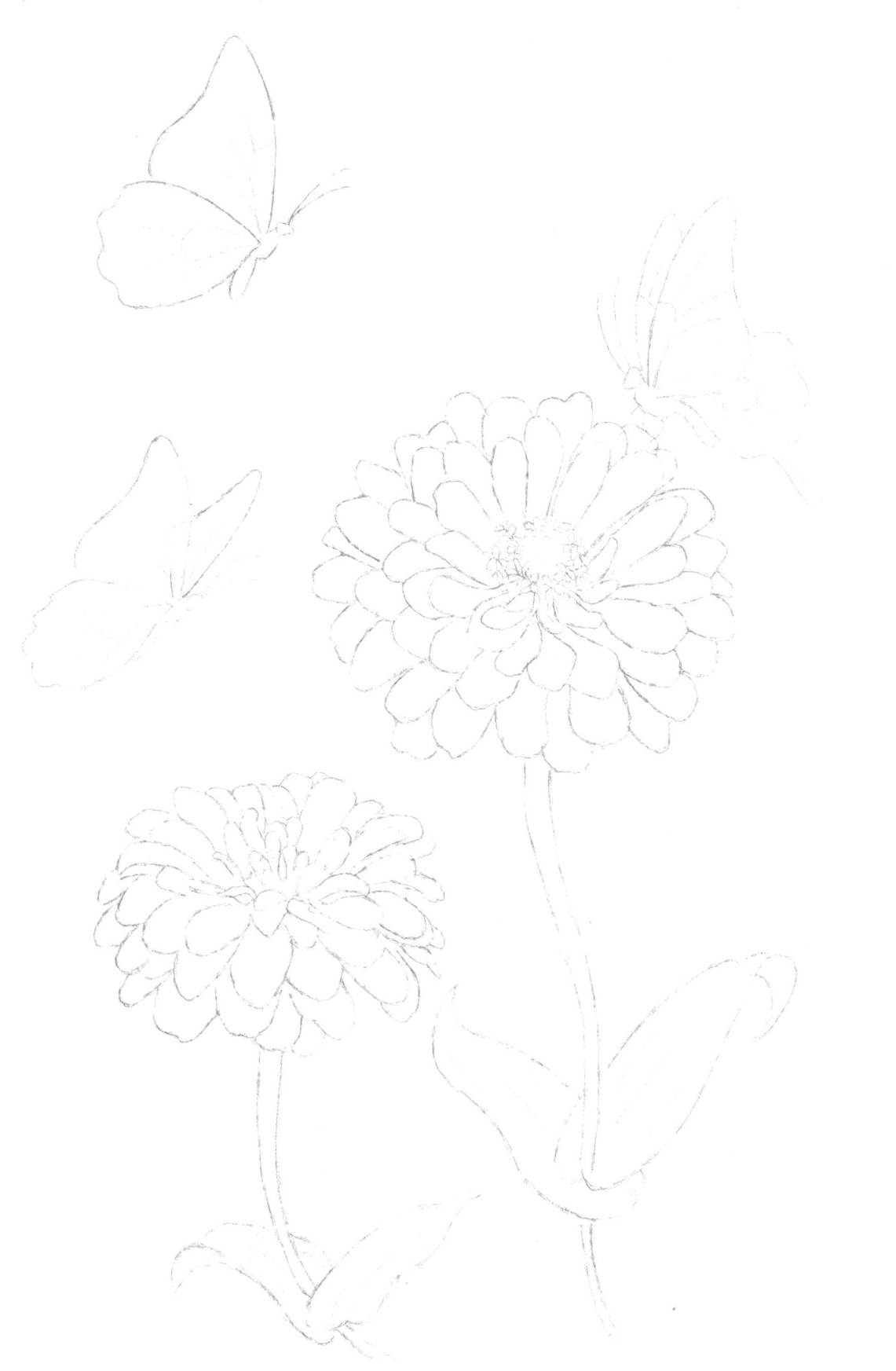

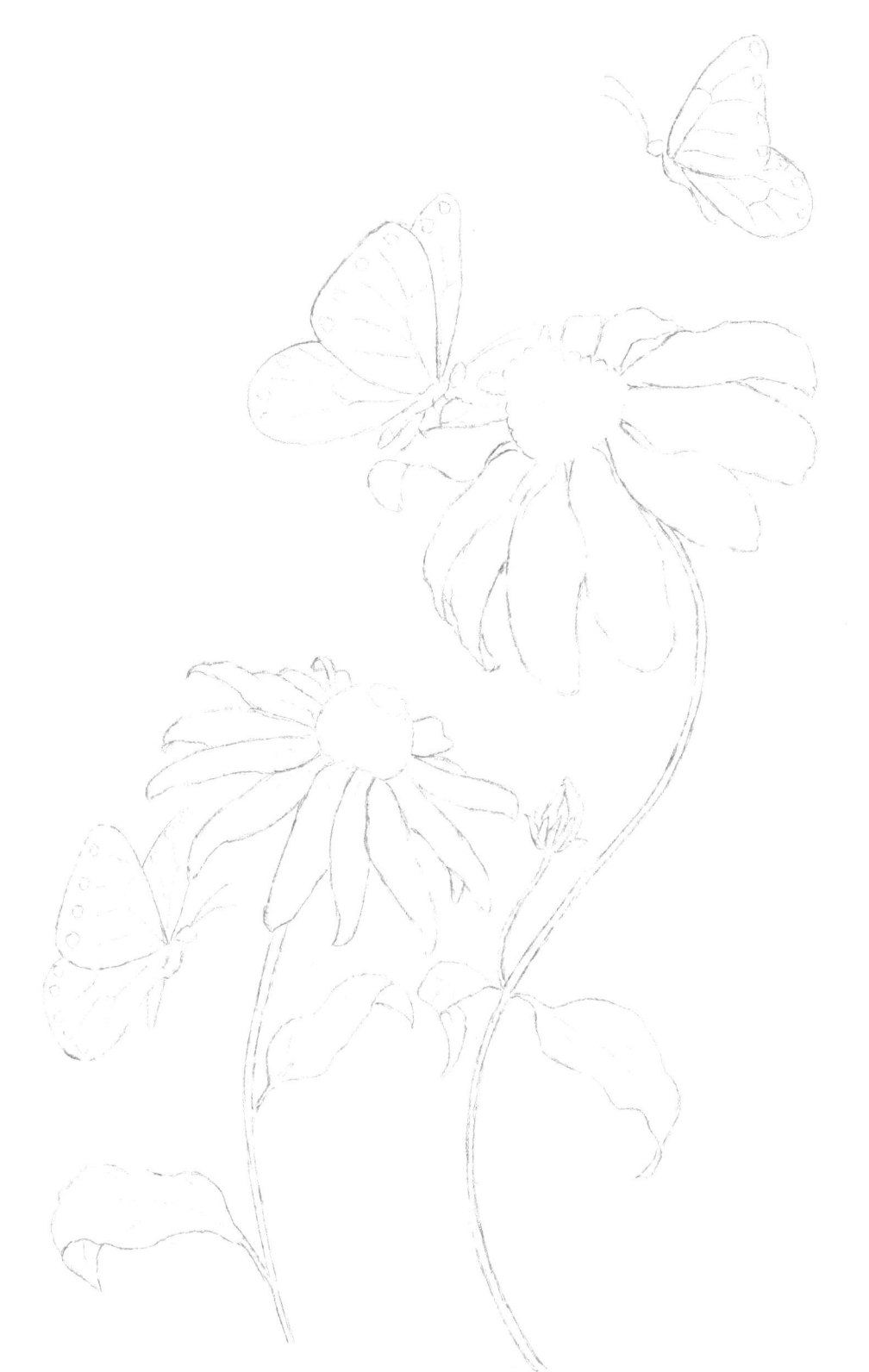